Echo Horizon

December 2001
For Lisa
Bert Howe

Echo Horizon

By

Bert Howe

Copyright © 2001 by Bert Howe
All rights reserved. No part of this book may be reproduced, stored in a retrieval system, or transmitted by any means, electronic, mechanical, photocopying, recording, or otherwise, without written permission from the author.

ISBN: 0-75960-293-X

This is printed on acid free paper.

1stBooks - rev. 1/18/01

For Jean, who never stopped believing.

Echo Horizon

1

The big carrier's crew was this moment standing down from General Quarters and rounds from the final bursts of 20 and 40 millimeter fire tore up the surface of the Sea of Japan. An aircraft, now deemed friendly with gear down, banked into final on its way to making early acquaintance with the great ship's *Fly Three*. The Landing Signal Officer guided the pilot down the middle toward the pitching flight deck and stood his position without resort to the net as the prop plane yanked on the third arresting cable and released. Reduction gear had whined all the way in.

A flight deck crewman was on the starboard wing stub before the canope opened and the big Pratt and Whitney R-2800 was shut down.

"You OK, Sir? Need a hand?" He noticed a scar under the right eye, the odd togs.

"Boats?"

"Aviation Bos'n's Mate Second, Ensign."

"Boats, I know this isn't the Morris, but what are these aircraft? Where in the old hell am I?" The pilot stood stiffly and started a leg over the rim of the cockpit.

"Easy does it, Sir, you sure you're OK. I noticed your guns have been fired. Six in the wings…sure don't see these anymore."

"Yeah, I got into a scrap or two. What's so strange about this F6?"

"Just thought they were retired to training squadrons. I've seen some F8s…Marines may have some F7-Fs on the mainland."

"Retired, hell no, the Morris has an air group of six's."

"Don't know the ship, Sir…that officer over there will show you to the wardroom. Welcome aboard." With that, the petty officer threw a salute.

"At ease, Boats. What's your name?"

"Korza, Sir, Nick Korza."

"John Alport, Korza. I sure hope someone can explain what in hell's going on. This has been one hell of a day." The officer with 'OOD' on his sleeve walked over to the new comer. Ensign Alport saluted the ship's ensign, then the OOD. "Ensign John Alport requesting permission to visit and refuel on your ship."

"Permission granted, Ensign. Lieutenant Will Hale at your service. Pardon me, but where in hell have you come from in that old F6?" A Pantherjet at that moment took the fourth cable and stretched it like a huge bow. A second was lining on final.

"Took off from the *Morris* at 0600."

"The *Robert Morris*? The hell you say. Wasn't that scrapped five, six years back?"

"They didn't tell me about it if it was. I was trying but couldn't pick up the "Y" beacon when I spotted you. My IFF was on the fritz…"

"It sure was. Sorry about the reception. Our guys don't get much practise…thought they had a real live bogie." The pilot from the first Panther trotted up to the OOD. The ensign stared at his tightly laced flight suit.

"Where in hell is he? Jesus Christ, let me talk to that six pilot!"

"Here he is, Halloran."

"Holy shit. Ensign, name it..anything. I owe you. Pete's on his way down. You saved our friggin' asses!"

"Wait, slow down, Lieutenant. What the Christ happened with you guys? Commander Dahlgren's comin' right down. He'll want a fresh debrief."

"They caught us with our pants down, out o' fuel so we were on the fumes and no ammo. Two MIG-15s….Ensign here splashed one maybe both. The second was takin' the express home trailing smoke. Here comes Pete."

The second Pantherjet pilot strode up and threw his salute. "This the guy? I see the F6 headed for the elevator."

"Ensign Alport, Ensign Pete Kane…oh, Kane, grab Korza for me and make sure the gunsight camera film is brought to the commander muy pronto."

"Aye aye."

"Jesus, give me strength. I think this is going to be one of those days my mom told me about."

"Or your old da, Hale," replied Lt. Halloran.

"Sure could use some coffee and anything adrift in the wardroom, Lieutenants."

"Right this way, Alport." Lt. Halloran was scratching his head. "This has got to be a first. I never heard of a prop plane bringing down a jet in Korea."

"Korea?" pleaded Ensign Alport. "We fighting them, too?"

"We sure as hell are mixing it up with North Korea and the Chinese."

"The Chinese…our friends?"

"Not any pukin' more they ain't. Those were Chinese communist, Russian built Migoyan fifteens you pounded. How the hell did you do it, I'm askin'?" Lt. Hale was beginning to relax.

"Yeah, what are they teaching you Hellcat pilots, now?" chided Ensign Kane just rejoined.

"Well, I was high. I was lookin' for my carrier which wasn't anywhere it should have been, and I knew I was way off my plot. I looked down, saw these queer swept wing jobs…saw the white stars on your wings and let fly with the rest of my rounds. I was empty in seconds."

"Attention on deck!"

"At ease, Gents. Commander Dahlgren's going to be a while in the information center. I'm told we have a visitor, Lieutenant Hale?"

"Yes, Sir, Commander Jenson, Ensign Alport…seems he made a good account of himself on the way in. Ensign, the commander's our air officer."

"I guess to hell he did, Commander, he…"

Bert Howe

"Thank you, Lieutenant Halloran..one at a time, please. What ship, Ensign, or are you land based? I mean, where are you still using the Hellcat?"

"Sir, I left the *Morris* at 0600 this morning on a Kamikaze patrol.."

"Hold it. Am I missing something? We crossing the equator, Gentlemen? Ensign, get serious."

"Begging the commander's pardon, I am very serious; but I'll admit, confused, also."

"A moment, Alport. Halloran, what went on during your patrol?"

"We were at 12,000 feet, Kane flying above me and to the starboard. We were on the home leg of a relative sector pattern when these two fifteens jumped us. We were out of ammo, having torn up traffic and supply dumps just south of the Yalu. I told my wingman to put his nose down and go for the deck, get up some speed. Next thing I know one of the gooks is in the drink. The other one was trailing smoke on the way to the barn. I caught a glimpse of the F6 and couldn't believe my eyes, but I didn't feel very fussy where help came from. Our fuel was registering in tens of pounds, so we cut back on the speed's why he beat us to *Antietam*."

"So, an F6 cut out two MIG-15s. Now, Alport, we got your secret weapon, whatever it is, and we're mighty glad you happened along, but I can't buy this Robert Morris, CV bit. What's the date, Ensign?"

"7 July, 1945, Sir. I had no idea when I left my carrier the line up of allies had changed so in this theater." The OOD saw Nick Korza hesitate at the entrance to the wardroom. His and the commander's universe was coming unzipped.

"Good, Korza, thanks. Carry on. Gentlemen, if you care to we could repair to the CIC and run this film through. Our lab's jiffy service is second to none."

A photographer's mate set up a projector, and the officers settled down to view Ensign Alport's film taken from the gunsight-aiming-point camera, a 16 mm movie camera which ran when the guns were firing. What the young ensign had thought to be a routine patrol when he started out proved to be a shooting spree. To him nothing seemed right from the moment he made his text book landing on the pitching stern of the *Antietam*. Forward, the deck was lined with strange aircraft; but for years the CASUs and CASDs were upgrading aircraft on carriers. The Wildcat must have looked strange to crews accustomed to the Brewster Buffalo at the war's beginning; but the swept wing craft he had shot with the red star on the wing…that was strange. Someone told him the *Robert Morris* had been scrapped. Now he was sitting facing a projection screen, and the Air Officer of the *Antietam* was staring at him.

A blurred image of an aircraft disintegrating appeared jumping on the screen.

"Christ, that's an old Zeke. This guy's right out of the second world war."

The next was a twin engine midwing bomber type, bobbing and weaving with one engine flamed. Suddenly, a gas tank exploded, and the viewer appeared to be hurled through the wreckage." Flame one Betty."

Next was a Val, followed by a Tony and another Zeke. "The guy's an ace! What the hell, Alport!? Lights. Christ!"

"There's more, Commander. Look at that. What in the name of Jesus is that thing jumping up and down? What, Kane?"

"Looks like a ship..an old square rigged ship, but the color…could be sunset or sunrise. Look at it comin' at us. Jesus, what a dive! It's getting shot to shreds."

"There's another ship off to the side…got a glimpse of a flag. Can't tell about it. Holy shit!"

"That's all. All right, Alport, what gives? I've seen Japanese planes shot to hell and at least one sailing vessel. This is 1951, for Christ's sake, July, 1951." Lt. Hale jumped to his feet.

"You alright, Commander?"

"Get the captain down here, Hale…."

Bert Howe

2

<u>Thirty years later</u>

She ran through the sea fog with the grace of a forest sprite, her shape and motions the result of a young life devoted to sports. Marna could completely lose herself on these early morning odysseys as she was this day on Cobbets Neck. Fog drifted in shrouds from the sea to soften ledge and tree, and all that could be heard was her foot fall and the spaced piping of a fog signal.

She needed to periodically lose herself, as the scene of the last moments of her parents' lives, played out the previous December, was etched as back drop to her every day thoughts. Her breath was measured and deep, a part of the abridged reality her aerobic running allowed. The moist air entering her lungs was real; the impact of each foot in turn was real. So was the arm thrust in her face which attempted to arrest her flight

She seized the threat and, taking full advantage of her momentum and rising right knee, slammed it down and twisted, eliciting a scream and a concatenation of curses. Now her heart raced as she realized the attacker was not alone. A snapping of branches gave signal to another closing on her path. Was her dreamscape to become transformed to her killing field? Gone, now, was the image that tormented her waking hours and terrified her in her dreams. Gone was the fireball which had erupted on her retinas a thousand times with the realization of finality.

She ran like a deer, wanted to return to her car and be out of here, but she needed distance. Where could she run? The lighthouse was automated and a mile distant. No human help. Her lead shortened when a balsam branch took her full in the face and sent her to all fours. This wasn't happening to her. Muggings just didn't happen in these parts, but the course voices to her rear put doubt to flight. If only she had a weapon which could bring her pursuers to a common ruin.

A rocky shore with steep drop offs lay just beyond a break in the trees, and she thought to move more swiftly on ledge, her way some fifteen feet above breaking waves washing through kelp. She leaped to a sloping ledge and teetered there before regaining balance, then jumped to a still lower shelf. With throat burning she darted nearer to barnacles and seaweed. She still believed she could outdistance her antagonists, and an extreme leap landed her on a smooth face of shale. Water swirled in a chasm wide of her ability to spring to the far side. Uncautiously she turned and slipped, and the continent slid beneath her, scraping her back and shoulder. She fought to arrest her slide and was in the ocean quicker than the telling.

Reason fled when she plunged beneath the icy Atlantic, hardly warmed by the May sun from its winter temperature. She was bumped against rocks, drawn back through repulsive, kelpy fronds and slammed back again on the barnacle-encrusted shield. She failed in an attempt to grab anything; her hands bled. With the next surge of the sea she was yards away from land and becoming dreadfully cold. Even as she was blinded and numbed by the salty cold, she knew the end was near; but she fought with the last of her strength to hold her head above water. She cried out but heard only a rushing in her ears. Why was this happening to her? Why now? Her struggles ceased, and she was oblivious to the hands that lifted her until she was brought against a hard surface and heard a voice, not hers.

"Easy, Mate. We'll 'av' ye safe and dry with not a moment to lose an 'oim' a sinner."

She squirmed, barely conscious, in response to the heaving that brought her over the side of a large rowboat. Strong arms propped her inert body against a pile of canvas and covered her with a sail. Though numb, she began to hear voices and felt the boat lurch, was aware of her proximity to a stout soul who pulled on an oar. A voice cursed the fog with a lexicon of vituperation not unlike that of the fishermen of Saxtons Harbor. She tried to speak and know her rescuers and where they were taking her. She shivered in her cramped position, jeans icy on her legs. At least feeling was being restored. She was certain of clearing vision but saw beyond the gunn'l nothing but a gray void.

Pushing to sit the straighter and ease her breathing, numbness became a tingle, and her thoughts widened.

"Easy, mind you, Laddie." The voice was deep and resonant. At last oars were shipped, and the boat bumped to a halt. A voice boomed from above.

"What 'av' ye lads? Ye set out as three, and ye return as four." Stout hands yielded her up and up, hands grasping indiscriminately. She knew she was being taken aboard a vessel, but little except two large masts materialized on the scene. Smoke she knew must come from the Charlie Noble, but it wasn't oil burning or alcohol or coal. No, it was more like wood smoke…charcoal.

A lift line slapped against a mast. Now, she could make out gaff and boom with sail untidily sprawled. Men were moving about the deck of what must be a fair sized schooner. Then she noticed the rake back of the masts. What was missing? For one, no fog signal could be heard. Possible but unlikely given the Coast guard's rapid response in-spite-of a paltry budget. No machinery of any sort did she hear…no auxiliary, no generator or pumps. Much of her wet hair which had been rattily twisted and stuck to her head and face was falling away in dark cascades. Surprise registered in a voice which proclaimed, "Aye, it be no laddie, but a lass," this from one who had helped pass her over a broad rail onto the deck.

A commanding voice issued from the far end of the vessel. She was shivering violently and leaving a trail of water such as a child on the path of mischance.

"What be, MacNab?" In not above seconds past her arrival on board, a tall figure bounded to her side, black hair to his shoulders and a voice as of velvet. "The lass be near froze!" whereupon he flung off his cloak and wrapped her gently within its warmth. Someone was blowing on a foghorn; a bell was struck. Slowly her wits took in the deck scene of what could have been a movie set depicting a period vessel. Another voice joined.

"In my quarters, Mr. MacLean, dry raiment lest the maid expire. I like not her color. Go, MacNab, desire cook to prepare something warming to the belly and pleasing to the taste. This is a fish shall not see her kelpie this day." The man called MacLean drew her to him and guided her to a companionway, thence below to a cabin beneath the stern deck, as best she could determine. She was responsive to the simple human goodness shown her so far, but the man who held her against any sudden imbalance stirred sensations in her to which she was not accustomed. Marna was restored sufficient to know this was the beginning of an acquaintance she did not wish to see end.

He was tall and solid, but he spoke to her in soft accents to know her immediate discomfort. This was the captain's cabin he told her; and she was to disrobe so as to don the articles of clothing he would produce from a chest near a bunk bed. She protested his presence, and he shook it off and advised he would leave her and see her in the wardroom to which he directed, it being slightly forward and along a passage on the larboard

Before his departure he drew forth trousers and a blouse, both of wool and near their natural color. "You must depart your wet clothing with haste." He laid the items on the bunk and stopped back over the chest and pulled out wool stockings, probably hand knitted she thought. "I leave you, now. You will be all right? Your shivering has ceased."

She thanked him as he left and looked about the compact stateroom. What a job somebody had done, making this stately schooner appear as if out of the eighteenth century. She knew of the endeavors of many history buffs; and these guys must be having a blast, except she hadn't heard any female voices. If women were aboard they had been well hidden.

Close over her head was a lantern of brass in brass gimbals. A thermometer and barometer, both old, graced a bulkhead, and on the bunk was spread a handsome hand crafted quilt. She

Echo Horizon

reached in a pocket of her jeans and realized how clammy she felt. The wet kerchief she withdrew was wrapped around a gold charm bracelet missing one of the tiny pendants which she intended to take to a jeweler for repair.

She placed it on the chest and shuddered as the nightmare replayed across her inner eye. A small twin engine aircraft lifted toward the bay until a second sun cast a reflected path from the wave fronts. Her mother and dad were departing on vacation in his plane which exploded before her. Just before embarking. Her mom had placed the bracelet in her hand with the request to have it repaired, then hugged her and told her they'd see her in a blue moon.

Thus her thoughts depressed to that tearful day of tragedy as her soaked clothing thudded to the floor. The sight of her underthings undermined her spirits a little more when she realized the wool pants and blouse were going next to her skin. The row of buttons on one side of the pants convinced her women were not anticipated aboard. Then things began to go her way. The blouse didn't scratch. She could smell the lanolin and did wonder at the total lack of wash and wear or any man made fibers. Her curiosity was inflamed at this point even to flaring to a peek under a tarp covering a large mass extending from the center window of the stern into the room. "Good God!" she exclaimed to herself, it was a gun, a huge gun...but old. Whoever these men were, wherever they had come from, they had documented this ship and appointments to the letter. They rated an "A".

She could smell the aroma of cooking and hastened past the door in the direction instructed and found Mr. MacLean and another tall man seated at a table which just fit into the tiny room. She was glad she had made use of the partial reflection from a window to, at least, marshal some directive over the directions in which her hair strayed. This had to be a movie set up. This was a production unit charged with the task of generating lifelike scenes aboard ship...had to be it.

"Come in..come in." The tall man stood, and she looked at the mainly dark hair and beard with graying streaks. He had a scar under his right eye, just as her father had. He was as tall, too, but at least ten years younger than her dad...striking resemblance, though. Mr. MacLean had stepped into the galley to fetch her a plate of whatever. "Allow me to introduce myself. You've met my first officer, Lieutenant Comfort MacLean. I trust he was able to clothe you. Your color is better, and you are finding relief from your ordeal? I am John Alport, master of the private armed schooner *ARCHER*. We are in these waters for a short time, it is hoped. This damnable fog has lengthened our stay as it is."

"Oh, wonderful," she exclaimed to herself. He was perfectly cast. 'Private armed schooner...the best of schmalz. The fog horn continued, but there was no sound from the lighthouse. Footsteps stirred on deck, and she heard fragments of conversation, not like any talk she would expect from vacationers or Hollywood people

She was served a steaming brew in a mug that was referred to as coffee unsubstantiated by taste. Mr. MacLean ladled something into a bowl from a tub size container, a stewlike substance he called martingale stew. Tasting it, she recognized beef stew. But it all felt wonderful going down. The warmth could become addictive.

What were they discussing up above? She made out something about a foundered vessel, remains in a cove somewhere on the coast...badly hulled. A voice expressed doubt all the gold was removed. Probably rehearsing their lines. She just knew she had lucked out. Did she dare ask? Better wait and see if they tipped her off to anything real hush hush.

"I trust our mermaid has recovered from the ordeal."

"Quite fine, thank you, Sir. I guess I would have been gone if it weren't for your people." Mr. MacLean offered that they were thankful the men were where they were at the time of her immersion. "I'm Marna Gantry of Saxtons Harbor. I teach school and write." This fascinated them, a woman teaching school.

"Was it accounts you write, Mistress?" Asked the first officer.

"I write stories and historical accounts and hope people read them."

"Well, this is indeed an eye opener. How came you to your plight in the water?"

"I was running through the woods..love the fog 'cause you can feel so alone and secure. I wasn't alone this morning, and I wasn't secure, because I was attacked." This straightened them in their seats. "I surprised one, painfully, I think and slowed them up, but I was careless and fell into the bay from a slippery ledge." Both men were silent for a moment, then expressed surprise at the notion of a young woman running alone in the woods unchaperoned, unprotected, footpads abroad and unhung.

"You are not far from home, then?"

"Not far, twelve miles at most."

"You have a carriage…?" This was getting to her. They were going beyond play acting. And, why for her benefit? Hey, guys, she shouted in her head, leveling time. "You bear a resemblance to a member of my family," offered the captain. "Doesn't she, Comfort, save for the color of hair?"

"Aye, It shows. Move nearer the stove, Mistress, you must be completely comforted before you be returned to land." She felt the movement of the hull, a shift of wind direction. Lines slapped against a mast. Mr. MacLean leaned back and peered through what served as a skylight overhead. "The fog lifts or I'm a Dutchman."

She wanted nothing so much as a chance to stay and converse with Mr. MacLean, get to know him. Never had she met anyone even remotely his equal in appeal. But so far he hadn't asked her if he could call sometime, hadn't even asked for her phone number.

"Time to return Mistress Gantry to the shore, MacLean. Arm the men, and carry your cutlass. We had best be departing,

Mistress. It is my pleasure to receive your visitation. My men will see that no harm comes to you ashore." Was this to be all? What she beheld was more than met the eye. Now, her imagination was running wild. She thought she must be dreaming and expected to waken in her bed at any moment. But this young man who cared for her, was concerned at her discomfort...no wisecracks, no coming onto her. She was losing her heart, and she knew it. She didn't want to go.

"Will I see you again? I'm in the phone directory." They looked at each other. Weren't they going to ask for her number? Comfort gently guided her up to the deck and, having retrieved his boat cloak, wrapped her in it once more. Then he helped her down into the stern of the long boat and held her closely to him while the oarsmen looked at their feet and rowed. The boat nosed onto a tiny beach where she remembered skinny dipping during summers in high school; and only after the men ranged widely in both directions did Comfort consent to her departure, when he told her they'd meet in a blue moon.

She watched the little boat long after it left her, then started to sprint in the direction of her car. She was just building up to a sweat again and a good heart rate when she crested a height of land bare of trees and affording a fine view of the bay. The fog had retreated almost to the point of land on which sat the lighthouse, and the fog signal was pealing forth. Search as she might, the view offered water and islands...no row boat and no schooner. Her heart dumped in that nostalgic, longing loneliness known only to the young. Where had they gone?

It was simply not possible for a sailboat, waiting for its tender, to then weigh anchor and tack to sea the two miles to the edge of the fog and lose itself in the short time she had been running. She turned in sadness toward her car once more and ran like a deer. When the faithful blazer came in sight she swept into a panic. She had left her wet things in the captain's quarters, her jeans, sweatshirt and unmentionables and the bracelet and *her car keys*. If there was a god in Heaven, she had left a spare under the floor mat.

She halted and looked all around..didn't know whether someone was lurking, waiting for her return. What had those bastards wanted? She didn't want to guess. Well, she had to try it sooner or later. She started and ran like the wind for the car, yanked the door open and tore up the mat. The key.

The drive to her home was as nothing, she taken up in thoughtful reflection. So many questions; so little time. They were so remote from her ability to communicate. The reference to a blue moon. Her mother had told her that in her last words to her. Where was the schooner? Where had she been for what...two, three hours? The sun was bright, and much of the day remained for her.

The blazer swerved into the drive under the huge spruce trees and stopped behind a house snug in its location just behind a rocky bluff overlooking the ocean. It was a product of the brief period between colonial and federal with carpentered pilasters at the corners, topped with simple cornices and box eaves on an "L" shaped floor plan with porches front and back.

Once changed she made haste with her notebook and pencils to the edge of the bluff where a natural seat was worn into the granite. She could sit unseen, feet dangling above the breaking waves and think. And in this state she busied herself. Since it was Saturday and no messages except one left by Nancy on her answering machine, suggesting they get together soon to select the direction in which their joint thesis would go, she didn't expect to be interrupted.

Gulls wheeled overhead. She spotted two loons and a seal. The birds would be leaving for the northern lakes after wintering on the bay; the seal had just moved in from down by Buzzard's Bay. No one could take this from her, the return of the spring. True, the black flies and mosquitoes would exact their toll, but all around, the earth was budding and blooming.

Softly, her name was called. The voice came closer. It was Nancy. If she saw the car in the yard and found no one in the house, she knew where to look. Marna looked up into the peaches and cream complexion of her friend Nancy Marsh. Blonde ringlets danced in the breeze. She never used make up.

"Marna, aren't those waves coming a bit close, you want to come up out of there?

"Hi, Nan. Thought you'd be in the library on Saturday."

"Partying again, was it? Marna, it's Sunday. Remember we were going to nail the topic?"

"Give me a break…Sunday." She took the offered hand and climbed back to level ground. "I always jog early Saturday." She put her hand to her forehead to shield her eyes from the noon sun. "And was this a wild session..Nan, you'll never believe…"

"C'mon, let's get some lunch. I brought fixin's. You can tell me all about it."

The kitchen was bright, and lunch involved a lot of salad, vegetable juice and cottage cheese. Marna could have eaten a horse but said nothing.

"….And when they brought me back to shore, the guys were carrying these wicked huge pistols, nothing like my .380, these were muzzle loaders; and he.."

"Who..?"

"Comfort carried his cutlass."

"Who all was at this party, Marn, and what were they serving?"

"Well, it coulda been a movie company or something.."

"But you don't think it was, do you?"

"I don't know what to think." She looked straight at her friend. "Nan, what a hulk! Like someone from your dreams…well, you wouldn't dream except about Erik."

"He'll call you, Marn. No guy's going to let a find like you get away if.."

"Nancy, he didn't even ask me for my phone number!"

"This is too much. C'mon, let's get to work."

"You really don't believe me, do you?"

"It's Sunday, you thought it was Saturday. You know, you've come up with some pretty imaginative stuff. I've read some of your short stories. Maybe it is a movie company. They'll come around; we'll see 'em."

"Like nothing I've seen ever."

"Look, we've got a huge break, the committee letting us do a joint thesis. Can't imagine what's come over Fenster."

"Not easy for a department chairman in a small college with a wife like he's got..sooo, where do we want to go with the history research?"

"I'm out of ideas, Marn. I thought of women in the Civil War, but actually, women played a bigger role in the Revolution, carried water, cared for the sick, washed and actually fought the big guns. Women've had a bad rap…camp followers indeed."

"Want to go with that?"

"Done to death. Tell you what, I'll just..no, that's it. Marna, I think I've found the perfect little void where there should be some history and maybe, just maybe, nobody can find it. Why haven't we come up with this before? I think it is so obvious." She paced around the kitchen, opening cupboards, pulling out drawers."

"For Christ's sake, light and tell me about it."

"OK, don't tell me I'm crazy or anything. England bungled the job of hanging onto the colonies, right?"

"History maintains they really didn't want them enough to spend the effort."

"Baloney! I'm going to take the stand that they tried some very dirty tricks, well, maybe one, anyway. What if they had contrived to bribe or assassinate as many of the trouble makers as they could? It was a right small portion of the population really supported the rebellion. Let's argue they set out in a single vessel with a huge amount of gold, under orders from Lord North to hire for substantial wages in gold a flock of Tories to go after all the big shipping interests…"

"The smugglers.."

"OK, smugglers, Sam Adams, Rob Morris, John Jay, Paine, Hancock…oh hell, the whole establishment and the Continental Congress and buy their defection, or terminate them."

"Get real."

"So, you've never heard of such an idea. What if it actually happened and a yankee privateer intercepted, vanquished and took charge of the gold? Oh, you don't think they'd tell anyone, do you? No history. That's where we come in."

"Nancy, that would make a great movie script, but no one's going to believe.."

"Let's make 'em believe."

3

As the taxi swung onto a roadway of the old naval air station outside Washington D.C. its headlights cut across a runway and reflected from parked aircraft on the far side, shadows radiating from weeds adorning cracks in the tarmac. The officer reached for his wallet, and the cab halted before a brick administration building built during the rush to readiness of World War II. Once outside, he made for the steps to the front entrance.

Spring was everywhere well advanced, and he stood outside the door for a moment and breathed deeply. Jim Starr was regular navy, trained as a SEAL and did two tours in Nam. He stood there straight and lean, two and a half stripes on his cuff, dark hair grown to the limit of length regs but well groomed around the ears. Jim had been enjoying leave at his Shenandoah Valley home, only just now called back to duty by the man to whom he reported, Admiral Pete Rankin. For three years Jim had been a special investigator, first for the Judge Advocate General and, recently, for Office of Special Accounts.

He continued to the office and proceeded inside without knocking as prearranged.

"Thanks, Commander for obliging me. I've interrupted your short but well deserved rest and relaxation; but I think you will concur with my urgency when you learn of this most unusual situation." The admiral threw most of navy officers' protocol to the winds in his eagerness to put his subordinate at ease while moving swiftly to the crux of the matter.

"You haven't disappointed me yet." Jim settled into an overstuffed sofa and watched his host pour from one of several single malt scotch bottles at a small bar. The suite was comfortably furnished with an air of permanence, walls displaying color prints of naval action out of World War II.

"There you are, Commander, just as you like it, neat." Rankin wore a plain business suit, and the commercial quality of the surroundings appeared to contradict his career as an air and, later, bridge officer.

"Thanks, Sir."

"Dinner will be coming in shortly, so let's get right down to the reason for the unceremonious interruption of your R&R. Incidentally, you might like to know we are funded for another year. Guess they can't get on without us after all. The professional spooks take themselves too seriously and don't seem to get much co-operation from folks. By the way, there is a special commendation coming your way beyond the usual *well done*. We were able to nail down two shipments of weapons before the cartel knew what hit them. Taxpayers were saved a few lengthy trials, too." Jim looked up from his seat at the pacing Rankin.

"Thanks, Sir; can't wait to see what's going down this time."

"Oh, you'll like this one." Jim was accustomed to the waving finger, but the voice inflection was higher this time, and it was as if the admiral were addressing others as well, though unseen. He finished his pacing and took his seat at the big desk. "On the table before you is a file. You can study it later. The subject is a captain, a flier.." He paused, rose and started again his tour of the room. "Jim, how well do you think you know me?"

"You really want me to answer that one, Sir?"

"Please, and knock off the "Sir". Somehow I am certain this is going to work better if we knock off the protocol. Can you handle it?"

"I'm all right with it…" Almost, but he managed to leave off the formal address. "What've we got?"

"Bear with me. I have to tell you a story that goes way back." He surrendered to a chair. "July, 1951…Sea of Japan. I was exec of the old *Antietam*. We were cruising near the thirty-eighth parallel about a hundred miles off the Korean coast. Our boys were hitting roads and bridges pretty hard, flying ADs and F9s. We'd had some losses. Thanks to our chopper crews all but two men were recovered that month. One day general quarters

Echo Horizon

was sounded and our five inch and all the forties and twenties on one side opened up on what turned out to be an F6-F, gear down, trying for a landing pattern. We stood down and took the aircraft aboard; and no sooner had the pilot gotten in to debrief when a division of F9s were recovered. Seems they were both out of ammo and flying on fumes when they were jumped by two MIG-15s, but before either worked up a sweat one MIG was flamed and going in, then the second trailed smoke and headed for the exits."

"I think I know where this is going, and I don't buy it already. Are you saying F6-Fs were operational at that time?"

"Not on my watch…though quite a few were used in training squadrons in the states. At least one carrier included a squadron of 6s in its wing for low level stuff. But this one was sure as hell operational. It jumped the MIGs. Pilot told us he had the altitude advantage and the sun behind him when he saw the swept wing craft pounce on unfamiliar aircraft but with white stars on them."

"You've got me, Admiral. What was an F6 doing in the area at all? Where was his base?

"You asked. Thank you. He told Commander Jensen the air officer he was on patrol for Kamikaze aircraft."

"That did it. What was his next stop, section eight?" The admiral returned to the bar and poured himself another drink, then picked up Jim Starr's glass and freshened it also.

"You're going to get a look at his gun sight camera film. He was at altitude because he was looking for his carrier, seems his "Y" beacon equipment malfunctioned and his IFF."

"Which flat top?"

"The *Robert Morris*."

"Couldn't be..not possible. You said this was 1951. The *Morris* had been scrapped years before."

"Ahh-h, seeing the light, I see, plus the Japs made a headstart on it."

"Well, there was a damn good reason his "Y" beacon was out. The ship wasn't there." Jim Starr had spent too many days in enemy territory and escaped to tell the story to let much get by him. He was having trouble with what he was hearing. Long sessions with suspected account ledgers and stakeouts made him wary of minute details.

A knock at the door preceded two stewards with the promised dinner. "Oh, good, Rollins. Commander, we have a treat in store for us, finest commissary crew in the district." When the men had departed a table stood burdened with repast. "Dig in, Jim, then we'll continue."

"So, he was above the two MIGs when he spotted them."

"Right, he was able to see the white stars on the Pantherjets, said he didn't remember seeing any such aircraft in the theater of operations. He said he put his nose down, hit terminal velocity and let fly with what ammo he had left."

"And…"

"We reviewed the film from his gun-sight-aiming-point camera…he'd had good hunting that day, no doubt an ace."

"Kamikazes, the *Morris*, F6-F, 1951, gotta be more to this."

"Eat up, you're going to see the film." With the fine meal for fortification, Jim left the table and took a seat at the indicated far end of the room where a movie screen was ready. The projector was focused, and Jim watched the parade of unfortunate Japanese aircraft followed by the sunrise scene with the ocean surface sweeping up toward the viewer and a square rigged ship undergoing defoliation, a brief look at what resembled a Baltimore Clipper nearby.

"No way, Pete,[no protocol, now] I didn't see what I just didn't see. What in hell is going on?"

"Tell me about it. You can't handle it. The officers in CIC couldn't handle it either. They called in Captain Woods and our visiting ensign nearly went to Section Eight in a straight jacket. Ensign Alport, that was his name, swore he took off from *Morris* that morning on a kamikaze patrol. He tangled with some Japs and the Chinese pilots and handled them rather roughly. He called the date as July, 1945. What he had trouble with was being told he had landed on the *Antietam* six years later. Guys in engineering reported they couldn't understand how the old F6 could stay in the air." Jim ran his hand through his hair."

"Jesus Christ!"

"Of course in good old navy fashion, those that couldn't handle it chalked it up to good old navy *SNAFU*. We checked with BuPers and discovered they had the officer listed as killed in action, no next of kin. He'd been an orphan, joined the navy in '43. But we had a hell of a time. Personnel would go as far as missing in action and agreed to reactivate his pay account, had a bundle of dough due him even in those times. So BuPers ground along. They wanted to try POW for a while, then desertion. Would you believe those idiots in Washington wanted him courts martialed. Meanwhile, he was shooting up North Korea for us after a few check rides in the Panther. Finally, after some creative history writing by our chief yeoman warrant and the medical staff, we got through to Washington with POW and escape 1945 with loss of memory and living in hiding in Hokkaido and the Kuriles. He got his back pay, and we had a fine replacement pilot."

"Excuse me, Admiral, what in hell really happened? I've got big problems with this."

"Join the club. I don't think he knew either. This is where you come in. Belief mechanism is not the issue..."

"You said 'knew'?"

"I'm getting to that. What we need is answers. You see, someone arranged for him and his wife to be blown out of the sky a few months back.."

"Ohh, no!"

"I want to know who. I want him or them. He was a fine officer, retired with four stripes. He even flew combat in Nam. Naturally, when I had the opportunity, I gave him every chance to talk to me. He said he found it easier to talk to me about his paradox and he needed to talk with someone. He had no answers, but he told me of a dream, a dream so vivid in every detail it was as if he were present in the dreamscape. I don't think he told anyone else."

"Dead..after all this, he's dead, and you want me to find the 'perps'." Jim's mental deployment was drifting off to a point of wider scope. The conversation had been serious, but a rear admiral of the United States Navy was describing a scene out of pure fantasy...except, every possible evidence existed that those involved believed it had happened. The film he had just witnessed. A carrier based fighter plane landed in 1951 on an American flat top with visual evidence of several Japanese aircraft in the process of destruction. But the most bewildering of all was the two vessels. The camera recorded only during the time the firing button was pressed, and the vessel fired on displayed a British ensign or he had lost all ability to distinguish or reason.

"You got it, Jim. Everything's in that file. I want you to read it, then tell me if you are ready for a new job. He was a smart cookie, Jim. He had two Nam cruises in the late sixties, then I lost him. For years I couldn't locate him until I found he'd changed his name to Gantry. He was retired, and his checks went to a post office box. Cancelled checks returned from a bank in a different city with an endorsement always showing his name written in a feminine hand, then counter-signed Betsy Gantry. Bank was happy; navy was happy, but I never could locate him. No reason, of course, but curiosity. The man had done nothing wrong. I think I would just like to have seen him one more time."

That rang a bell with Jim Starr. Of all the emotions, sentiment was least likely to surface in Pete Rankin. He listened with rapt attention, wondering, should he embark on some wild cloak and dagger expedition, how far afield the admiral's personal involvement would take him, but his own curiosity was taking the upper hand.

"Then he surfaced in Saxtons Harbor, Maine several years ago. I was there for a summer of R&R doing a little fishing...guy named Beal knew his way around..."

"Thank you, no, Admiral, I want to be able to find my way home...very good hooch."

"Talk was a guy named John Gantry came into town and bought the old Alport place. That was his name when I knew him, Alport. Gorgeous place it is...on the shore...couple hundred acres. Would have cost a fortune then, and I had no reason to believe he ever had that kind of money. Too bad about him and Mrs. Gantry. They left a daughter about...oh, somewhere in her twenties."

Jim continued eating, saying little but thinking hugely. The story as laid before him lacked definition. Legal and investigative activity over the years had honed his thinking process to adapt to most any definable system of logic; but he was not comfortable with what he had been told. His thought process kept tossing bits and pieces of the story out the window. But the tale assumed a life of its own, no matter it didn't fit with known co-ordinates. A man had lived, functioned superbly as a fighting machine, married and participated in giving life

He wondered what he wasn't being told. Something about the business was more romantic than just seeking out a killer. That was straight police work. Maybe it was the single malt, he reasoned later, but he charged ahead all the same.

"Admiral, I've got another two weeks on the farm. No problem with cutting it short, but I don't understand yet what it is you really want accomplished here. I expect the Transportation Safety Board and the FBI have made some progress running down the culprit."

"Russ, they haven't found any wreckage. Oh, we'll see to it they remain as a presence plugging away while we attend to our business. What I think is this. The girl knows something..."

"What the hell, you saying she's implicated?"

"No..no, what I'm saying is, I think she can offer background..maybe even has some information she doesn't piece together, unrelated facts and experiences.."

"You mean she may know something she doesn't even know she knows."

"That'd cover it."

"Then, Admiral, what is it exactly you want me to do?" Jim had been in some tight places, had inadvertently appeared with egg on his face, even carried a few scars before he literally had landed on his feet one day and realized he was going to pin down any working orders and mechanisms before he jumped into the 'rough' ever again.

"Very sensitive, Jim, because there's a murderer on the loose. I think the girl is the key. I want you to get to know her, Commander." Formality, thought Jim. Now, things would get serious.

"You don't mean interview her, do you?" He pulled on his tie.

"Right, date her. You'll be there a while. I don't need to tell a young buck the drill. Let her tell you things. Jim, it may be the only route we have."

"Tell me about this young woman." Jim would now gain insight into the extent the admiral had extended his snooping.

"Name's Marna, never married, about twenty-seven. She's a hell of a woman, Jim..flies, swims, skis..has a real mechanical bent."

"She know any of this story about her dad?"

"I don't think so, even so she and her parents were close; but I have no evidence she knows much about either parent's life before she was born. They've lived in that place only some ten years..hers, now. But where did he come up with that kinda loot? That has to be part of the puzzle. You're not buying into that time paradox bit, are you?"

"Open mind, Admiral..can't afford to close up. I don't believe in gravity or dowsing but use both. Something happened in 1951. I wasn't there, only heard what you told me. Whatever went down, we work with the results. Now, do I have this assignment straight? I'm to get acquainted with Marna. Gantry? I'm to operate short of courting her?"

"Nothing short of, Jim. I shouldn't need to show an eagle how to fly. ..Now, you come and go as you see fit. Come home when you want, but live a normal life based in Saxtons Harbor."

"What can I disclose?"

"No secrets, you make the scenario. Navy officer on leave, investigator. You wing it." Rankin went to the desk and took from a drawer a packet. "Here, ID for TSB...FAA. Want an FBI shield? No I didn't think so. Here, how about Treasury or Federal Marshall." Jim took them all. "You really want the FBI?"

"Might come in handy. You never know..maybe if I need a porter or some other leg work the bureau will oblige a little more willingly."

"Boy, you don't forget, do you?"

"Forgive, yes...forget, never!"

"You've got all the financial backing you want. Jim, you may be up to your ass in no time. I don't know how many know how much about what. Something went down in 1951...45 for that matter. Others know and may know a lot more than we can guess." At this point the admiral wiped the back of his neck with a bar towel, and Jim knew he was headed for a ride.

"Can you tell me any more about the girl...make that young woman?"

"Writer..career going nowhere..may have taken a job as instructor of history at the local college. She's about as striking appearing a young woman as you will find...don't think her dance card's filled, though. As I say, she has the commanding beauty of form that only activity in sports will generate; but she'll get under the hood of a truck and trouble shoot, or a plane or a tank for Christs sake."

"You going to pull your spooks in?"

"Wh-what?"

"Pull your dogs off, please. If I run into any, I'll lean hard."

"Jesus, Jim.."

"Just do it, Admiral, please." Jim was not going to be a ping pong ball.

"Yeah, sure."

Jim felt it in his gut the old man wanted something beyond running to ground a killer. The story related thus far was too utterly fantastic; and to be sure putting a bomb in somebody's aircraft was not the sort of prank you let a perp get away with. Just what in hell was it Pete Rankin wanted thirty years after he met a young navy flier under circumstances beyond understanding?

"Any of those serving on *Antietam* surface since?"

"Dahlgren, poor slob, couldn't hold his liquor. Right after Korea he was in trouble for falsifying accounts and was forced to resign. He came to light on the east coast, New York, I think."

"New York, you think," Jim whispered under his breath. The admiral knew damn well.

"What did you say?"

"Just thinking out loud what we know. You've got your man. I'll leave any time."

"Fine, seventy-two hours…get your home affairs in order. Take your car on per diem, and you can call up air transportation on site any time."

"Guess that's it. Permission to leave."

"Wise guy, when did you ever need permission to leave or for anything else?" Jim was on his feet. The admiral rose and extended his hand. "She's a sweetheart, Jim, be nice to her."

4

An annoyance to her dreams resolved to her ringing phone, and repeated probes with her left hand revealed it already under her covers with her.

"Marna...I know it's early..no, wake up and talk to Nancy. Breakfast, can you smell the coffee..see the pancakes at Beals? Meet me in half an hour. We've got to talk. Classes are over, thanks be. We've got to nail our field of dissertation."

Dressing, for Marna, was a simple affair. Maine's rugged beauty inspired a colorful and wear resistant garb, boots, pants, shirt, which kept the wearer secure against the elements of Maine weather, while bearing a native attractiveness. Clerks behind the scene at Solly's Outfitters' Boutique rolled their eyes at the singular magnificence taken on by their shirts and jeans during Marna's try-on sessions.

A native American trading center provided her with accessories and any décor which she chose to wear. So it was this morning, she gave her long, dark hair a toss and simply tied it back, secured a beaded choker at the neck and placed one silver and turquoise bracelet on her left wrist.

As always she drove onto Beal's Wharf and walked as quietly as she knew how into the restaurant known as Beal's Cuddy; and, as usual, forks clattered on plates as male faces looked onto her passing as she moved to the booth where waited Nancy. She at an earlier appearance had been piped aboard with similar fanfare and greeted her friend with a mug of coffee in hand. Nan had to tilt her head slightly back to look into Marna's eyes, and blonde ringlets swung accordingly as she did so.

A slight difference in character, more appropriately named social graces, was built into each young woman's guidance system. Nancy knew she was a fine figure of a woman and responded with ease and gratifying familiarity with the young fishermen, contractors and seasonal rusticators who frequented the Cuddy.

Marna was totally unconscious of "looks". Her physical endowment allowed her to swim, dive, ski and run. She tried to eat right, except at blowouts at the Cuddy, during those times when everyone was having a good time laughing and singing. So, she wasn't self conscious when she strode into the restaurant. Her mind's eye saw the scene as good natured people who simply liked her.

"I had no idea, Nan, it was so late when you called. Thanks, we do have to get on with this." It was then six o' clock. Katie knew what both wanted, and had it ready. Both were served a breakfast with which Maine woodsmen and fishermen are familiar. The reader who isn't familiar had best leave it there, for consuming such a breakfast is an art form as demanding as the article itself.

"I'm on fire with our idea, Marn, but where in hell do we start?"

"General Court archives, historical societies...maybe private solicitation.."

"But we have nothing to start with or from..."

"Well, my thinking steers me to 1777 after the battle of Saratoga...not much going on, Howe blundering into Chesapeake Bay trying to find the Delaware River and Philadelphia. I don't think what might be available as public knowledge will be much help. If a Continental Navy vessel actually interdicted such a plot, we'd have nothing for our thesis. My contention is....." She took a long drag from her coffee mug. "...A privateer would have been the agency for deflecting the shot."

"Seems like such a long shot. How do we even know such a privateer worked out of Maine, er-r, Massachusetts? Why not Virginia, or Connecticut?"

"Start somewhere. Hey, we aren't committed. Give me some other suggestions for a thesis."

"No, I like it. You sure you're ready for this, Marna?" Nancy's voice dropped in pitch, and Marna didn't want to be fawned over. She was over it. It was five months ago.

"Think what a lot of fun it could be; we'll meet a lot of people, and there's got to be old letters and documents somebody's held onto, genealogies. I wish I could explain the feeling that has come over me, well like…since I ran into those people on the old schooner…"

"Marna, I still think you were dreaming."

"You won't when I show you the clothing they loaned me." Finally the meal was over.

"You had enough? I'm going to follow you home, then you come with me to the Meadows. Gotta pick someone up there, the new Pyschology Chair."

"Now?"

"Yeah, we can toss Katie some money on the way out."

Nancy put the top and the accelerator down. Marna fought the backdraft which bunched her hair about her face, while Nancy drove unencumbered by flailing hair. The scenery flew by on the road inland and to the small country airport.

"You know, Marn, this could be the craziest idea for a dissertation. I can hear Lennie Fenster, now."

"He can't find his way across the sidewalk. Lennie's the least of our concerns. At worst. We will have a heck of a story. "What's this up ahead, a fire?" They had rounded a turn and were straightening when they came in sight of a line of mostly pickup trucks parked along the road. Nancy swerved into the first available parking space between a Ram Charger and a Jimmy. They were beside a level field, and what was happening was a demonstration of close order drill and parade ground maneuvers.

"Tricorn hats, Nan, and look at the crossed white belts. " Marna stood on her seat. "Those are powderhorns, and they're not carrying broomsticks."

"Those are real, Marna." If Nancy were the more urbane of the two, Marna was the more traveled. Her life until her high school years at Saxtons Harbor were spent in one naval air station after another, following her dad's rise in rank and responsibility. Nancy had been raised on the Philadelphia Main Line and chose Ossipee University at the Harbor, where the two girls met and were now teaching.

Nancy saw the parade ground as a sporting event of ambitious fellows and proudly announced to her friend that Erik Lehn, her one and only, was captain of the militia company, his cousin, the guidon bearer of the platoon now executing silent drill.

Marna saw the period costumes and flourishes in the romantic past. In fact her mental construct placed six drummers beating cadence where none marched. She heard fifes. She saw and felt more as Nancy went on.

There's all ages out there. Some of the guys remember the Twenty-ninth Division at St. Lo, the Twenty-eighth at the Ardennes. Wives and sweethearts play a big part, making uniforms and cheering the lads on. See? Quite a few of 'em turned out. That was the way it was in the battles, but women got a bad rap as camp followers from historians who couldn't tell their ass from second base. That's why I wanted to get into the part played by women in the Revolution."

"No reason we can't find something and play it up big, Nan."

"I can't get over your confidence. You know something?"

"I have some ideas." Marna's ideas always seemed to come from some strange inner intuition that men and women have joked about for years. As she watched the flanking moves she could see the fields of Townsend up the coast where the Penobscot Expedition of 1779 hoped to enlist a couple thousand militia. They found less than half that number in Colonel McCobb's regiment, rousing to go to Bagaduce. She could all but hear the commands that would march the men down the wagon road to waiting ships in the harbor.

British fortification of the heights at what is now Castine threatened the activities of privateers from Townsend eastward, and Massachusetts's General Court thought to end this threat forthwith, enlisting General Peleg Wadsworth in charge of troops, Paul Revere, artillery officer and Commodore Saltonstall in charge of a fleet of some forty-two ships and sloops. It turned into a fiasco the likes of which would not beset an American navy until December 1941, all ships lost or scuttled ahead of a force of six British ships which simply outgunned the Americans.

Marna was lost in this event trip through her head, and Nancy had to shout to be heard over the crash of gunfire that marna imagined. " Got to get going, Marn. Boy, you really go underground, Girl."

"We're going to do just fine, I know it. The dirty tricks is the thesis."

On the road to the airport once more, the going was quiet until a stretch limo bulleted past them so close, Nancy decried another coat of paint.

"Son of a bitch…I'll kill him! Did you see that?"

"Nancy, slow down, you're not getting anywhere taking after him. We don't need to be wrecked, now." Nancy plowed ahead in her little convertible until the grassy reaches of the Meadows appeared up ahead. "I could sure do a coffee and a donut, maybe."

"Marna, you're always doing that! You eat a horse, then want to eat the harness and never gain a pound." Nancy was at odds with always having to watch out for her intake of food. She hung a right on the gravel without slowing, then onto a grassy knoll showing evidence of recent tire marks. She stopped, and they sat a moment looking about without speaking. Nothing stirred in the breeze but an old wind sock and nearby grasses.

Two Cessnas, a North American SNJ-5 trainer and a Stearman N2S biplane sat tethered against a chance blow. Sun glistened from shiny wing planes across the parking strip. The control tower perched atop an old henhouse, and a radar antenna rotated above green tinted windows. Marna's mouth went dry. It had been such a day last December the Earth stopped turning beneath her feet.

"Must be he's late. Good." Nancy was glad they hadn't kept him waiting.

"Wouldn't he be more comfy on a commuter flight?" One wasn't due 'til afternoon.

"You gotta be kidding," blurted Nancy. "Roni?"

"Roni, is it?" Marna was ready to pounce

"He's made his own arrangement for a plane, wouldn't have it any other way."

"Something you're not telling me, Duckie. I'm convinced you get around, but why these older types?"

"What older…?" The roar came from barely above their heads like a crashing wave, and a shiny wing passed yards above the car. Marna screamed and slid off the seat. Nancy gasped, "Good God, that's him!" Marna crawled back up on the seat and gazed ahead as the aircraft, a twin Beech, climbed steeply. She was blown out of her reverie, reviewing the men on the strange schooner as some sort of maritime re-enactment society such as the Continental muster down the road when the Beechcraft twin flathatted them.

"He sure did toss his airfield approach guide out the window. Look at him climb! Oh, I can't look. The aircraft isn't stressed for that. He's making a split "S" to final approach." She drew the back of her hand across her forehead. "Nancy, did you tell me this guy is the Pyschology Chair?"

"Yeah, but I think you ought to know he is also Colonel Ronen Dayan of the Israeli Airforce on leave of absence."

Marna stood on her seat, looking all about her as if expecting some sudden onrush. "Any more little surprises, Miss Marsh? Holy Hannah!"

The glossy, red lightning bolt trim on the twin Beech glistened as the plane taxied to park beside the SNJ and stopped, propellors coming to a halt with a final jerk. The two sprang from the car as if catapulted and approached the aircraft as a large figure of a man heaved himself from the confines of the cabin and stood facing them.

He was big as a tree, wore a light blue jump suit and laced cordovan boots; and Marna found herself staring dumbly at his craggy features and brown, wavy hair...part of the aircraft reflecting from mirror sunglasses.

"Marna, this is Roni." Marna, this is Roni, her mind mimicked. Just like Nancy to omit all titles. Marna wished she had dressed this morning with a little more sophistication...wondered if Roni Whatever watched her through his shades. She was, on top of nonplused, tongue-tied and feeling foolish. Wasn't he going to remove those mirrors? Suddenly, he spoke to her, then everyone was speaking. He held up a hand.

"Gossip we do later..first to lock up the aircraft." He poked into the cabin of the plane and looked about. "Where did Bernie say to look for gust locks?" he spoke out the hatch to no one in particular. Furious activity ended with wingtips tethered to stakes pounded in the turf and wheels chocked. No sooner in the car, Roni asked, "Where do we get pizza?"

"Pizza it will be, Ron; Marna and I will take you to our favorite place at the harbor after we get you to your quarters and you are settled."

"I'm for getting a sandwich and coffee here at the grille...."

"Yeah, right. You know, she's hardly eaten a thing all morning." Nancy drove the short distance to what served as a terminal and led the way into the breezy little site of the Airport Grille. They found the counter empty and handy.

"Hi, folks..Nan. What'll it be?" A hefty young man made a single swipe along the counter with a towel.

"Roni? Just coffee for me."

"Lobster roll."

"Marna? I can hardly wait."

"Oh, coffee." Nancy saw the vacant look in the eyes and feared the worst. Marna was for sure reacting to her presence once more at this fateful location. This time, voices, recorded permanently in her subconscious, began to replay.... "..once again in a blue moon, Dear. Engines revved, pushed to firewall, and the blue Navajo started down the field on its take off roll, lifted and proceeded out over the bay in a steady climb to seaward. Then another sun appeared in the sky. "...Yeah, and I'll have a lobster roll, too...is that pumpkin pie I see over there?" Nancy rolled her eyes.

A youngish man joined them at the counter with a familiar greeting. "Oh, hi, Al. Roni Dayan, Al Brandon. Al's one of the top fishermen on the coast. We'll most likely be eating lobster taken by him. Al, Roni's going to teach at Ossipee.."

"That so? What's your thing?"

"Pschology."

"Well, there..works for me. Prob'ly a good thing someone understands something about it. Most folks 'round heah take theirselves too seriously...most likely mistakes to begin with."

"That's a good one. I'll need to remember that one."

"Oh, Marna, by the way, day or so back...or was it yesterday? Well, couple fellas was askin' after you."

"Who was that, Al?"

"Never seen 'em before. No one I'm aware saw 'em come in to harbor..they was some fog makin' in; but they left the dock in a long row boat..whitehall design..you know, with the wineglass stern. What is it, Marn..you know 'em, then?"

"Nan, it has to be them. I knew it; they're still around. They give a name, Al..?"

"Yeah, I guess. Let's see. One called the other MacNab."

"You tell 'em I'd be around..they ask for my number?"

"Nope. Ask me, they was more interested to know that you was safe than actually finding you...not like guys on the make or anything like that. Never seen 'em around before."

"They're here, Nan, or never left. They say anything about a big schooner, Al?"

"Nope, just asked a few questions and was gone..like that."

The ride back to town started off in carefree fashion. "What kept you, Ron?"

"So, I make a little detour to pass over those hills west of here I think I see snow. Is this usual, Nancy?"

"Not unusual in the White Mountains even in midsummer. You got the charts I sent you?" The stretch limo was holding back and as yet unnoticed. "Any trouble with the flight plan? You fly *OMNI, VFR,* or what?"

"Must have left the charts with Bernie in Teterboro." Nancy put a hand to her head. "How about a certificate? Bernie did manage a certificate or a student permit or something, didn't he?"

"What certificate? Bernie says I fly here, no trouble." He waved a hand in a gesture of dismissal. "Some day I should fly back to Teterboro, no problem. Now, if I would have taken a right turn at…at.." He squirmed to reach into a pocket while residing in the cramped, for him, front passenger seat. Marna tugged on her hair in the back seat. He produced an auto club road map. "Here, I-95, yes, I should have followed more closely." This time Nancy slapped her forehead, then hauled on the wheel to wrench her right front tire from the soft berm.

"OK, let's take Roni to Faculty Row and, what…about three o' clock we'll take him to Beal's for that pizza. Then, why don't we go to your place for dessert and that nice walk you've been promising? When…what in hell is he doing….?" The stretch began to pull abeam, and Marna saw the tinted front window begin to open.

"He's got a gun, the freakin' raghead!" What happened next took place so quickly there was no time for panic. The three lowered their profiles automatically, and Nancy hit the brake, the gas, the horn and the wheel all at about the same time, starting the convertible into a four wheel drift. Nan had still been slightly in the lead, and the other driver didn't expect what she did to him, over corrected and his front wheel was pulled by the soft berm into the grass and saplings. A lot of bark was ripped from a stand of oaks, and the big Linc heaved over on its beam ends

The three occupants of the little car were not long silent and began trying to figure out just what had happened. Roni had the final word when he announced that he didn't think the hostiles were after his friends. "They wanted me, I think."

"But how can they think they can get away with trying to kill us? Let's get the cops!"

"That will be an humanitarian gesture, but all they will get from the police is help no matter what charges you bring against them."

"The hell you say!"

"Your country allows them to enter with armed body guards with diplomatic immunity. You can do nothing. Let it pass."

It was late afternoon when Nancy and Marna brought Roni to Marna's house by the shore. A chill came off the Atlantic, and Marna was soon at work starting a fire on the hearth but not without Roni's help bringing firewood in from the porch. "You say this gray appearing wood is driftwood? That could be an endless supply of fuel."

"It is about endless, as long as someone puts the time and effort dragging it up to the house and cuts it." She saw the results of careful arrangement of kindling as the smoke drew upward.

"Marna, what is this marvelous little boat on the stone shelf? Did someone in your family make this? Oh, forgive..you are maybe not ready..?"

"It's OK, Ron. I'm OK with it, really." She looked up at him from arranging larger wood on her masterwork. "Dad made it. Oh. I guess he was real young when he did."

"Your fire..it feels already very good..right to the soul. I was about to ask you if you thought it would snow tonight. You will tell me something of the little vessel?"

She was relieved to know she was comfortable with the explanation. "...Has to be a privateer schooner, probably of a type used during the War of 1812 with Great Britain."

"He has crafted every pulley and these..belaying pins." It became obvious to Marna that he knew far more of American History than one might suspect right off. "The guns..can we guess at the weight of metal fired from one?"

Echo Horizon

"My guess is nine or twelve pound ball." Nancy joined them and advised her very special pudding and hard sauce would need an hour and a half and why not have that walk while waiting?

On their way to the rocky rim of the great cove Marna explained that her family's land extended on both sides of the cove, about two hundred acres in all, "and all for sale to the highest bidder." That outburst surprised Nancy who assumed her friend would settle in given time. She started to speak, but they had reached a rather abrupt drop off, so she concentrated on the safe placement of each footfall on the rough edge.

Resident fishing boats at mooring pointed into the wind, silent sentinels contemplating sea marks and courses run that day. Much larger vessels could shelter here and probably did, Marna stated. Roni studied grades and depths as they jumped and climbed along the way to the head of the cove.

"Is all your land as rough and tree covered as appears looking back from the house?"

"Strange as it may seem, I don't know," she offered with a shrug. "I've never really explored..always busy with something else. In school it was..well, Dad only bought the place less than ten years ago."

"We should maybe make up for time lost." They arrived at the upper end of the cove a little battered..sun at treetop level barely lighting a stream entering the intertidal zone over pebbles and broken seashells. Where water ran from a marshy region, large, flat rocks deeply embedded made a straight line across the stream. Steep ground on either side would have made this a perfect location for a dam, Marna thought.

"What of the flat stones?"

"Local legend has it a mill stood here a long time ago. They were probably footings for a dam. Looks like a lot of water could be blocked in back there." The flood gates parted. He wanted to talk history, so Marna spoke of the activities of privateers in the time of the American Revolution, how a seafaring people lived on these shores. "Farmers and fishermen owned a sloop, a brig or schooner just as their modern counterparts own a pick up truck today."

She told of the Penobscot Expedition and how the disaster put an end to privateering on this immediate coast. Nancy and Roni absorbed themselves in little mysteries, and Marna noticed she was experiencing some kind of identification with the surrounding scene that was at once eerie and fascinating. They had skirted the edge of the shore, virtually forced away from the upland by thick bayberry and moose maple and wild dogwood. As she looked away in the direction of her house she might as well have been experiencing a different time plane, since her mind had cleared the acres of trees and replaced them with pasture and mowing fields. But strangely, though lacking in definition, the outline of a manse serenely juxtaposed with a barn appeared to her, sited facing the sea. Time stood still and she dared not breath while gazing past the manse on a large sailing hull, masts stepped, posed on blocks and awaiting a launching tide. Just as quickly as the scene had materialized it dissolved and would be dismissed as a sort of reverie were it not for the detail and stimuli of other senses. She imagined the aroma of tar and oakum. The vessel had not its suit of sail, but lift lines drummed on the masts in the light breeze. All about had been new mown fields.

"Marna, you OK? Marna?"

"Sure..yeah. I'm OK. Lets bushwhack to the house sort of over that way. You guys up for it?" They traversed a hillside given over to oak and yellow birch, and once away from the edge of the shore the way was remarkably clear of tangling brush. She remembered her father mentioning that he'd never found poison ivy on the place...now her place, her mind emphasized. Roni was looking toward the brightest point in the west and noted a tall treetop for reference. When they broke into a grassy glade, he found his reference point once more. Nancy lamented the fate of her chocolate bread pudding they tarry much longer in their return quest.

Immediately in their path was a line of boulders as if the remains of a foundation which it very likely was once they established the location of the other three sides of a large rectangle. "Could this have been a barn?" Nancy threw in reluctantly.

"Sure might have been if that were the house beyond," added Roni. "We couldn't be far from the water's edge. My guess would be the house faced south, Marna, you agree?"

"That was the custom if this site is as old as it appears to be. A whole culture in New England was based on optimum use of sun and drainage of air and water. Ground was the storage place for root crops and fruit." They stood at the edge of a cellar hole only partially filled, in which a long dead pine trunk stood broken about twelve feet above grade. The tree by any reasonable inspection had been dead fifty years and took a couple hundred years to attain its size.

By this time they knew they had their work cut out for them to return to the house before dark and unscathed. Nancy remarked on the circle of stones which had to be a well curb, and Marna described for them what she perceived to have been a well sweep for the raising of water.

"What are the large shrubs that have found their way into the cellar?"

"Oh, Ron, we're a month early, but those are lilacs, most probably planted from imported stock two hundred years ago. I'll bet they're purple, and the fragrance is like nothing you've ever experienced." Their departure was by what could have been a once maintained roadway beyond sight of a few badly tumbled slates and marble slabs tucked back from their way beneath two huge red oaks.

Nancy flew to the kitchen on their return and rescued a well browned pudding while Marna and Roni prodded and refueled the fire. The first stars showed through the afterglow, and with the pudding pronounced a success, Roni asked that they have a look outside at the stars.

"Mind the ledges; it's a long drop to the water." The moon had set hours ahead of the sun, and the tide was filling the cove. Suddenly Marna recalled the fragments of conversation from the deck of the schooner. She recalled grumbling about something buried in the cove. By their reference to an island lying outside the mouth of that embayment, she knew a possibility existed they referred to this one. But why not references to a charted position? She wondered if they would ever come by, for, obviously they were still in the vicinity.

Starlight revealed the positions of her friends. She wished she had thought to bring a flashlight, but the porch light gave some glow to the area. Surf growled, washed seaweed and assaulterd barnacle encrusted ledge. She continued. "My dad used to say stars are guides for those who know them."

"I salute your Atlantic stars. Have you ever viewed the Heavens from a desert? The stars are each a fiery ball. We have even all that sophisticated stuff in the Mirage-3, but so many times I come home by the stars and that good horizon at the nose...wait. What's that? No, above the cove." Marna and Nancy looked where he pointed and Nancy told him they were looking at Scorpio.

"The bright red star in the neck is Antares." Roni indicated another group of stars. "Which, that one on the left? Oh, down to the left, that's Sagittarius the Archer or the teapot because it makes a perfect teapot. Later in the summer it'll be higher and upright, more like it's getting ready to pour."

"When is the tide at its lowest, Marna?"

"About three tomorrow morning."

"When can we dig clams? I am told the clams from Maine are the most tasty in the world.

"Sure, in a few days the tide will be low in the forenoon. How about Saturday? Want to go clamming, Nancy?"

"Count me out...plans Saturday."

"We could pick another day, Nan."

"That's OK..not into clams. You guys dig."

"Well, Roni, Saturday, then...nine o'clock?"

Echo Horizon

"Good, we dig clams."

"Careful, Ron, that's an awful drop to the water." Even as she cautioned, a wave broke with threatening violence too close. Her words attenuated on the wind as he moved away in the starlight, ledge to ledge as only a mountain goat should. But soon he stopped and leaned on some monstrous slabs of stone raised upon others and providing an opening to the sea.

"Shine the light this way. See, these rocks are strangers to the area and must be transported. Just room for a great gun, two maybe."

"Dad had a notion this spot had been fortified, probably for the war of 1812. No telling, no records that I know of."

"We could give that some serious attention, Marna," offered Nancy. "I've collected some fascinating material"

"Perhaps privateers have used this cove as a base," suggested Roni. He straightened from his examination of the stones and faced south toward an eerie glow from breaking surf. The constant roar sifted their voices. He indicated a line of reefs forming a crescent from the opposite side of the cove's mouth. Then his composure vanished. "Did you see that!?"

"See what ?" inquired Nancy unmoved by a change in tenor.

"Scorpio! It disappears before my eyes." Marna glanced skyward in time to see Antares blink out. Her blood chilled at the very unreasonableness of the event. Her heart felt poised ready to take flight as she stood shivering.

"The whole thing is disappearing!" As Nancy spoke Scorpio seemed to erase itself a star at a time right to left, then the right corner of Sagittarius.

"It's like…maybe..a passing ship, and its sails are blocking the stars."

"Get real, Marn." Nancy put on an indifference she didn't feel. "Gotta be a passing cloud."

"Ladies, please, have you seen a cloud defy the wind?" They fell silent as Sagittarius quietly occulted. Fully as disturbing as the dissolution of Scorpio was its return.

"But, Roni, there wasn't any vessel," whispered Nancy.

Bert Howe

5

"I think you really meant it when you said you wanted an early start. You did just great finding the place after one visit. We've time before the tide is out far enough. How about some breakfast?" Roni made a face, and she realized he didn't wish to appear too forward. "Won't take any time at all..oranges and grapefruit in the fridge. Grab what you like. Coffee's on. We can have pancakes, ham and eggs, bacon and eggs….ooh, Roni, I'm so sorry…"

"My new friend, do not carry on. Lighten up. Not to worry. For me is no problem…eat what I like. You say what you want; it will be fine."

This guy is incredible, she thought to herself. "OK, why not? Let's have at it."

"You are in good cheer today. Let me guess. You were chosen for the Dart Series Lectures in the fall term. I think."

"You know, don't you? Yeah, I bit the bullet, but I still don't know. I'm a little.."

"Allow me to say this for you. You have encountered some weirdos, and I mean this sincerely. In Tel Aviv would have been a much different approach to university study. But here is the indoctrination. A student should have a road map to know where the genuine learning opportunities lie."

Marna whistled. "You don't pull any punches, do you?"

"Isn't it always time for truth? I can't believe the number of faculty here who must hate their country! Everything is wrong. Hatred is fomented among conjured classes for other groups, social and economic. The government must heal and pay for all society's ills. With all this the student must agree with the mentor's demented ideals or…"

"Or fail. Roni, is this going on in summer session?"

"I think it will make no difference." He spoke hurriedly around bites of breakfast, enjoying his coffee. "In my little country a college student would build on that learned in earlier years. He has been taught much to prepare him to preserve his country, not tear it down. Here the undergraduates march in lock step to someone else's political zeal. Everything is political...clothes, whom one dates, what one thinks, says."

Finally, laden with clam hoe and hod, they wended their way on a bayberry lined path to where mud flats glistened in the late spring sun. "Yes, look for small holes in the mud. As we step you can see the squirts of water. Clams are digging their way down from threat..not so dumb. But we're going to dig them out." As she spoke she was having trouble removing her feet from the mud without leaving her boots behind. She drove the tines of a short handled fork into the muck at an angle and drew back. Five good size clams made the short lift to the hod. This was a simple basket made of laths with a bent alder sapling for a handle. "Dig beyond the clams. Try not to put the tines through the clam like I did this one. We'll keep it, though."

"They had their work cut out for them when the tide turned. They wanted a goodly mess for supper and conjured visions of clams steamed or fried in batter and hot clam broth or chowder. No breeze refreshed them, only an occasional splash of cold water in the face from a settled pool. The work was not easy.

"Like I should walk around shaped like a "U"? Who will bend us straight again?"

"Look there. You missed three big ones. Gotta work faster before water fills the holes and you can't see them." Marna dug while other thoughts insinuated her mind. This had to be the cove she heard the men discuss when she was below decks on the schooner. Could something be lurking here beneath the silt of ages? What were they talking about? They hadn't seemed very pleased, whatever it was. They obviously were historians and archaeologists and could have referred to anything during the last three centuries.

By noon they agreed to stop; they had dug enough for a feast. Marna rammed her fork into the mud once more where it fetched up hard, throwing her off balance onto her side in the mud. She was a mess, and she allowed the world to be first audience to her opinion of the situation.

Echo Horizon

She worked the fork free, and curiosity drove her to scrape at whatever it was beneath the surface. Had to be something like an old tree trunk. Roni added his effort when they decided on other tools from the house. They each grabbed a beer from the cooler and blew at the suds on the way up. Whatever else was down there they scraped with hoe and shovel to reveal a large square timber and cleaned off enough mud and debris so they could see it was hand hewn. Another was close beside it, then others. Lying there in the mud, one end slightly sloping down into the depths, was the remains of a very old vessel. Roni was fascinated to distraction as he worked the shovel. Unmindful of the proximity of lunch time, but satisfied himself with another beer. Very thick planking was fastened to the underside of the ribs and appeared to Roni to be in line with the length of the cove. The ends of the ribs were away from shore and, far from clearing away from the entire structure, they knew it to be a large vessel.

"The keel must be much deeper in the mud in that direction. What of these holes in the planks? They are oak, maybe?"

"Must be worm holes, Roni."

"Such worms, they are fifteen, twenty millimeters across, and such dense wood."

So, something was in the cove after all. She wanted to know more, but water steadily claimed their find and covering the flats quickly. "Tide's coming, Roni, we could go to the house and make lunch."

Lunch assumed a life when they decided to steam the clams after only a modest rinse and the risk of some grit. Clams are generally left in salt water long enough for them to eject the sandy particles from their being. Marna found some wine, put the butter on to melt and carried luncheon settings to the porch facing the sea.

Ron was obsessed with the historic possibilities surrounding their find, and she paused between bites and mused on a connection between their discovery and the words she had heard on the schooner. It was then she regaled him with the accounts of that day, jogging in the fog. He listened attentively to her relating of the experience on the very odd vessel. He reserved comment. She found she enjoyed his company. She noted something gentle in his repartee wherein he found it unnecessary to come up with a fast opinion, or jump on her lines or offer up a parallel experience. His psyche seemed to be nourished by her offerings without thumping his own chest. She was at a loss to explain fully for her satisfaction.

They cleared away the dishes and pans, but in her imagination stars occulted. She couldn't concentrate; something controlled her thoughts, and she forced her attention back to respond to his comments relating to the boat model on her mantel. The sun reflected from something he dangled in front of his face. It was a small gold ornament. "My God, where did you find that?"

"Tucked in the stern of the little boat."

"I couldn't imagine where it had been lost. That's the Sagittarius charm from my mother's zodiac bracelet." She stopped short of continuing that she had meant to take the bracelet to a jewelers for repair, then fell into despair on recalling where she had left it.

Roni had left his lights on with the resulting dead battery, so she urged him into her blazer. On the way to Faculty Row, he congratulated her again on the new assignment upcoming. "Rumor has it the department head is thinking of stepping down. I have heard Mrs. Fenster causes talk behind his back, she is what do you say...the lush. You are acquainted by chance with...she is named Nadine?"

Marna drew a quick breath while rounding a corner and came out on the straight with, "That...!" She successfully stopped her expostulation. This was not a conversation she wanted to continue.

"Precisely."

That surprised her.

Late Saturday afternoon activity exhibited nothing on campus to call attention. She had taken notice of two stretch limousines with tinted windows parked on the town street. Two vans with similarly colored windows were parked farther along. Roni studied them as she drove along but said nothing.

On leaving campus, she gave vent to rage that had been building within her for months. "CHRIST!" She didn't understand what it was had caused her to be so passive in that space of time and was determined to reverse it. A yearning to explore, to discover, had its genesis that morning on the flats. She knew next to nothing about the property her parents had left her, and it was time to learn. She had been a loser long enough.

What was that clown up to? One of the vans turned broad on in front of her as if to block the way. It stopped. She reacted swiftly, turning her blazer onto the sidewalk by driving skillfully between trees and hydrant.. Coming to a driveway she swung back onto the road and didn't look back. She fingered the .380 Colt on the seat beside her.

She could have caused severe injury or death to the occupants if she had rammed the van. That had been her first sparking impulse and she wished on reflection she had the brass to do just that. Well, she could go home and sleep peacefully because she didn't have to explain anything to anyone.

Soon her mind drew calmer thoughts, and she recalled the old stone foundations they had found and imagined the spot cleared and farmed with animals in abundance. When she drove up her lane, the sun was low and promised a beautiful sunset and a chilly evening. She got out and walked and looked into the cove. That was something she would give further attention..that old ship's remains. Would she be able to keep the curious away, particularly those new owners of everyones' land, the EPA?

Her immediate surroundings and reference faded as she imagined a great activity upland from the cove. Remembering the vision she had on the recent walk, she wondered if a vessel had actually ever been built here. If so there must be evidence. The tangle of brush could be hiding something. She walked as if seeing people in her mind's eye. She imagined they spoke to her. She felt as one of them, as part of a community. A feeling washed over her that she was a hurried person, trying to propel herself to an objective, and it was important. But how dreamlike, always a hindrance to keep her from where she wanted to be.

Just as quickly the scene vanished, but strangely, she no longer felt the morose sensation of being alone. Marna had always been a whole person before her life was trashed. Now, she could feel the effect of being that person once more. Her world widened as she looked toward her house, determined to possess it, rather than be possessed. Now they would become acquainted.

She charged up onto the porch and went inside to prepare supper, thinking the while of the changes that she would make, starting with the kitchen. She placed a whole frozen pizza in the oven and made plans for the next day, or what would be left of it after she had made a thorough exploration of the old wreck in the mud. How could she best describe her new and enthusiastic outlook? Even the incident with van hadn't dampened her flair. Friends, friends, that was it. She knew she had friends, and that made all the difference.

6

The sun was hot on the flats the next day. She'd had to wait almost an additional hour for the lag in tides and had collected an arsenal of tools at the banking. The holes she and Roni dug the day before were filled with water and silt. Mussel shells glistened as did bits and pieces of stones.

About an hour into scraping mud from between ribs and working farther down the side and deeper toward the keel, as she assumed it had to be positioned, she paused and gazed aimlessly into a pool of water between two ribs while regaining her breath. She wiped a muddy hand across her face. No breeze refreshed her labor, and sun beat hotter. It glinted off two bright reflections close together, brass, perhaps. She reached without thought to pick one up and examine it. The realization came milliseconds before the screech. It was a bright disk with stamped ornamentation partly worn..a gold coin. She grasped the second, a twin of the first, and matter of factly held and examined them before the full impact hit. Excitement burst, and she leaped into the air. She jumped up and down, shouting for several moments before she realized she wasn't clearing the mud, but had hammered her way down, leaving as the only avenue of escape abandonment of her boots and a stocking-footed search for other coins.

There had to be more. Where had they come from? Was she the only one who knew they were there? The design on each coin was strange to her. It depicted an ancient ship, and shields seemed to be lettered. She was certain of an "A" on one shield and a "K" or "H" on the other. They were bigger than a half dollar, a bit smaller than a dollar. She wondered how long they had lain in the mud inside the vessel.

By the time a flooding tide drove her from the flats, she had hoed and raked for four hours, retrieved her boots, muscled the tools up the bank on all fours and consumed a six pack of beer. For her labors and pain of limb she brought to the house a dozen steamer clams and seventeen more coins, seven more like the first two and ten smaller ones differing in size and design. Close examination of one coin showed a rose on the face of it.

That night she slept with the gold under her pillow, if it could be called sleep. By morning her bed looked like a nine mile walk. Her excitement never abated. She started coffee at an early hour and set about a task she had never before undertaken...the thorough cleaning of a whole house. She ate lightly of toast and fruit and worked the morning through. A week before she was ready to place the property on the market. Now she was consumed with visions of a restored farm with a beautiful restoration of a manse, the way it must have appeared, back from the cove in a cluster of buildings and gardens. She would rebuild the dam and the mill to perform again its important tasks of a bygone era. Her new found wealth gave her the confidence she could afford her aims. She had some notion of the collector value of her treasure.

By late afternoon an astonishing thing happened. While stepping on the end of the hearth to dust the length of the mantel, she moved the boat. When she made a slight push against a panel just above, it gave way inward. She stepped to peer inside the resultant opening, and the panel closed. She pushed again and realized quickly that a slightly loose stone in the hearth operated a catch.

On further examination she realized a secure hiding place existed behind the panel, and she was quick in taking up her treasure and placing it in the vault. What a wonderful sense of relief to have her coins in a safe place.

A clean house and a nest egg of value beyond her knowing, these were affecting her thoughts, replacing recent depression, and she was rising to the surface. Her fractionated view of the universe was coming all of a piece.

Slowly she withdrew her hand from the trove, and it brushed against a smooth protrusion which moved slightly. She pressed her body to the cold stones of the fireplace at the first scraping noise, and a section of the wall to one side moved inward to reveal a compact entry. Curiosity was always big with Marna, but first she stepped to a table and withdrew a flashlight from a drawer.

Narrow steps led up and turned left. Between the steps and chimney was a small doorway beyond which she discovered that descent along the base of the chimney was possible but perilous by way of large, flat stones protruding from the chimney as steps. The chimney was huge. She chose to venture upward.

She had not known of this crypt and wondered if her dad had. The house had just begun to take on an identity as something beyond a cold and lonesome existence for her. The possibility of a sinister turn had so far not caught up with her passion for exploration. Her light turned orange, prompting her to retreat to the kitchen for a more reliable torch. She was determined to know where those steps led.

Marna thought she was circling the chimney. The dusty steps didn't creak. She sneezed. Thinking back, one of the bedrooms on the second floor seemed smaller than it should. Was she passing the second floor on the way to an attic? She continued on her eerie way, determined at this late date to learn of her house, paying no heed to the increasing moan of windsong in the eaves.

Her light gave detail to a space under the roof, and she was aware of the "el" shape of the building. From the intensity of cobwebs and dust, no one had been through this space in eons. She continued on with shuffling steps until she stumbled against an ancient trunk which she felt compelled to open regardless of sore shins.

Even a pile of artifacts from another era lying next to the trunk held little fascination as she wrenched open the lid, nearly tearing it from rusty hinges. Layers of ledgers, books, and rolled parchment reposed free of a lifetime of dust which covered the surrounding area. She took up as much as she could carry and headed for the daylight.

On impulse she had brought back to the kitchen what she perceived to be an historic treasure trove of information. Her next impulse, on viewing the pile of crumbling leather bindings, was to reduce the chill in the house by throwing the whole lot in the fireplace. She fought the impulse, not a good idea.

On the plain of indecision she noticed a name on what seemed to her to be an accounts ledger.

J.D.Skimpe, Mercantile

It didn't jump at her, rather more insinuated her thoughts. Its binding gave up the ghost as she separated pages bearing the stains of centuries. It was a list of credit entries under the heading

McCobb Cove

Marna guessed the ink was concocted from rusty horse shoe nails soaked in vinegar, good enough for drafting the Declaration of Independence. The next name did jump. It wasn't possible, but there it was.

J^{no} Alport Mill at McCobb Cove

She was aware neither of elation nor unease. But she continued more patiently with the pile before her. Until recently she had valued nothing tangible in her life and would be two thousand miles away in a heartbeat if a simple phone call would make it possible. Now, that name before her on the ledger induced a compulsion to find and return on board that schooner. What had the captain called it, the private armed schooner *Archer*? That was too much. Here was his very name. Could it be an ancestor?

The first officer had really gotten to her. She was drawn to him as if by a nostalgic something from a childhood dream. It was indefinable.

Who were they?

Items in the old ledger did amount to credits. Perhaps money was owed and services were rendered. This could be a ledger from an old counting house which preceded banks in America. In time bits and pieces fit together and she gained insight into a "now" which was every bit as real as the present.

She noticed the darkening, heard distant thunder. She was glad she had no plans to be working outside. What a good day to pull secrets from her find? Well, not much day remained and it was time to stoke the fire. She read well into the evening, unmindful of thunder and pelting rain until a chill caught her attention to hunger and the need for wood on the fire again. That attended to she went in the kitchen to throw a cold cut salad together and return to the living room. The tea would join in time.

Week by week accounts measured the pace of fortune. Fascination moved her beyond an ache growing behind her eyes. She unfolded the chronicles of a settler on these shores who started out to support life's maintenance with fishing and farming. He cut and shipped firewood to the Boston market for hard specie, then took up iron mongering.

He extended his estate by building a dam and mill on land purchased from the Kennebec Proprietors with privilege on a stream. McCobb's Cove. Where on Earth was McCobb's Cove? She had thought a mill existed at some time at the head of her cove, but she didn't make a connection.

She moved the books closer to the hearth, knowing she really wanted to retire for the night but unable to tear herself away. A date stood out, 1767, something about nether stones and dancers. Was she ready to share this find with the world? Who would care? Nancy would. What *had* she found! Nothing here might in the least aid in their thesis; and, yet, there might be the foundation for a thesis here which was far better. She began to hear the haunting words "..again in a blue moon". She knew she had found the reason for being.

The pile drew her on though her eyes were mere slits. Leather bindings, brittle with antiquity, crumbled in her hands. She craved every word and fought against frustrating mounting desire to sleep. She nearly came unglued when she held in her hands the log of a vessel and realized with a start she gazed upon the name *Archer*.

She had been aboard *Archer* just days ago, but yacht owners were forever borrowing names from stars or constellations, as well as from antiquity.

Bert Howe

The binding's gold leaf was nearly gone, and letters had been traced with something sharp. She had difficulty at first with the master's name, but no mistake, there it was. It resolved to Alport. This was too much for coincidence and she had a problem with intuition. The pages blurred, and she wiped tears from her eyes. Tragedy lurked behind the words and teased her sensors. Her genes might possess the key to when or what, but the who might lie forever undisclosed.

Those eccentric yachtsmen, what had they discovered which motivated them to build their vessel and so name it. She moved fragile pages and read from faded script.

> 29 April slushed the masts in morning watch & manned Pump 2 hrs. Gripes and does not pass stays smartly. Moved crates to aft hold theby easing sit'n Wind makes off westerly by seven bells. Thicken up thin and likely clear off cloudy. Spoke no sayl Florida straits northard.

Not tierces, not pipes nor casks, but crates. She scribbled a note on a paper napkin, then put aside the log in favor of a packet of letters, tied with what once might have been trawl line. It powdered in her fingers. She picked a letter, then went off in search of a reading glass and note pad.

The missive bore an impression in sealing wax after all these years. Local craftsmen had likely produced the crude paper. Fifteen minutes with the glass concluded the date of the letter to be 1772. Then her heart did flips at the revelation of the addressee, none other than J^{no} Alport. So, he built a mill, she thought; way to go J^{no}. Produce a product, then construct a vessel to carry it to a good market.

Probably produced some jobs along the way, she mused. Her country had been built by men such as this. She could understand Captain Alport, she knew. But where else had he made an appearance in historic context? Where had others found

Echo Horizon

reference to him? She remembered every moment she had spent on that run down replica of an ancient vessel. They must have laughed their heads off when they came upon her wet clothes. Bummer.

Aging script revealed reluctantly the text of a town grant.

> The Towen have voted and given liberty
> To J^{no} Alport yeoman of McCobbs Cove
> to dam the brook and seate up a mill therby
> next the toen landding and near the Parsioneg
> Fearm, Whear they shall see meet & to
> Hav a Convenient yard Rouem with way to
> S^d mill & to hav all the Towens right
> And interest in s^d Convenient sies for thorty
> Years after this tiem without enny molestation
> From the towen the s^d J^{no} Alport allowing for
> The damieg that May be don by reason of s^d
> Mill as Rasional men shall Judg.

With infinite care she studied the signature.

Caleb Gordon, Selecman

With eager enthusiasm she was swept up in the swirl of discovery. She wondered what possible aspirations drove the first Captain Alport. Her own world was not so gentle as it was easy, anything at the flip of a switch. Were people now basically any different than people living in 1772? Possibly she, as she felt like both eyeballs were looking out the same socket.

What of life and attitudes in earlier times? She needed to feel a presence, to know of the existence and struggles of people on this shore when these documents were trail markers of commerce. In her model she must exclude, radio, TV, petroleum power, electricity or steam.

She explored an account of conveyance of a tract of land by the Kennebec Proprietors to J.D. Skimpe, Esq. While her mind wove a tapestry of a reality within a time frame. Included in the transfer of title:

All and Several privileg on s^d stream
From headd of land to entry in McCobbe Cove.

Must have been some discussion on that issue. Such privilege was not easily given up. So then, she reasoned, the neighborhood needed a facility to grind corn, mill wheat and saw lumber. Neighbors supported one another in building a house and barn, if for no other reason, for mutual security and survival. If a neighbor were industrious to the extent of constructing a vessel to carry farm produce and lumber to profitable markets in-spite-of the Navigation Acts, the cargo represented the industry of many. She pondered what she thought such ambition would be met with in her time.

She sat back and gazed past her window at a darkened sea and decided to take just a short nap on a very inviting sofa at the far end of the room, but first a phone call.

"Nancy, how about breakfast at Beal's...sixish? Yeah, I think I've found something."

She stepped to a light switch and turned off all but two sconces on king posts which faced the sofa. She held every intention of getting right up, making tea, and returning to the documents.

Her eyes fixed on the small lamps, then ever so slowly rolled back in her head. She moved and refocused on the sconces lighted by tapers. She watched the tiny flames swaying in a draft, knew they were smoking and that her tapers required trimming. She knew she was dreaming. Marna expected to waken from this dream momentarily. An element of anxiety persisted. She was aggravated, almost irritated but knew she kept a pleasant countenance. She must dip more bayberry candles as she fancied them simply fine. But it was Sister who fashioned the finest of soaps. Mehitabel did squeal so when first the egg did float in her potash.

Spring was on the land, and Sister had awakened first again and pottered noisily in the buttery, nearly drowning out the strident call of the blackbird from the alders by the impound. Again Sister had prepared the early meal by the time she had entered the summer kitchen, adjusting her green muslin skirt. She joined Sister and Mother.

Father had departed for the schooner's stocks, and a full day of milling awaited her and Mother. Porridge with biscuits and tea must keep them the day long, for they would not stop to eat again until day's end.

She walked to the mill and inhaled the aroma of sweet grass, looking on the green all about. She was barefoot, though her father had worked long at the joinery to buy her shoes with buckle of iron. She had fashioned her own skirt, blouse and apron.

She climbed nimbly as a sixteen year old can to the dam. The mill wheel was turning and belts made a "thwacketa" sound as lacings struck wooden pulleys. She felt the sun on her face as she watched water race from the sluice and splash on rocks beneath her. She turned at the sound of a trout rising in the impound.

Her mother called out to Sarah, and she knew it was time for her to carry cider to the men working on the vessel that they wet the eye. Deadwood rose on blocks extending from the edge of the cove all the way to the blueberry. It would be a fine schooner, and the men were kindly toward her and Sister. How they labored even with the joys of companionship. All had worked at sledging timber to the site all through the last terrible winter.

Asa and the Pritchard brothers told the most ribald stories, of a certain not for gentler ears. And Caleb's big ox, Herschel, the beast would fair stop at his draft whilst Master Gordon marched to the fore, looked the brute in the eye and called attention to all and sundry invitations to industry on either side.

A voice called "Sarah" once more. Maul rang against iron, and men hoisted a balk with an "A" frame. She raised a jug from the cool water of the pond and looked down from the walkway. They had all worked to move these massive stones, rafted them on the tide, then laid them up a magnificent dam. Hadn't Squire said so when he visited to view progress and give Father his acquittance?

If she could manage it, there was one over whose thirst she would like to linger. Comfort MacLean was young and had always a look and a smile for her. At such a time she knew she blushed, fussed with her hair and averted her eyes. Why did she need to bite her lip? How could she ever explain to Mother the feeling which gripped her whenever he looked at her? Mustn't say a word to Sister. She was afraid she was going to be tongue tied again today, but she was happy he was here.

She knew this was a dream and the scene would fade. The vision buoyed her but did dissolve and deposited her with many questions in her dimly lit living room. Out the window dawn had defined the horizon. She pinched herself and staggered to the bathroom and reached without thought for the light switch. The face she saw in the mirror was not that of a teenager, nor was the body that of a sixteen year old. She returned to her living room and stood in the light from two sconces; she turned up the thermostat. She was really in her own home in the twentieth century, but she pinched herself once more. It was only a dream.

She asked herself what is it with dreams. Wasn't she simply overly stimulated by the events of the past two days? What had the night of reading from old records contributed to responses in her head? Weren't the characters simply there because of some reference to them in the reading? But there was no answer for the deep and abiding feeling of lonesome longing. That really nice handsome guy that was so gentle with her on the yacht...she'd included him in her dream. His eyes had held her..she could not turn away. It was all so real. She wondered if a dream could actually leave you with the notion you were really visiting another plane. She wanted to see him again, and the next time she didn't want him to go away.

Echo Horizon

With no warning she was suddenly gushing tears, losing it. Losing it over a phantom. Had she dreamed or could it be she was swept up in someone else's dream? Had she actually experienced another place and another time? She let go any attempt at further rationalizing. No rules explained her state of being at this moment, and she contemplated the likelihood of consciousness of time and a presence through the agency of another soul. Could that be Sarah?

She was experiencing love's pangs, and nerve centers resonated. That much was real; but here was that unfinished, unresolved dream of youth abandoning her to a state of lonesome anxiety. If she had seen, felt, even existed through the senses of another girl from another time, who was she? Who is Sarah? Could this house, her place she called home be next to McCobbs Cove?

She checked her watch and lit off to have a shower and get dressed. She'd just make it to the Cuddy in time for breakfast with Nancy. As she rolled onto the wharf she could see she had arrived first. Some of the fishermen were already out of the harbor or boarding their boats. She was not early by their standards.

She wasn't long at a table when Nancy arrived looking like she had been active for hours. Katie had started for the table with coffee. "Hi, Katie. Hi, Marna. Were you burning the midnight oil, or what?"

"That's what I want to talk about....yeah, Katie, sounds good..eggs, the works." Hardly able to contain herself, she continued. "I've found something that could be highly significant."

"Germane to our subject?"

"Don't know yet, but it blows the roof off anything I've found to date, and right in my own attic."

"Well.."

"A whole community, its development, accounts, shipping, milling and farming."

"When do I get a look?"

"Sure, afternoon?" Nancy looked up just as a large figure familiar to both strode up to the table. Hi, Dave."

"Well, Nancy, ain't you a lookin' thing. Hi, Marna. Say, Marna, I got a sort of message for you..don't know much about it.."

"Sit down, Dave. Have a donut."

"Don't mind if I do. I"ll just shag my mug, too." He swung back to the counter and returned. "Kinda strange fellers they were. Don't know what kinda company you're keeping.."

"C'mon, Dave, the best, you oughta know."

"Well, these guys don't come from around here..rugged customers if I can gauge. I was down to the boat last night after the rain, checkin' 'er out when these birds, three of 'em pulls up alongside in a long boat, no lights or nuthin', asked if I knew a Mistress Marna..I'm not kidding, that's how he spoke. Seems all the guy wanted to know was that you was all right. I tell him as far as I know you are OK and that we're friends and all, went to school."

"He give a name?"

"One of the guys on the oars called him Bos'n MacNab, sounded like..What's the matter? You're pale as a ghost, Marn. Have some water."

"I've met them Dave. They saved my life a week ago, pulled me out of the ocean." She told him her story. "Have you seen anything like the schooner I've described? I lost sight of it when I ran back to the car…Hold it, Al Brandon said he ran into them and they asked after me. So they do exist."

"What do you mean, exist, Marna?" Nancy wanted to know.

"I mean the whole lot disappeared once, looked like they'd come from another world. They certainly came to my rescue, and I'd like to thank them properly plus"..She stopped short of the wet clothing left on board.

"I've seen 'em around, but I'll keep an eye out and ask around, Marn." Dave rose. "Gotta get goin'."

The girls finished up breakfast, made plans for the afternoon and parted.

Marna could not resist a renewed plunge into the papers and opened randomly to a page in the log. Something touched the deepest recesses of her being.

> First officer keeps a steady hand.
> 30 April sticky block forstays'l port
> Have at it next calm. Wind north
> Glass not worrisome. Come about 315
> At 8 bells. No sayl all points. Mr.
> Dighton entertain all hands last eve.
> As good story teller as can find.
> Asked Mr. Ruck exercise forward guns
> Before sunset. Uncertain waters.
> Billy taken noon sight. Able seaman one
> Day. Eve watch sound holds
> 			Alport Captn

His name was actually there. She stared. Something in this entry agitated her. A hand had produced the script two centuries ago and presented her with a bridge across that gulf in time that became an obsession to her. The pressure built. Not accounting for a dislocation of centuries, she could have been brought aboard this very vessel. Of this she was certain. But when? She had heard the names, the voices. She left her soggy clothes and her mother's bracelet in the captain's quarters, for had she not returned home in clothes offered from a chest in his very cabin by a very real Comfort MacLean? She had already spoken with the captain and a very much alive first officer; and that dream in the night…she wondered if she were losing it.

During the walk around her land with Roni and Nancy, she had managed to conjure a vision of an imaginable community where trees and shrubs hid the remains of a homestead from passing eyes. Her dream was an invitation to be part of that scene. Perhaps she would just take her newly acquired clothing to the Archaeology Department one day.

Now, she sat where she looked out on a sparkling seascape, poking through a pile of history. She took in hand a small book which opened stiffly to verses. On examination she found the back cover thicker than the front. The paper cover on the inside was loose and revealed a sheet of paper, small and folded twice. While carefully extracting the paper, she noticed an inscription on the inside front cover. Faintly, barely this side of imagination the writing came to definition.

1777   To Sarah   Comfort

To Sarah…Comfort. Was this an expression of sentiment, or was Comfort a name? Then it hit her. She had been called Sarah in her dream, and Comfort..her heart raced as pieces fell together and she began to identify. Something significant was in her hands. She'd dreamt; she'd heard, and here it was coming together.

She grew fearful of handling the paper which appeared to be a letter, for if it crumbled, its message would be lost forever. But she couldn't leave it alone, curiosity relentless. As it turned out, script and paper were remarkably preserved, and she found it not brittle.

What she found inside were words so profound and evocative of feeling that she was moved as nothing had ever moved her. Anxiety and longing were unlocked from centuries old words committed to paper on far off seas and pervaded her mood at once. This same page, surviving the ravages of time, had been held with tenderness by a girl named Sarah while she read with aching heart these words from her lover. His name was Comfort MacLean.

As musical notations put down by a long ago master carry in their system creative passions to be released by a latter day virtuoso and audience, so did those words distill from Marna's sequestered yearnings an unprecedented rush. Written in the month of December, in the year 1776, the lines of pathos spoke of another three months before the return of his vessel to McCobbs Cove.

A word lay hidden from her beneath a small, round stain as might be left by a teardrop. It was presently joined by another before Marna turned brimming eyes from the missive of love sundered by war.

Unlike haunting refrains from a lost rhapsody, the scribed words, having transited centuries, elicited from Marna only unresolved dissonance as she wept uncontrollably for the lovers. A tenuous trail of delivery was suggested by names of two vessels' masters who participated withal.

December reflections prompted the shivers as Marna pictured her house without central heat or stoves, only fireplaces. She imagined thundering surf raging before a gale, sleet rattling on bottle glass windows and feet cozied up to warming stones beneath feather quilts. She fancied one secret to warmth on such a night was a light supper and two bodies under the covers.

With glass and perseverance she urged forth each line and was drawn behind what her mind's eye saw as shadow. Despair found new dimension. Beyond anything she might glean from faded ink, she knew separation for the two had been arduous, fortunes of war exacting. She fathomed the heart and soul of Sarah, the circumstances of her life, its bounds of reality. Her own horizon in the waning years of the twentieth century was suspended above that of Sarah's. She went on laboriously with a line near the letter's end.

"...so, Dearest Light, I carry your portrait always in company with stars in the night and on rise of sun each day..."

Marna turned her eyes toward the sea, glimmering through her window while the words continued in her mind.

"...and I desire you not to change a hair while yet I wait upon our tryst on a blue moon hence..."

She looked then at the chimney and dabbed her eyes with a napkin before gasping at words written on the page as she had conjured them. Marna's horizon conjoined at that moment with that of Sarah's, and she saw down dim corridors of time that which Sarah saw and felt what Sarah felt.

7

<u>Summer afternoon at Meadows Airfield</u>

The sun played shadows around a parked white Porsche and around a cream and blue vintage North American SNJ trainer. A short, thick set man, hair cut short, crouched on the wing stub in conversation with a tall, lean and casually dressed man with rather comfortably groomed dark hair. Shifting breezes had just let a hank of it settle back as the lean one continued in praise of the first class restoration and then entered a more general exchange involving flying experiences, techniques, and more specifically, flying conditions in the vicinity.

Jim Starr came on as an intensely interested and ingenuous visitor from Virginia who was enjoying his contemplation of beginning life anew in these parts. Ben Lane crept off the wing in the same crouched position, and Jim was a little surprised to be looking down at a figure a half a foot shorter than he and whose eyes seemed to smile in a round face. The wind had little affect on Ben's hair which resembled a pile of short straw.

"You know, Mr. Starr…"

"Jim will do just nicely."

"Well, if you're lookin' to settl'in' in these parts, you might want to have a look around from up there. I'll be happy to take you up."

"That's capital generous, Sir. I just may take you up on your offer. Now, why don't we go in the grille for some coffee and something, my treat. My old stomach reminds me I've been up for a long time." Jim had entered the first phase of his investigation and had offered no identification. His method was simple enough. Most investigators are a new face in town with never enough time in the budget to blend with the community, become an accepted part of the scenery.

It continued to work in the grille where Ben introduced Jim around. He wondered if his Shenandoah drawl raised any curiosity; he found the chopped speech of the Mainers a fascination. He found the sandwich he was devouring unusually savory, coffee was real coffee and the atmosphere contagious. With all, Ben was a catalyst. Jim knew he would have required infinitely more time to break the social ice without this genial companion.

Two ladies found his accent a thing to fawn over and offered to show him eligible realty properties, and Jim replied, "A most kindly gesture." Before he was finished with his second sandwich, he managed to ignite a conversation between Ben and another airplane chap on the state of security at the Meadows Field and the safety of general aviation. That, in turn, led to the Gantry disaster of last December. Jim learned one unforgettable fact. Anyone on almost any night could wander among the parked planes and place a device aboard.

At one point he felt compelled to defend the transportation safety board in its failure to find wreckage. He didn't, however and decried to himself the lack of organization and reporting.

Ben walked him back to his Porsche and glanced approvingly at the sleek, little car. Its top was down, and on the small rear seat, reposed in a box a remarkable wood likeness of a fair size bird.

"What's this, Jim?"

"That's a northern pileated woodpecker; he's almost finished, then…"

"You carve that?"

"I sort of got into it a while back; good for the nerves."

"Mind if I have a closer look?" Jim indicated to pick it up, and Ben held it and whistled, turning it in his hands. It was a full size replica of the big bird, standing twenty inches high. "Man, you know, almost tempted to blow and lift the feathers." He handed it to Jim. "That is something. Keep in touch, Jim, glad you're thinkin' of settling in with us."

Echo Horizon

The Porsche glided out of the grassy area and onto the road to Saxtons Harbor. Jim found he enjoyed the casual chat with the Mainers he had met, the easy put-downs they had for one another. He wanted to meet the man the admiral had mentioned that had shown him around. In good time he would find the young Gantry woman but decided against any direct inquiry.

He waited in the car some minutes after parking on the wharf. It was no task to find. His map had suggested an intricately broken coastline with hidden coves and backwaters; but what lay before him was a majesty of land and seascape. Moored boats of all sizes, moving boats, buoys, lighthouses, church spire, spruce trees to the water's edge, brilliant blue waters under a blue sky all brought forth a whistle. Truly this was a scene uncommon to him

Men moved on the wharf, carrying fishing gear. Some wore high rubber boots turned at the knee and clumped back and forth. One or two waved at the stranger in the little white car from away.

It was late morning, the restaurant nearly empty. A big sign announced *Beal's Cuddy* over the door, and he went in, took a seat at the bar. It wasn't lunch time and breakfast was certainly over, but he was ready for lunch.

Katie appeared at the bar without delay with a big smile and asked, "What'll it be?"

"I think I'm ready for a big meal, but I'd like to start off with a pitcher of beer, one of your microbreweries, if you don't mind."

She stood for a second, and Jim wasn't sure he'd made himself clear and started to repeat. "You got it. Mister, you're certainly not from around here. Tell me, I gotta know. Where's your home?" He told her. She turned away and started to fill his request. Jim immediately took to Katie's matter of fact address and watched her with her short, brown hair as she filled a pitcher. She wore a lumberman's shirt over a denim skirt and had on the high flying running shoes so many wore now, claiming unusual foot comfort when on the go all day.

"There, you're gonna like that. Now, Mister, let's you and Katie start work buildin' that big meal you've got on your mind." He was absorbed with her dialect, classic throwback to Elizabethan west coastal Britain with a little early 1700s Scot/Irish.

"Why don't we first start things off right and you call me Jim, you all right with that?"

"Finest kind. Now, you like sea food?"

"Katie, I have brought with me one of my greatest joys, my appetite. I am told that Beal's Cuddy specializes in food that best puts the beauty and bounty of Maine in front of its guests. You recommend, please."

"Well, I don't know about that; but I'll bring you a seafood platter, couple ears of corn and some blueberry muffins. How's that suit you?"

"Lead on."

Moments later a big man with a white beard and crown of white hair strode to the bar wearing moccasins. He dried his hands on a towel hanging from an apron pocket. "Couldn't help overhearin' my niece chatting with someone with a delightful western Virginia accent. You findin' things to your likin'?"

"So far I'm liking. In fact, Sir.."

"Names Beal, just call me Syl."

"Well, Syl, I don't think I've ever been in a more beautiful, more relaxing spot in the world aside from my little farm in the Shenandoah Valley. Call me Jim, Jim Starr."

"A long river, what town?"

"Little crossroads near Staunton."

"Here comes Katie with your dinner. And my Lord, you must have sweet talked her. She's bringing the crown and glory of the Cuddy. Enjoy your meal. Look, Jim, when you're done, come on back and visit, that is if you have the time. I'm an old cuss, but I like to see new faces in town. I think there could be a number of reasons why you're here, and I don't want to appear nosey or anythin'. But maybe I can be of help."

Echo Horizon

"That is right kind, Syl. I will look in on you if I can get up off the stool after all this." Katie was just unloading the tray in front of him. Lobsters, crab roll, French fries, corn, muffins, even steamers on another plate. "Katie, surely you're planning on helping me with this or finding help."

"I guess we could if you think you need it. I guess you brought along some of that fine Blue Ridge Mountain weather I've heard about. What a day!"

Jim was well along in the process of breaking open a lobster claw and was enjoying the exchange with the young woman who had served him. "How does that there rank with you expert lobster eaters?"

"You've done this before. OK."

"You know, you folks can be right proud of your weather. I feel a breeze off the ocean. Folks where I come from will miss the airs as the sun goes down and won't sleep as well as I expect to tonight."

"Doesn't it cool off some at night?"

"Some, but not near enough 'til October and November."

"Are you joining us on a vacation, you plan to stick around?"

"That's my plan. I like it so well in these parts, I'm looking for a place to buy so I can settle here."

"Great, well, maybe we can show you around. Ohh, gotta go..customers."

A well figured blonde with short curls headed for a table to his left, followed by a dark haired girl whose appearance caused him to drop his fork on the floor. She came close to taking his breath away. She is gorgeous, he mused to himself, the way she carries herself...the confident air. He noticed she was glancing around the room, then at him as she passed to her table. He noticed, too, that Katie whatever was right by their side in a flash. Here was a pecking order he couldn't overlook.

He reasoned they had probably just come from some office and had just so much time for lunch. Mustn't stare. The sudden averting of eyes is as raucous as a swinging baseball bat to someone who is skilled in observation. He was unable to hear their conversation against so many voices. The place was filling, and he recognized a gold mine.

"Did you see him, Nan?"

"See whom?"

"The guy eating at the bar alone. He looks so much... My God!" she squealed, trying to squelch the noise, "That's him. That's the one I told you about on the boat. It has to be him. Oh, do you think he's seen us?"

Nancy didn't turn to look. "Seen us and heard us. People will be in off the street to see what's got you rattled."

"I know I shouldn't look, but that's him. I know it." Marna froze. "He's looking this way. He's smiling."

"Smile back."

"He'll think I'm a pick up."

"If he recognizes you as the one he pulled out of the ocean, he'll come over. Won't he?"

"I don't know what I'll do if he does."

"Marna, get a grip. He's more interested in that shore dinner than he is in us." Just then Katie stepped to their table with lunches that would delight a rabbit. Before thinking it through Marna beckoned her close and spoke barely a whisper; and discreetly, Katie went in and out of the kitchen before checking on her patron at the bar. Marna incautiously watched Katie approach and saw the man turn toward her before her eyes snapped back to the table and Nancy.

"Honestly, I don't believe I've ever seen you so bubbly. What's come over you? Anyone would think you've struck gold somewhere."

Marna was ill at ease.

Jim Starr had finished two lobster claws and was looking to other parts when Katie filled his water glass and asked if he'd like more muffins, to which she got a yes.

"If you'll forgive me...ohh, I don't want to sound like a total idiot."

"Not at all. What's up?"

Echo Horizon

Katie stood with her back to Marna and Nancy. "One of the ladies...at the table over there..." She made a slight motion with her head..."wants to know if you were on a yacht on the waters here earlier this summer. She thinks she met you on a schooner, I think it was."

"No..no, but I'm charmed." He noticed Marna's eyes suddenly turn away again. "No inference taken. I'm sorry to tell you I've not cruised these waters this summer or any; but you tell...pray, what is her name?"

"Marna, Marna Gantry, the one with the dark hair."

"Jim's benign mask slipped. If Katie noticed, she didn't register it. "Kindly convey to Ms Gantry that I am flattered and honored that she would take me for someone who could ever invite her attention." He put it on a bit, couldn't help it, hoped his admiral didn't get wind of how much he was beginning to enjoy his assignment and decided then and there he was going to spend some of that financial back up.

That quickly, here she was; he'd made contact with his assignment. What he really wanted was to walk over and introduce himself and thought better of it just as Syl placed a substantial piece of apple pie in front of him, which took several minutes to disappear. The ice was already broken. Surely they'd invite him to sit and join them. He paid his bill with a generous remembrance for Katie. No, he mused, he would not resort to a phony come-on. If he were to learn anything of substance from her, a meeting must follow genuine acceptance, no longer a new face. But, already, she thought he might be somebody she knew.

He stood up from the bar, found his cap, looked toward the table and tossed a salute. Neither looked up, but he knew they were aware of his leaving. The motionless hands on the table told him that.

He drove to his seaside motel and changed into dungarees and a shirt more in keeping with downeast Maine and a chill east wind off the ocean. He lifted a uniform shirt from his duffel and fingered the silver oakleaves on the collar points. The admiral had come through with Jim's third full stripe before leaving for

Bert Howe

Maine. It felt good. He planned to walk the shore for a while, then return to the Cuddy during the afternoon slack if there were such a period, have a beer and a visit with the old man.

Marna lamented to Nancy that she would probably never see the guy again. If he wasn't Comfort MacLean then a twin brother. Katie's description of polished southern gentleman really turned on her curiosity. Nancy was all dispatch and expedition.

"Look, Marna, he was unattached. If a guy has his wife with him on a vacation, he sure as hell doesn't go off alone at noon to bust up a boiled lobster. He saves it for dining with her in the evening. So, if he likes what he saw, he'll be back."

"Ohh, Nancy, I don't mean I'm..."

"Well, you sure as hell ought to be. That one's so far ahead of the losers I've watched you sigh over, they wouldn't catch up this century. This one must be a gentleman. He sure as hell knew you were here, and he tossed a goodbye when he left. Breeding, Marna, breeding...he didn't want you to feel like a pick-up. If you're interested, give the guy a break and go half way, make it a little easier for him.

Jim noticed the uncomplicated layout of the village. Mast Road ran up the hill directly away from the waterfront. Parallel to the shore were Water Street, next Front Street, then Commercial Street. Streets parallel to Mast carried the names of local heroes, he was sure. Jim was intrigued with the pace of the town. The air was grand, and he knew he could quickly grow accustomed to this.

He drove back to the wharf, now nearly empty of cars except, he figured for those of people who worked for Beal. Again, he waited and gazed into the harbor scene. Marna's image wouldn't leave him, and he knew his blood pressure was elevated. He didn't even know the girl and he was reacting thus. The investigation was quickly taking a back seat. Couldn't he just chuck the life he had been leading? After the years alone and never knowing what lurked around the next corner he could

Echo Horizon

imagine settling down with a girl like that. Wouldn't matter what he did for a living.

Once more he entered the Cuddy and was greeted by Katie. Jim motioned toward the office, and she gave him the high sign. Beal sat a desk with a picture window behind him. He stood and gave Jim his hand, then reached for a box of cigars. Jim declined and he took one. "Wondered when you'd be back."

"Not if?"

"Not if. I think we may have one or two topics in common. Er.."

"Jim, Mr. Beal, Jim Starr."

"I'm Syl to you, Jim."

Jim removed his ID wallet and extended it to the other. What the hell, he was going to confide in this man because he needed a strong friendly presence if his work was to go as he wanted it to. He wanted to be a friendly face. Besides, he reasoned, Beal didn't get where he obviously was by divulging information recklessly. He accumulated it. "I'm here to study the Gantry tragedy."

Sylvanus looked up suddenly and handed back the wallet. "Commander, welcome to Beal's Cuddy and Saxtons Harbor. How can I be of help? I guess at least three government agencies have been around back and forth. I don't think they've accomplished much of anything." All trace of accent was missing from the man's speech, Jim observed.

"They haven't. What do you think of if someone starts shoving questions down your throat one after the other?"

"Why, I'd forget anything I ever knew and stiffen up wicked."

"Exactly."

"You've got some ideas, then?"

"Syl, I'm not going to pull punches or waste your time. I need you. I need the influence which I think you represent. A body of knowledge exists in this area. No knowing in how many pieces it may exist, and it will come forward only in a relaxed atmosphere. I plan to be here a long time. Actually, I've about made up my mind I want to settle here.

"You have a place in Virginia?"

"That little farm in the Shenandoah Valley near Staunton. I've offers on it already."

"I think we'll have no trouble finding suitable digs, maybe a rent for the present unless you're over fond of that motel." Jim looked up.

"Here, Syl, is a number you can call. My superior is a rear admiral and can verify anything I've said today if that will ease your mind toward me." The older man handed the card back with a smile.

"No need, Jim. Again, how can I help?" Jim stood and walked to the window, taking a visual sweep of the harbor and its myriad vessels of all color and shape.

"I guess Captain Gantry must have loved it here." Jim remained standing and looked at Beal. "Will you tell me what you know about the man? That's where I should start. I'm not going to ask you questions, but I'd appreciate it if you'd just ramble."

"Well, for all life! I guess I can ramble, sure as the next tide." Jim took his seat again. "Oh, I guess it was back in the 70s sometime. He brought his family into town for a short vacation, his wife Betsy and his little girl. I guess you seen her this noon time.

"The captain was a fighter pilot, been two tours in Nam. I guess you know he also flew in the Korean mess." And was probably in WWII, Jim mused. "That was a couple years before he retired from active service. He was here every summer after that and seemed to have an uncommon interest in the coves along the shore in the region, loved to fish, but he liked treasure hunting, too. Wasn't too uncommon to see him with a shovel and one of those magnetometer contraptions walkin' along the shore.

"There was this old property had been tied up for a generation in trust came on the market ten or twelve years ago; and damned if he didn't bid on it and buy it. It surprised a lot of folks, because he didn't make any show of that kind of money. I don't know what a four striper retires on, but it can't be much. You got no questions? Well, that's about all I can come up with. He was a fine gent, lovely missus. And that Marna is a star. The family loved to sail. Hell, they was into winter sports, all of it. She went to high school and college right here, quite a water sports girl. You'll want to meet her, and we can arrange that."

Jim would have given anything to say yes, the sooner the better. He wanted to pursue her, court her; but he would follow up on the investigation, and instinct dictated that the core of what information she might divulge lay deep in her mind. He would learn nothing in a half hour interview. And then what?

"Syl, hold off, please. I'd like any meeting with Miss Gantry to happen in a matter of fact manner. I would enjoy being looked on by her socially rather than officially." He saw the raised eyebrow. "Listen, old timer, whatever is going on in that brain of yours is correct. I am smitten and will leave it there."

"I sure was right about you from the first. Most any visitor to town would have let little time slip by before he put the move on our local miss."

"Thanks, Syl…permanence."

"How about a drink, a single malt suit you?"

"What did Katie say? Yeah, finest kind, neat if you please." He took the drink offered.

"You fly, Jim?"

"A little, general aviation, not navy."

"I flew some, long time ago, Korea."

"I thought I caught a picture of an F-86 on the wall; but you found where you wanted to be."

"Sure did. Tourists think I'm native. Fishermen know better. I feel bad for that lot."

"Why is that?"

"Fishing's gone to hell. Give it five more years, it'll be done. Access to the shore is drying up as more folks from away are buying it up and building. Must be twenty accounts use this dock. Course I buy all their catch."

"Fishing's one of the state's big industries, close to forest products?"

"One of the largest is money laundering. You take the…No, that's another whole subject. We got our hands full."

Jim looked at his watch. He'd been with Syl an hour and a half. "Syl, thanks. I'll stay in touch. Watch me try to blend into the environment." They shook hands, and Jim stepped out into the restaurant. Things were picking up in the late afternoon, and Katie had a girl helping her, and a school kid was bussing the tables.

There she was. Marna Gantry was alone at a table, same one. Her back was to him, and she had a drink in front of her. He wanted to speak and took a few steps nearer, was about to clear his throat in a cliché prelude when a large man muscled past him and threw a look that would take an hour to melt. As she looked up at the newcomer, she saw Jim. A smile started on her face before the man boomed out, "You lookin' for the mens' room, Jack? It's back there." Jim thanked the man and moved on.

8

For two days and nights rains were torn from low flying clouds by wind gusts which ripped the crests from surf and sent sheets of water and foam into the tops of seaward standing trees. Finally, with the advent of a clearing wind from the northwest, Marna walked and continued an exploration of her land for the first time in a week.

She accepted the futility of hoping ever to hear from the man she met on the schooner what seemed eons ago. He obviously had better things to do and no intention of contacting her, and that was doing nothing for her self esteem. She had arrived at that resignation to the facts when he or a double had shown up at Beal's. Damn! Charades. She expostulated to herself. She was sick of it. No matter that he denied it to Katie, he had to be that man.

Good old Sandy sure put the kibosh on meeting him. That was the last time he would bully her and stand in the way of her social life. She was so positive that the one Katie referred to as a southern gentleman was on the verge of speaking to her when Sandy appeared. What was a gentleman to suppose but that she was taken? What could she ever see in Sandy, no polish? Her ideal man comported himself in a manner totally alien to Sandy's small world of fishing and beer drinking.

She scrambled into the thick, bushy growth surrounding her old foundation stones for no other reason than she had tied up her hair and was wearing old jeans and shirt. No, that wasn't exactly right, she had to admit. She was aware, and quite distracted by that awareness, that she was drawn here. Something about the old place, the site of an early homestead, intrigued her. She couldn't explain why, but she was just simply happy in this place. It was as if a happy spirit were sharing the spot with her and trying to impart something to her. That was the best way she could describe it beyond its physical features, and they were surrounded by dense growth. How she wished to change that.

Between her desire to restore the site and her reclusive preoccupation with her old documents, she had gone crackers, she was certain. Maybe she would do better making some progress with her story of a young girl living right here on this site two hundred years ago. Her discovery of Sarah had become an enigma, and she was determined to know who she was and decided to write about her, making up what she couldn't know. Thus her thoughts had flowed into her word processor with an ease she had not before experienced.

Sun brightened a patch of katherina moss next a boulder, and she sat and stared, caring not in which direction so long as the sun warmed her face. At one with her surroundings, Marna's mind withdrew a curtain of undergrowth except for two huge maples, a mass of lilacs and an herb garden. She sensed the mass of a house at her back and smelled new mown hay scythed all the way to the shore. She knew the two large maples stood at the other side of the manse, and she heard the mill wheel working. A deep mist slowly cleared at the back of her mind.

At the grist...that was where she was supposed to be, not gawking at the vessel rising from its ways with masts stepped. All that was required was a launching tide. She knew she was caught in a time between reality and reverie.

The labors had gone on all through the winter months. Whenever she was at her chores or at the mill with the grist, she felt awed by the stately hull rising in shape from baulks and timbers. The men had worked at saw pit and forge, and here the vessel finally loomed waiting for the maul's ring as wedges were loosed that it might slide to its watery element. It was large, for father planned to sail to the Antilles to trade lumber and farm stuffs, cooperage and textiles for a return lading of coffee, sugar, rum, exotic wood and spices, all the sweet abundance of the tropics.

She carried the cider jug, cool from the pond, as she had done so many times, and the men thanked her. Of a moment she might be asked, "Sarah, mot ye foind me pipe loosed from me hand? There, by the keel block, lew side, girl. Thankee." These all were friends and neighbors. Some would sign to sail with Father on the first voyage.

Then there was a call and a whistle. She heard the ring of maul on iron and wood. They were knocking away the wedges to let the hull's cradle down to the greased ways and soon the proud vessel must slide to the tide. Her mother broke a rum jug on the prow, and cheers echoed as the hull moved.

Squire's *Coral Empress* fired her battery of six pounders before the stern of *Archer* flung white spray to glisten in the sunlight. Arresting lines came taut, and the kedge was let go. She had never felt so proud. Sister jumped up and down as the schooner's graceful shape swung on her cable and put her eye to the sea breeze. *Empress* fired a final salute which gave Sister a start for she liked not the great guns.

Marna found herself stooped to tie a shoelace, her foot on a ledge at water's edge. She couldn't remember walking from the old foundation, but she was several hundred feet away from the spot at which she had been sitting. Shoelaces tied, she remained in that position while examining hands which were chapped and red. Some spots were sore to her touch; she really needed to get to her hand cream. She couldn't imagine why her shoulders and back were so lame.

A final confirming glance along the shore told her no vessel existed; but the scene had been so detailed for her, so real. Her senses told her she had been present at a launching. She guessed it was about time to get in her Blazer and drive into town and mingle.

On arriving in town, a parking spot uncharacteristically availed itself to her, and she had change for the meter, a combination of events which rarely occurred on the same day. She sat parked by the hardware store on the left side of a one way street with the motor running and didn't see Roni and two seniors from the college coming along the opposite sidewalk behind her. What she did see was the last thing she expected.

Suddenly, there he was. Why couldn't he have walked over to her table the other day at Beal's just to say "Hi"? As he approached her from the post office, he couldn't miss seeing her sitting there totally unoccupied and accessible with the window down.

What to do? Twice he had passed her by at the restaurant. Sandy was no help, the animal. Her mind raced. He was coming nearer. Her engine idled, and her radio played softly; it was a beautiful day. He was looking right at her, and her eyes were trained on him. Don't look away. The question leaped from her soul. Would he speak to her? Why did she have to bite her lower lip? He stopped at her window and leaned down to speak. The Earth stopped.

"Your motor's running."

"I know, but you didn't start it."

He straightened slowly and moved on down the sidewalk, diminishing in her side mirror. She didn't hear his chuckle.

Before Roni burst on her space, her spirits were in free fall. "How about a lift back to the campus, my two friends and I?"

"Yeah, get in, sure."

"Well, good day to you, too. Is everything not all right?"

"Everything is not all right, Roni. I'd just like to find a deep hole, jump into it and ask someone to fill it in." Her words ended in a sob.

The two companions climbed in back, and Roni settled into the bucket seat beside Marna. "Talk to Dr. Dayan, my mussel schlepping friend. Students, not to take notes, not to listen yet. Hang from the windows and talk to tourists. So, Marna, you were the possessor of the light heart so soon ago." His attention was fully invested in her.

"Oh, I don't know. Maybe I shouldn't take on the teaching job."

"The instruction of inattentive undergraduates is not, I think, the root of your present unease." He turned suddenly. "Here, Gert, direct the hot breath away from my neck. Lotta, assist your friend to occupy herself with the passing scene. No, Marna, I believe the source of your soul's distress still ambles aimlessly along Front Street, having, what do you say, struck out. Alas, I thought I was the cause of your accelerated heart beat.'"

"Roni, what am I to do with you?"

"What happened back there with that young man?"

"Nothing, dammit!"

"Nothing, dammit." Roni rearranged himself as best he could in the confining seat.

Jim Starr had visited most of the stores on Front Street. He made a purchase in each one. A couple items he requested to be shipped to the admiral as keepsakes. Conversation would be easier later on with these several people who would remember him.

He had not expected to see Marna Gantry in her car, parked on the same street. He noticed that she was watching him through her windshield. Even as he neared, he couldn't discern the color of her eyes, green, brown or hazel through the glass. Why he had mentioned her motor he didn't know, but it sure ticked her off. It was quite evident to him that Marna was not going to be easy to meet on his terms. She knew he was around, and he had the notion she might even like his attention, but there were always others around. The guy with the mirrored sunglasses and the two kids, who next? He was determined to be patient. This was, after all, a professional assignment. Why did he have to remind himself of that?

Jim was awakened by the telephone at bedside. Light-emitting diodes on his watch told him 4:00 a.m. It was Beal.

"Don't usually do this, Jim; but a car's been parked by your motel with two guys watching your doorway. They're over here, now. Been watching your place most of the night, the lads tell me. Look, you got a fishing pole, grab it, get dressed and meet me over here right away. Mackerel are schoolin' wicked. You'll find me on the wharf. Somethin' you oughtta see." The phone clicked off. He sure didn't waste words on the phone. Didn't say we'll talk, but the lads?

Jim was out of his room in ten minutes, fishing gear and all. He darted back and picked up a candy bar against hunger. He parked the Porsche facing the harbor, and there was Syl, rod in one hand, coffee mug in the other. The sun was just beginning to break the tree line, but Jim had light enough to see a mug of coffee and a plate of donuts on a bench. Beal already had a half dozen mackerel in a pail.

"You were saying, Mr. Beal."

"Don't turn your head. See that Buick backed in against the toe rail. They just pulled in. That's the car the lads saw at your motel."

"These lads sleep?"

"More'n you might guess. Donnie Whitemoon saw the same car parked off the road under some trees by Marna's place the other night. Dark green or blue, would you say? D.C. Motor Pool's letting some nicer stuff out these days, but these birds are up to no good, and they've got a surprise coming. Hear that motor?"

"Yup". Jim could hear a faint rap in the diesel's exhaust.

"That's *Candy Lou*. She's about to head for sea. Watch the Buick." Jim started to turn his head just as a two pound mackerel hit one of his multiple hooks. The diesel roared to full bore, and the Buick swayed slightly at the toe rail, then hurtled over the edge, settling stern first into the harbor.

9

The midsummer crowd had the town's accommodations packed. Any available room sold at a premium. The weather co-operated with clear skies and temperature at midday in the 80s until the afternoon sea breeze cooled things down.

Jim had picked himself a comfortable bench on Beal's wharf, had his carving tools beside him and was going at the almost finished bird with a vengeance. He hadn't gotten anything going with the chief reason he was in Saxtons Harbor spending the taxpayers' money. He had chatted with dozens of folks in his homespun manner and found little of interest.

His suspicions grew as to the real objective of the admiral, for it could be that there just wasn't going to be anything to find out in the vicinity. The NTSB, the FBI and the FAA all seemed to have packed up with no visible results for their pains. His mind went over it and over. What was it the admiral was really after? It was a cinch he had turned the two hoods loose to find something or to check up on him. At any rate, if they crossed his path, he was going to lean hard.

The breeze was off the water and carried the shavings and chips away from him. A little more work on the breast, primaries and tail coverts and he had a bird which he would paint or not. He heard the footsteps and knew right off a woman approached, but he didn't turn until he heard the squeal.

"My God, what a beautiful thing! Is that what I think it is? It is. It's a pileated woodpecker!"

He was looking into hazel eyes, the most gorgeous, limpid pools of eyes he had ever wanted to simply fall into; and they were her eyes, Marna Gantry. Lightning crazed the clear sky.

"I don't wish to butt in, only it seems like I almost know you, we've nearly met so many times. I'm Marna, Marna Gantry." She extended her hand. She wore jeans and a casual white blouse.

He wanted to speak, but his breath was in the way, and his heart pounded. "Jim Starr, Marna."

"Hi, Jim, may I join you?"

Hi, Jim, may I join you? The sky had opened, and Heaven had fallen all around him. "Oh please do."

"Where did you ever learn to make anything so true to life, Jim? He's preening, isn't he?"

Her voice was like tinkling bells. Was his heart coming through his ribs, or what? "My grand dad taught me when I was very young back on the farm in Virginia."

"So that's where you got that delightful accent."

"Sure is, but what happened to yours? You could have come from California or Colorado."

"All the years travelling from one navy flying station to another. You don't pick up the downeast way of speech in a hurry."

His mind raced. How could he capture her and have her with him for the day? But the problem was taken from him in seconds. "Oh my look at the time. Jim, would you consider having lunch with me? You know how good the food is here."

"Dear lady, lead on. I'd be honored."

If Katie had any compelling thoughts as the two appeared to float past her to an empty booth, her body language divulged nothing untoward. "Nice view of the water, guys. Shall I bring you something to drink?"

"Jim, what's your pleasure?"

"I'd like to defer to you, Marna."

"Well, OK. Katie, how about that delicious house special wine you served the other day?"

"Coming right along." Jim returned the gaze which was taking all of him in, nothing furtive, simply an honest appraisal. At first he had been swept off his feet but was now feeling increasingly at ease. Never, he told himself, had he been in the company of such a woman. She displayed no effort at posturing and spoke straight from the gut.

"I hope you'll not joust with me as to whose treat this is," he spoke.

"Certainly not, wouldn't think of it. It's mine; I asked you to lunch."

"But I just think…"

"Jim, this is the 80s in Maine. I'm an 80s woman. You're my guest, and that's an end to it."

"Alright, but on one condition."

"What?"

"You let it be my treat soon." He watched her eyelids flicker just a bit closer together as she leaned slightly toward him.

"How soon?

"This evening."

"Done. Now, that gives us the whole afternoon. Can I show you the town? We can swim at the college pool, fish and explore. Tell me you'll let me show you my town."

"I am enchanted with the idea."

Katie came up to the table with the wine. "You're going to eat, also?"

"You start, Marna."

"That wonderful chef's salad that Syl has already put together this morning."

"Nacho sidedoor, Katie, and plenty of salsa, please."

"Got it."

"Alright, Jim, I simply have to know. What brings you to this place? Do you mind my asking? We have almost met so many times, and I'm so sorry about my behavior in the car the other day on Front Street. What must you think?"

"I think I was pretty much of a wise guy, but I couldn't but think you might be breathing a lot of that exhaust."

"And I was so forward that first time I saw you in here and I sent Katie to ask you if you had been on a cruise nearby."

"Marna, I was really moved, but it sure wasn't easy to get to meet you, always surrounded by people."

"I know, and I was getting a little bit concerned that you didn't like me or something."

"Perish that thought, but as to why I'm here..." He paused. Tell her straight, he counseled himself. You'll be glad of it later, and you're not going to give her a barrage of questions. "Marna, I don't want to cause you any discomfort. You probably don't want to talk to me about your parents, but I have to tell you I have been sent by the navy to attempt to discover who was behind the tragedy, if anyone. I am with Naval Intelligence, though various branches have differing titles. It's joke time if you wish. But, Marna, then I came and I saw you; and if you think that wasn't about the grandest thing that's ever happened to this Virginia farmer, think again."

"Thanks, Jim, that was forthright, and I appreciate it. I want to get to know you, and I have so much to tell you, it's hard to know where to start. Could you stand that?"

"Try me."

"How will I know when you are on business and when you're being social?"

"There is no "business" between you and me, Marna, except if ever something comes up, something you wish to tell me. I have no questions for you, and you are not, repeat, not suspect. Here comes lunch, and I proclaim myself on vacation for the term and looking forward to the rest of the day while you show me around. I don't know if Katie here or Sylvanus has said anything, but I have every intention of settling in these parts. I'm sort of on terminal leave and will retire."

"He'll sure raise the quality of this town if he does," put in Katie. "Chef's salad for the lady and nacho sidedoor for the gent. More wine? I take that as approval, Marna."

"Get out of town, you'll retire. You're so young."

"Lied about my age with my dad's help and went into the navy when I was sixteen. Was trained in the SEALs, two tours in Nam, then the Naval Academy. I've had twenty years."

"And you are a.."

"Three striper. I can probably make ends meet if I get a job, too." They ate with gusto and she told him about the jogging adventure and all that followed on the schooner, the first officer who could be Jim's twin, the gentle treatment and the disappearance of all when the fog lifted. She stopped short of her visions but told him of her plans to restore what she took to be an old farmstead and mill with its dam and impound.

"Whew, what a program! Can you use help?"

"Paid help?"

"I wouldn't want a dime. The whole idea just appeals to me, and I'd like to be a part of it."

"You're on. I'll feed you, though."

"We'll talk about it."

"I guess you really do like making things with your hands after seeing that bird. How do you do it. Is it true you just remove all the wood that's holding the bird captive?

"That's about it, except that you have to visualize the finished creature in your mind, see every detail. The tool lies dead in your hand if you've forgotten the shape and dimension of the part on which you are then working. You have to do a lot of looking."

When lunch was finished, they agreed to leave Marna's Blazer on the wharf and ride in the Porsche to Cobbetts Neck and walk the trail in stead of jog with lunch so recent.

"Just up ahead is where I was attacked that morning, I'm pretty sure. Was kinda foggy. Seems ages ago, now."

"Marna did you get a look at them? Could you in any way identify at least one?"

"You can laugh, but I think I would recognize the arm of one and his aroma. That's about it."

"Clothes, anything come back to you with clothing?"

"I didn't actually see the second one, but I gave one a good kick to the groin; and I think something is coming back to me about his trousers. He was not dressed for the rough. I don't know what he was wearing, but it was more suited to office wear."

Something gnawed in the back of Jim's mind, and it had to do with the two stiffs watching his motel room in the wee hours and who later received a ducking at the hands of a couple fishermen. That Sylvanus was a strange bird. What galled him was why they were here and if there was any connection with the attack on Marna. He was plain angry at that news and was ready for retaliation in any form that made itself handy.

Walking on, she gave him an account of the chase. With each recount of the progress of the misadventure, the details returned more hotly clear until, finally, she brought him to the point where she descended to the rocks and continued a perilous series of leaps while all the while hearing her pursuers. She recognized the fateful ledge immediately. Jim looked at the height of the drop, even with tide near full, and the void beyond which she hadn't been able to negotiate.

The breeze had placed cotton puffs along lines of waves on the bay, and fleecy clouds streamed from the northwest. Gulls and terns made a racket, and here and there a seal bobbed on the surface. Jim gazed in silence at the seascape with far off racing sloops leaning into a reach, a glittering summer scene to his eyes.

Marna strained to see through the influence of recall, the terror that had gripped her in these very waters, a cold hopelessness. Her mind gave her a studied outline of a schooner, anchored a half mile out, raked masts, about ninety to a hundred feet overall. So began her account to Jim of her ordeal climaxed with a zany visit to an eccentric's yacht.

"Whoa, hoss, hold up, this is more'n one farm boy can take in all at once. You say the guys who pulled you out were in a rowboat?" She nodded. "...a rowboat and no outboard. You're telling me there was no power on the schooner. OK, OK, now, tell me this. Didn't you see some fancy bright work, like stainless steel winches on the gunn'ls for raising and lowering sail? No?"

"Nothing like that, Jim. Everything was plain. Even the clothing of the crew was about as plain and homespun as I could imagine." She described the raiment she had been given.

"Vessel that size would cost into the millions to build, wood or otherwise, particularly wood. I can't imagine who would put that kind of money into a vessel to be deliberately old fashioned. Lotta work sailing one of those things. You remember if it had a clipper or a spoon bow?"

"I couldn't notice. I know the difference, though."

"And you have the impression the guys on board weren't having that good a time?"

"Quite a bit of grumbling about some old foundered wreck down the coast. I heard *prize* mentioned. The fog was all around; I heard more than I saw.

She told of the meeting with the captain and his archaic quarters and the great muzzle loader cannon. Jim listened with rapt attention as his mind went back to his recent meeting with the admiral. The information given him then was strange. Marna was telling him more strange facts. Wanting to believe, however, couldn't overcome years of rational deduction in the case of mysterious undertakings.

His short time with this enchanting woman had carried him beyond his original mission, and his enjoyment of her company was magnified each hour. The walk back to the car became a jaunt, which became a sprint, which left them in a perfect mood for a splash in the college pool. The wind dropped as the day warmed. When they were completely cooled down, Marna suggested they gather up both their cars and go back to her place for some cool drinks and some points of interest she hoped he would like to see. Jim was tempted to pinch himself. Marna was making this spot on the globe about the most fascinating place he had ever seen. As he followed her into her drive and saw the prominence overlooking the ocean and felt the breeze on his face he knew he had found the place on Earth which would suit him for the rest of his life.

They spent time sitting by the shore talking, then she took him on a short tour of the surroundings until they came on the remains of the old farm home. He surprised her by exclaiming to her that he was experiencing a reaction to the scene which was much as she had when first she came on the spot.

He jumped into the cellar hole of the house and examined what appeared to be a path trampled in the grasses and pronounced it recently made. It led behind lilac bushes to a narrow confine by the wall.

"Looks like someone's been excavating. Let me give you a hand. See that?" A quantity of earth had been distributed among the lilacs and she saw evidence of digging. With the light available they were unable to make out clearly the opening of the cave or den or whatever it could be. "You haven't heard anything or seen a light at night? Appears to me someone thinks there's something in there."

"What next? I'm not going to sleep very soundly after this."

"There are ways to head this sort of situation off."

"I'll have to do something. I'm not about to let some stranger rearrange my property." They walked back to her favorite place for meditation on the edge of the cliff overlooking the waves, and he perched on one of the big flat rocks.

"Look at us, Jim. I just can't believe this. Yesterday we were strangers. I'd ordinarily be running around today with a dozen things to do and accomplishing nothing. I don't know what's come over me. I've babbled on about the highlights of Saxtons Harbor, and there's so much I'd like to know about you. I can't just barrage you with questions."

"Try me. I promise to divulge all if you'll tell me all about you. Let's get in the Porsche and drive around until we find the right place for dinner, and we'll talk."

Marna tossed her head in an effort to control blowing hair as they sped north off the long peninsula, finally balancing the tresses on either side and asked. "How did you learn to swim so long under water? You made at least three laps of an olympic pool."

"Lots of practise. How did you learn to do a Dutchman's pipe with a full twist from a six meter board?"

"Practise, I guess. I think I was in the water before I learned to walk. Jim, those scars are bullet wounds, aren't, they?"

"Keepsakes of Nam."

"You're in such good shape. Excuse me for being so personal."

"Please, don't stop. The navy takes pretty good care of me."

"Did Sandy bother you that other day at the Cuddy. Is he why you didn't come by and introduce yourself?"

"I think I told Katie there was no way I wanted you to think I regarded you or your friend as pick-ups. I know the difference. No. Sandy didn't bother me."

"I don't think much would."

Finally, they turned east until they came to another road heading out to sea on another long neck of land. Salt creeks passed under the rural highway and ran into extensive marshes as the miles ticked by. Quaint farm houses reflected from the calm flood tide. Osprey nests perched high on dead trees, the crowning achievements of pairs of the great hawks and near the size of a VW.

Hunger stirred as they saw the inviting sign indicating a country inn a mile farther on, and a well groomed drive invited them onto the grounds past acres of flower beds and fruit trees. The sun had a couple hours to setting as they made their way into a vast sitting room of a period house and were escorted onto a large dining veranda. The inn faced east and offered a land and waterscape across one of the hundreds of coves on the coast emptying a creek bubbling over huge rocks and under ancient hemlocks and oaks.

On the far side sat a manse with a low sloping roof and large central chimney, flanked by a huge barn and outbuildings. Marna sighed as she looked with envy at the very likeness of scene she wished to restore on her property.

Their waitress brought them a carafe of wine, a tray of cheese, crackers and pumpkin bread and left them to conversation. "OK, Jim, will you start and tell me about yourself?"

"I promised, didn't I? Right. I'm an orphan except for some distant relatives who don't even know I'm alive. My folks passed away while I was in Nam."

"Oh, that's awful. Do you have a special girl? Oh, oh, that's a bummer. I'm.."

"That's all right, but I'm going to reach way out here on a limb and say no, I've never found that special girl."

She knew she was blushing, and it worsened. He had to see that."

"Is there a man in your life?"

"Well, ahh-h, one particular or rather, I was...No." Her defenses were in shambles, but she wondered why she thought she needed a defense.

They eased into their meal as shadows compromised the emerald water of the cove, and moored boats pointed the rising presunset breeze. He told her of his childhood, of riding horses and hunting with his grandfather, work on the farm. Her left hand was on the table, and without thought, he grasped it. She looked at him and placed her other hand for a moment on his.

She spoke of learning to sail with her father when he was stationed near the water, or skiing when near mountains and snow. Her dad always had an airplane of his own and did much of the mechanical work on it and his car. He would always include her, and she grew skillful in the diagnosis of mechanical ills and curing them.

Their evening drew to an end, and Jim returned Marna to her home, thinking the while she was really isolated. He didn't want the dream to end, and dream it had been to him, for never had he been in the company of such a girl. His mission was growing dimmer compared to the brilliance she had brought to his life. She had her hand on the door latch and turned to him.

"Jim, will I see you again, soon?"

"Can you arrange tomorrow?"

"I think so. I...Do you mean it?"

"Sure, I mean it."

"It so happens I don't have a thing planned tomorrow. I know what. I'll make you dinner tomorrow night. And why don't you come here for breakfast, say eightish? We can dig clams. Oh, and there's something buried in the cove you may find interesting. How about it? Oh, God, am I a dreadful woman? If I'm out of line you tell me."

Jim picked up her hand, squeezed it and put it to his lips. "Marna, I'll be here around eightish; and if it makes you feel better, we won't call it dating.

"Just being together?"

"Works for me."

"Be sure and bring clothes for digging in the mud."

"Yes, M'am." He vaulted the side of his car and saw her to her door and inside and with a salute was gone.

Bert Howe

10

Marna was up and about by six a.m. Her hands were slightly chapped, and she had forgotten. What would she put on them? Jim would be here at eight to have breakfast with her. Finally, they had met, though she had nearly given up. There simply never was such a guy and she couldn't imagine a companion who was such fun to be with. She glanced out the door at the diminished area of grass as yet unmown. It wouldn't do for making hay, stems were all dry. Neglect she wasn't going to abide.

So intensely real had been the scene she had conjured yesterday morning. She had actually been present at a launching..no mistake. She could still hear the guns. Little sister…where had she come from, and the name Mehitabel? The guns had frightened her to death, poor little blonde thing. Marna's mind continued playing tricks on her as she turned back and searched high and low for glycerine and rose water. Where were these notions coming from?

What was surprising, she found some in her mother's bedroom. Now, to the coffee, and she'd make an omelet like never was that would go well with the pastries she bought. She felt as though this were the way life should be. Eight o' clock and he was here.

"How are these for playing in the mud?" He tossed a huge pair of rubber boots from his Porsche. He was dressed casually for breakfast and assured her he had his work clothes in the trunk. "What smells so good?"

"Just some frozen buns I tossed in the oven. We have three kinds of juice, or you can eat an orange or grapefruit, too, bacon, coffee, eggs any way you want."

"How about scrambled?" They had no difficulty with conversation while eating and lingered while the tide dropped a foot or more. They stacked the dishes, donned boots, grabbed shovels and hoe and headed for the cove.

"What can it be we're looking for? I see clam flats."

"Just a short way. Most of my digging has been covered over, so we'll need to move some mud."

They wasted no time, and finally they could make out the ship's futtock ends. "When did you find this?"

"It was back a spell. A friend and I were clam digging. Want to dig some for lunch?"

"Not too fond of clams, but I'll take you to lunch anywhere you like. Do you have any idea what vessel this is and when it met its end?"

"Haven't a clue. We noticed something strange, though. Let's see if we can find some." She dragged and scraped. "Here they are. See those holes? They go through the planking. I was able to run my hand under the other side and found some on the opposite side of these thick...what did you call them...that didn't come through. It's like someone shot a lot of bullets into the ship."

"Considering the probable age of the thing, I wonder. Could I take a piece of that wood up to the house? Would you mind, Marna?" His mind repeated her words—like someone shot a lot of bullets ...

"You are actually going to cut through that and pry a piece off its tree nails? In your dreams. This I have to see." They returned to the house for axe, crowbar, maul and wedges. She remarked her dad was prepared for anything. By noon, he was finished and sloshing in the water. "Jim, you're going to hurt yourself!" He placed a six foot section on his shoulder, walked to his car and laid it on the ground. "Time to hit the showers."

"Agreed, that will be nice."

"Make yourself at home," She directed him to the bath and towels and wiped her own face. "That notion may be catching."

She rejoined him in the living room twenty minutes later, hair done in a towel. "My appearance will change for the better, I hope; but I gotta show you something very special if you promise not to tell."

"Cross my heart..." She retrieved the box from her wall cache which contained her gold coins and spread them on the tablecloth. He stared and didn't speak until he asked permission to pick one up. Marna was amazed at his deference.

"Sweet lord, Elizabeth I, and over here I do believe Edward VI, and that one right by your finger tip has to be a Harry noble, only a fraction of a pound once, but now..." He whistled. "See the ship and those initials?" He grasped a pencil and pointed. "Looky here, "H" for Henry and "K" for Kate, Katherine of Aragon." He sat back and looked at Marna. "Lady Bug, I don't believe what I'm seeing. These pieces are antiquity itself, and you found them between the ribs, the futtock timbers." She nodded. "Hard to determine the vessel's nationality, even carrying English gold. But why was it rotting in an American cove if it were foreign?"

"Do you have any suggestion what I should do with this stuff? I'm sure it's valuable."

"I would keep them in safe deposit. Maybe there are more where you found these. It's a job for a museum, but always there's a security problem. Do you have any...no, you couldn't. Marna, there haven't been any of these found for ages. The value of that one coin there..." He used the pencil again. "Unimaginable, Marna." She turned her head slowly from side to side. "It's a gold noble, maybe six shillings originally, struck during the reign of Edward III. The ship with the king and shield, those were supposed to have been recalled for melt down when Elizabeth I came to the thrown. If there are any more, I tremble to think."

"Jim, I don't know what to think. The value would be to a museum, wouldn't it?"

"Not necessarily. People who get their kicks with this sort of collecting, and can afford it, would pay a fortune just to be able to tell their colleagues they own one. It's a game of one-upsmanship."

"No way am I about to trust these to a bank! I have control of them right here, but I really wonder what they could be worth."

"If you'll consider the opinion of a nonexpert, I suggest a figure somewhere between a half a million and two and a half mil."

"You've got to be kidding."

"Marna, for all practical purposes, in the coin world some of those don't exist. You've got a fortune. You aren't sure of a value extrinsically until you have a sale. Depends on who buys."

"Can I ever thank you?"

"Let's not worry about that, now. Put 'em back in your hiding place. Where do you want to have dinner tonight?"

"I'm going to prepare dinner for us right here if you'll join me; and while we're eating we can plan an exciting little trip we should make before the fall foliage brings crowds to the mountains."

"What do you have in mind?" He smiled back at her and looked into smiling hazel eyes. 'Nothing short of courting the girl', the admiral had exhorted, and advised that he was sure the girl had information she didn't know she had. That hadn't made complete sense to Jim then, but it was becoming clearer, now. What could Marna know of the exploding aircraft in which her parents were climbing out over the bay? Only the culprit could know.

If the admiral had something else in mind, and it would have to be money, then the pieces might fall into place. He was a tool, and so were the two hoods who were responsible for Marna's near tragedy in the water. He knew this wonderful woman had swiftly become the center of his life and needed his protection. Suddenly he felt cut off from his past, his whole foundation of operations; but he needed the military support. He'd just continue playing the part of investigator and close the perimeter of his operation.

"Penny for your thoughts. Have I shocked you? It's just..."

"Shocked? No. I've been running over the possibilities. Lead on."

"Well, you like your mountains in Virginia. I thought..how about a weekend hike in the northern Appalachians? I have Spectre Mountain in mind."

"That's one of your highest..over in the National Forest, I think."

"Right."

"I think that's a terrific idea. You're on. Now, I'm going to have to go back to D.C. for a few days, and I'll get myself outfitted. Maybe while I'm gone you'll find me a bungalow by the shore I can lease or buy."

"I'll find something."

"Marna?"

"What?" She sat up in her chair by the table.

"Promise me something. Hey, listen to that. I have no right to…"

"What is it you'd like me to promise?"

"Don't change anything about you, ever. I want to sit here a moment and just look at you." She reached for his hand.

That evening they lingered long by the fire and enjoyed their wine. Dinner was not hurried either. They chose a weekend in September for their odyssey in the mountains, neither having paid scant attention to the nearness of Labor Day. He would return to Washington and be back the next weekend.

"Marna, someone will be by to pick up that timber in the yard if that's all right with you. Close inspection may reveal something that's right interesting."

It was midnight when she stood by her door and watched the little Porsche's tail lights pass from view. The sudden silence, all alone—she felt she was deep inside a growing emptiness. Only a few days, he had told her. She had known him for just two days and so much of her was this moment whisked away. She felt more alive during the two days than at any time she could recall.

Marna decided to sleep on the first floor, so she locked her doors and made sure the windows were secure, then prepared for the short remainder of the night, her purse by the day bed. Sleep washed slowly over her senses, and she became aware she was dreaming, for hadn't she exclaimed already this evening over the sunset?

Once more the sun dropped low over her dream horizon, and the western sky reddened. A ship's bell, then the voice of the watch, "no sail all points" the duty officer acknowledged. Sea air was balmy on her face, and though the slight motion of the deck gave her cause to mind her balance, she would never fall under the weather.

Wind dropped off with the lowering sun one bell into the watch, and she struggled aft on legs more accustomed to a level deck. Lift lines and down hauls were less noisy in their catterings against the masts, but from under the counter came the sound of the wake. She knew well it was time for exercise of the great guns, and for her they held no fright. Sister huddled in her quarters at the booming of the twelve pounders, ordnance Father had secured at Guadeloupe, Grande Terre—contrary to the Navigation Acts, she was certain. Presently the command was heard to down helm and come to irons.

She felt the schooner steady herself with its change of heading and heard the rustle of slack canvas. The long boat was swiftly away to set a keg for the mark. Comfort knew just precisely how to back their square top gallants to ride through irons when the order was given to resume course. She was convinced he spoke a language to the sails known to no other. Her heart pounded.

"Sarah, whyn't ye lay below for the gunnery?" It was Mister Dighton, always kind and considerate, but she would not miss the excitement. Her fascination with guns was a mystery to all. Well did she know the voices of the forward firing twelves, the bark of the six pounders amidships, and the doom voice of the huge eighteen pounder beneath the quarter-deck in Father's cabin. It fired to the rear and could poison the day for any interest in hot pursuit.

She remained by the companionway when came the order to fire. The deck lurched, and a thunderous convulsion nearly cast her from her shoes. Mister Ruck must have touched off both at once. She saw Billy carry the long, pointed match for him. Billy was cabin boy but made a fine powder monkey.

The sails were retrimmed, and they were under way once more on a night heading. She retired to her quarters having witnessed the keg disintegrate on a far off wave top and the small burgee flying from the mark into the air. All around her was the soft, regular chop against the hull and a smell of tar, then nothing.

Blackness gave way to the faintest delineation at her windows, and she wasn't listening to hull sounds at sea but surf on the ledges beyond her home. Where she had been mattered less to her than the knowledge she was secure in her own bed and rather hungry.

In a short while the most desirable male company in the known world would be coming back to her and they would plan their trek in the beautiful back country. Now, she must get on with her life. So, swinging her legs over the side, her bed began to shake before she could make out the heavy beat of a moving wing aircraft. She was awake now, and she remembered he had said someone would be by for the hunk of wood in her yard.

What she needed was a visit with Nancy, not only a super friend but the greatest sounding board. She knew Nan had breakfast early on the wharf, her excuse being, it was convenient, and she could keep abreast of local comings and goings. Right. The only coming and going that was of any interest to that one was what's-his-face in the Continental Volunteers who ate an early breakfast there before going to work on his contracts.

All at once, while walking to the refrigerator for juice, she felt as if she were walking the deck of a vessel on a broad reach. The floor swayed. Sarah. She couldn't get Sarah out of her mind. Couldn't be the flu. She felt fine. She felt wonderful. Sarah was the name she would give the heroine of her story. Now, that perplexed her, because she still didn't know quite where she was going with her story. Would there ever be anything worth reading?

11

"Marna, where in Heaven's name have you been? I've phoned and phoned. No one's seen you since…I don't know when was the last time. I know, we were having lunch together. I've got it. That real cute hunk was at the bar, and you wigged out. Really, girl, you've got to get hold of yourself. You never throw yourself at a man like that."

"Listen to you. Wasn't it all-knowing smarty pants Nancy who told me I should at least cut him some slack, something about making it a little bit easier for him? Well, I've learned he just isn't the kind of guy who goes around putting the move on strange girls."

"Oh-h? And you're an authority on Mr. Southern Gentleman with the fancy drawl? Oh, no, you're holding out on your pal, aren't you? C'mon, that's not fair. So that's where you've been." Heads turned. Katie looked their way. Marna colored. Nancy worked at lowering her voice but barely approached the audible threshold. "Tell Nancy, that's it. You'll feel better for it," she coaxed.

"Nan, I don't know if I *could* feel better about anything." Katie swooped up to their table with flapjacks, sausage, more rolls and eggs up.

"You guys want to come in at 4 o' clock and audition for the floor show?"

"Thanks a bunch, Katie. How about some more coffee? Can you believe this girl, Katie? She's living an alter life, a secret love affair with her dreamboat."

Now, Marna blushed, and she didn't care. An alter life…Sarah. Suddenly, she knew where her story was taking her. It would be wild with adventure. Certainly Sarah was madly in love with *her* dreamboat. It was all falling into place.

"Nancy, how you exaggerate! Sure, we finally ran into each other." Her eyes took on a sparkle, and her flushed countenance broke into a wide grin. "And, Nancy, he's wonderful."

Nancy sat as wood, then stuffed a forkfull of pancakes into her mouth. Never taking her eyes from Marna, she gradually ingested. "You've finally gone off the deep end, Marna, I'm proud of you. What's he like? Any pillow talk?"

"Oh-h, Nancy," Marna demurred.

"C'mon, Marna."

"Physically or personality-wise?"

"Stop stalling. Both."

"Physically, he's the kind of man the navy SEALs would want. Personally? Ohh, well, he's probably the easiest man in the world to get to know."

"You did a lot of moping around after falling in the ocean and meeting that bunch on a yacht, and you thought your guy was one of those on the boat. What now?"

"I really thought Jim was that guy. He isn't, though they sure are alike. But he has a gentleness you don't forget in a man. Both were…are…gentle in their ways, anyway with me. No macho air about either."

"So what next? Gentle, huh?"

"He has to go to Washington for a few days and will be back this weekend." She exhaled a sigh. "And I'm counting the hours." She averted her glance. "We're going on a hike in the mountains in a couple weeks. Do you think I'm dreadful, too forward?"

"You? No, you've got some catching up to do. Watch your step, though; you never know. Be in control. It's your heart you're risking."

"Gee, Nan, I don't think it's gone that far…I.."

"Yes, it has, and it shows. I'm glad for you." Marna looked straight at Nancy but seeing nothing of her friend or the surroundings. Fragments of a knowing, the barest prelude of an idea glittered across the dark, shrouded folds of a curtain behind which either an enlightenment glowed or stark emptiness prevailed. What as yet had not become envisioned within her mind could manifest at the level of her genes. The world into which Marna had been born and to which she had become accustomed and took for granted was about to change.

"Thank you, Nan." She actually felt relieved, she told herself. She felt so much better after telling Nancy all. And hadn't she just dreamed of him, or was it the look-alike? Or was someone dreaming of her? In her private world of perceptions the two men were one and the same. That could govern the state of Sarah's id in the novel. "You won't believe what happened this morning. A helicopter dropped by this morning to pick something up, a big navy chopper."

"God amighty, you girls hear the news" Katie was near hysteria as she ran to their table, spilling coffee on the way. Heads turned. "Someone tried to kill one of the profs at the college...wounded an assistant in Di...Dayan's office. Somebody said a raghead with a machinegun shot up the place and got clean away like a shadow in the night."

"Christ, is Roni all right? About the guy that got shot, he OK?"

"A girl, grad student, maybe a senior...older than most seniors.."

"Well, hell, is *she* OK?"

"Flesh wound, they say. Professor Dayan was down the hall. Gert something, I think they said on the radio."

"Good God, exclaimed Marna. "That's the second time. Someone tried to run us off the road early this summer. He said he thought they were after him."

"Another time, Marna, last week."

"Some of that coffee, Katie before it's all on the floor. Last week, Nan, you sure? I just gave Ron and two girls a ride back from town three or four days ago. He didn't say anything."

"He wouldn't."

- - - - - - - - - - - - - - - - - -

Jim drove up to the dingy building on the old air station near the Pawtuxent River in full daylight dressed this time in civvies. Inside the admiral greeted him with a sweeping arm gesture toward a table covered with knickknacks.

"Got your souvenirs and your expense account. You're enjoying yourself, I see."

"You know how I work. Been successful before."

"This is all going somewhere, I presume."

"Door openers and conversation starters mostly. More in the car. That big package arrive yet?"

"Last night if you're referring to the stick-in-the-mud."

"You got it."

"Lab boys have it. Interesting stuff. They've carbon dated it. Sometime around 1750 that tree was cut down. They're running tests. What do you think made those holes."

"Exactly what you think did. I watched that film from the gun camera three times. I can't believe it; but let's say we're really off the deep end here, over our heads, and there's a shred of reality. We're talking time warp here, or maybe another term best suits the situation, time plane, parallel existence. We've got a situation here could shake the world."

"Right."

"But it's beyond our belief mechanism."

"Beyond anything that could be released as a statement."

"You got anything to eat or drink around here? I drove straight through, and I could start on one end of this sofa."

"Five minutes a whole breakfast, OK?"

"The coffee arrived in less than five. Then, when he had finished a substantial meal and the table was cleared away, Jim continued. "You have others on this case."

"You caught me. I was hoping they were smart enough so your paths didn't cross, civilian contractors, some of the stuff we have to work with these days."

"I think two of your 'contractors' may have attacked Marna and nearly cost her her life by drowning. Our paths cross again, they will be demoted maximally with prejudice."

"Commander..."

"This is serious, Admiral. Your two 'contractors' have an agenda of their own. I think they are bloody treasure hunters."

"I'll call them off. They've done a lot of preliminary investigation which helped me build a background before I called you in."

Jim looked squarely at his boss. Sure you will, he thought to himself.

"You are making progress." This was not a question.

"Way ahead of schedule. I believe she's comfortable with me, told me a lot of family stuff. She knows more than she thinks. You were right." He stiffened in his chair. This was Marna they were discussing like any business topic. This was the girl who made him feel ten feet tall, whom he had known two days and made their acquaintance timeless, as if he had known her through all of time, for whom he had fallen irrevocably in love. He was going to make no mention of the gold coins she showed him.

"Very well, where are we?"

"No one in that community placed a bomb on the captain's plane, but anyone could have. Field is wide open. I don't think a local would have for fear of recognition of himself or his vehicle."

"You will narrow this down."

"Someone wanted the captain out of the way because he wanted to look for something without interruption. He figured he could scare Marna. Only one factor upsets the balance of the equation. Except for it the waters would be smooth. Captain Gantry some dozen years ago came into enough money to buy a million dollar property. That's a good trick on a captain's pay and allowances or pension. At no time in Marna's and my discourse has she alluded to a lifestyle which could only result from a large amount of extra cash."

"Jim, I hadn't intended to send you on a hunt for buried treasure. My network has picked up rumors over time, but my intentions have been pure. You have an assignment; but you may as well be privy to what I think I know about the issue of the property. I think I told you, Ensign Alport and I became more friendly than an exec and a flying officer usually become. He had apparently had an unnerving history, and he told me much. I mentioned Commander Dahlgren, fallen from grace. My informants had it that at about the time Alport changed his name to Gantry, Dahlgren and some unholy colleagues helped the now late Captain Gantry to convert, under the table, a lot of gold specie. Some lives were lost. Dahlgren, even now, resides in a home for alcoholics in upstate New York. Any trail of information is lost."

"Jesus Christ!" Jim was on his feet. "Then anyone with a breath of this information would kill Marna or worse for what they think she knows."

"That could happen without our intervention. I hate to ask, but you have confined your investigation to the death of her parents?"

"I've walked the line." Jim wanted to flee the premises and return to Marna without delay. Admiral Rankin answered the knock at the door. Two deck grade line officers entered, one carrying a fat file.

"Thank you, gentlemen, you haven't let me down. Commander Starr is leaving the station today and needs to see what you have."

"Very straight forward, Sir." The two striper placed the file on the desk. "We confirmed the date of the wood with a process just down from the Naval Research Lab. We removed samples of metallic salts from six holes and isolated traces of lead, iron, copper and phosphorous. The admiral will note there is a slight amount of undecompositioned steel, high carbon steel, Sir. Our conclusion is consistent with target receiving several rounds standard .50 caliber armor piercing and tracer ammunition." The admiral didn't look up from the sheaf of papers in the open file. "Sir, considering the age of the wood, which is confirmed to be oak, a variety found in the Baltic area, could you explain…?"

Echo Horizon

"That will be all, Lieutenants; thank you." The officers left the room. "Well, what in hell are you waiting for? I don't want to see you again until you have some answers."

Jim bounced down the steps and sprinted to the Porsche, the spectacle stopping two petty officers in their tracks. It felt good to be out of uniform on a naval air station. Business in the Potomac area was finished, and he could turn his attention to I-95 northbound. The elation he experienced was entirely new.

As he headed for the beltway, a notion tugged at him to head for Georgetown and a little femme boutique he had heard about. Once there parking was nonexistent, so he drove onto the sidewalk and went inside.. Now, he was nervous. First inspecting suggestive mannequins, he was joined by a soft and breathy voice. His undisciplined fancies were augmented by her many outrageous notions until he was thoroughly embarrassed. Totally flustered, he left the svelte form in a mask of heavy makeup. He resolved to buy Marna a good shotgun and a set of tools.

Of one thing he was certain. He would drive straight through the five hundred miles, and it wasn't to continue any investigation. Marna had left no doubt in his mind that she was waiting for him to return, so he carried his heart like a high school junior on his way to pick up his prom date. He was focused on Marna and he was headed back.

Bert Howe

12

Through Grafton Notch the Porsche climbed like a feather on a thermal draft. Marna resigned herself to the wind tugging her hair for a while but finally employed a kerchief. She had insisted on the top down as everything looked so good to her. Nothing mattered, for she was where she most desired to be. They had no need to speak; when she turned her face to him she got a smile.

She had given little thought since to the manner in which they met. Things simply began to happen, and they were spending a lot of time together. She had heard her friends comment on the way men had hit on them. Jim hadn't approached her like that. Truth were known, she had made the first move; and from the beginning it was plain that he regarded her as an equal in every sense. All this was to her liking, but she was a woman who was not completely comforted in the knowledge he had not advanced any further demands on her. Now she was discontented with the direction her thoughts were taking her. What if he didn't find her that attractive, after all? Be in control. Yeah, right, Nancy, she bristled to herself. In control of what? When?

Well, here she was, she rationalized, in Jim's Porsche headed for a weekend in the mountains on as perfect a September day as one could pick for a hike. He stirred her into conversation, never forced it. They could have known each other for a year rather than the two weeks since they met. She made an inward shrug. Relax, she commanded herself.

At the eastern base of Spectre Mountain is a shelter complex – lodging and meals, souvenirs, equipment, weather and trail information. Several trails begin at this point. They left the car in a secure parking location while they went inside the lodge. Bunk space in a high trail hut by a stream was no problem, so they reserved it. The ambient tundra was but four walking hours away from their zone of trees.

Fine-tuning of pack straps was indicated before both moved out on short, measured paces.. This was not her companion's first trip east. Their physical condition was tested early on by two chimney ascents, one close upon the other, and she was relieved to learn he enjoyed a rest stop now and again. Conversation ensued as they had the breath.

Much leafy foliage was still retained by trees, but the scent of dry leaves under foot filled the air where the trail passed choke cherry, black alder, moose maple and poplar. Later, up the trail, huge yellow birches, as well as white and silver, gave a vaulted aura to their surroundings, but they gave way, higher on the path, to firs in abundance. Their way was strewn with rocks and crossed by dry beds of streamlets.

At times little air was there to stir branches and leaves, and they heard the hammering of woodpeckers. Nuthatches laughed their rustic greetings, and an audience of chickadees and golden-crowned kinglets followed along high in the tree tops.

In time, frost-flattened ferns lay far below on the east slope; and when the late afternoon became shaded by the mountain massif, they halted to add clothing and adjust pack straps. Marna needed to relieve two tender spots on her shoulders.

She couldn't remember such elation in a man's presence, and Jim gave her every reason to be sure he was enjoying her company. When they stopped to wet the whistle or gaze on a new vista, he had a word of encouragement for her. Then it dawned on her. He was learning more about her than she was of him. He had ensnared her in a social trap of going on about her universe. But they laughed easily, and she needed that.

"Jim, what really prompted you to take me up on my suggestion we take to the high hills?"

Without delay he replied, "The company." They were standing by a great boulder which had rolled that far down the mountain, probably at the time of the glacier. She started to turn away, but his gaze held her. She thought he smiled with his eyes,

Echo Horizon

and he didn't make her feel uncomfortable as he went on. "I guess we've seen each other for most of a week." She leaned back on the boulder not in a hurry to return to the trail and break from wherever this conversation was going. "From that first day you've made it easy to talk to you. A lady like you has to be attached to someone. It's always like that."

She bent a knee and slid her foot behind her flat against the rock. Sun shown on her dark, glossy hair.

"Forgive me. I'd be really embarrassed if you thought I sounded like I was coming on to you."

"Forgive you for, like, coming on to me? Should I be offended at...?"

Jim removed something from his pack, looking at her the while. "Marna, I wonder if you have any idea the difficulty a guy like me has meeting a woman he really wants to be with and can talk to?"

"So. Where do you get the idea it's easy for a woman? If she sees a guy she would like to get to know, the society of the times says OK, approach him. More than likely he gets scared off. No man, it seems, wants to make a commitment...and the lines...the macho identity are totally unlike the real guy."

"An attractive girl such as yourself is always surrounded by a bunch of guys."

"Don't we wish."

"And there's another thing, I'm hopeless at cocktail parties...don't have the small talk. I'm lost on a dance floor." Marna straightened and stepped toward him. This man was not sweet talking her. He was leveling. She began to see herself as that woman he really wanted to be with. He liked her so much he couldn't bear to be away from her. The thought warmed her. Suddenly she was very warm. She liked that, and her guard was all the way down. She wanted to hug him, anything to let him know how good she felt to be with him in their own world. She looked up into his eyes, put both hands on his chest.

"Jim, a wonderful man has just come into my life. I wonder if I dare say 'I'm here'." As they opened their packs his lingering touch on her shoulder reassured her.

They remained at the over look long enough for cold tea, crackers and cheese, but clear sky promised a cold night on the mountain, and a growing chill urged them on their way. As they climbed, their horizon broadened, and fields and villages took on a tapestry-like appearance.

"Look down there, Jim, it's as if we could move those farm buildings around with a toe."

Marna knew warm valley air would rush up slope around sunset as it was replaced by radiationally cooled mountain air running down slope, giving the unwary a false impression of weather to be expected. They stopped by an abyss. "What are those little flowers, Marna?"

"Wood asters, and that's a black sedge beside them." From there the trail began to deteriorate, and they scrambled from rock to rock. Tree growth spread out below their elevation, and ahead rose a rocky spur with yellow map lichen and grasses bending in a coverlet of color. Countless feet trod this trail, and as many eyes saw this mountain, but not as Marna saw it.

"There it is, Jim, in that col. You can just make out the end."

"Is that our hut?"

"That's it." Five hundred feet of elevation remained to them. They looked up at rock, straight ahead and down at rock, leaping from one to the other so that Marna thought her pack would pry her off the trail. Jim, behind her, called for a halt. He refastened her belly strap and seemed, so she thought, in no special hurry to continue. He was perspiring in-spite-of the cold, and she realized she was breathing in deeper gulps.

Within shouting distance of the hut their path leveled onto a plateau, and one of life's sweeter moments came when she dropped her pack and splashed spring water on her face. Inside was evidence of two other hikers; more should arrive before dark. Marna placed her pack on a bunk and changed into her warm-ups, legs tingling.

Echo Horizon

She lost touch with the moment as Jim held out her jacket for her upon noticing her first shiver, reaction to a rising breeze and rapidly cooling air. His manner was so like that of the man on the schooner who had wrapped her chilled body in his boat cloak. The nearness of Jim generated a stirring that brought her to the point of a tremble which she tried to mask with a sudden turn of her head and a thank you. Her voice reduced to a whisper when he swept her into his arms and just held her so she felt his warmth. She made no move to break away. Time stopped.

Definition to the east beyond the mountain was obscured by the massif's growing shadow, but light played still on their high range as Jim dropped two pre-sealed dinners into a pan on top of their alcohol stove. He placed their clanking eating ware on a table which had been brought to this place on someone's packboard years before. Then he rummaged and came up with two candles which he stuck to a piece of firewood and set alight on the table top.

Marna's eyes were riveted to him as he brought forth two wine glasses and a bottle of chardonnay. Dinner suddenly took on a formality she wouldn't have predicted. Jim kept surprising her. Little hope was left that she would figure him out. She was wild with good vibrations and anticipation, but she had to admit to herself her inability to figure him was a frustration. She wasn't uncomfortable; she was enjoying the time of her life with good companionship. But here was a man no one was going to second guess.

Cleaning up was simple, and though both were tired, sleep could wait. Sunset and light still remained. The summit was not visible from their location, but a bubbling brook invited them for a last stroll of the day. The sky was clear, and first stars appeared as they stretched out on a flat rock ledge where they could listen to the brook and gaze over distant valleys with pockets of lights showing near the horizon. They were barely aware of the return of two hikers.

Bert Howe

Neither spoke for the longest time until Jim brought out his flashlight and trail guide. "What route appeals to you for tomorrow, Marna?"

"How about the trail of the cascades? That way we go over the summit on our way to Meteor Mountain."

"Works for me. How about escape trails if we run into bad weather?"

"Any number of them, and they all pretty much descend to the same general location." The reverie was broken, and her thoughts prodded her. What should she expect? What did she expect, and where was this going? He was all business and for the most part kept his distance. She liked that, she thought...but only to a point. What point was that her inner self demanded?

What she wanted was to be cuddled, and she'd never felt like this in the company of a man. She wanted him to cuddle her, acknowledge she was a desirable woman, and she wanted to snuggle. Was that too much to ask? Why would he make her do all the work? If she had looked up, she would have seen him looking at her as she sat in the sunset's final burst of light.

The fear nagged her that she was not sufficiently attractive to him other than a good companion. Well, she'd just see about that. She started with a shivering noise and crossed her arms in front. He was already in the act of removing his jacket which he wrapped around her and took his place beside her.

"Now, you'll be cold."

"No. You're awfully quiet." She couldn't bear to have him know what she was thinking. "What a feeling of detachment up here, Marna. What have you been thinking?"

What had she been thinking? She felt trapped. Anything. Grasp at anything. "Dreams, mostly. Do you place any importance in dreams?"

"It depends. Some, I guess."

"Well, do you ever dream you're someone else, or living someone else's life?"

"I never gave it much attention until you just brought it up, but yeah, dreaming in the third person, that's what it is. I don't have much success calling up the details, doesn't happen that often. It's like the lights are turned way down."

She knew she wasn't directing the conversation. The words were leading her; they had led her before. She didn't know what she would say next, but she felt like everything had happened before. "Look at those fiery furnaces up above. What are we in comparison? They make me feel tiny. This mountain makes me feel of little consequence, but people still regard themselves as the center of the universe."

"Egocentricity may be the price of being."

"Don't you wonder, sometimes, Jim, what we are, who we really are? I wonder why there is such a person as me. How come I'm here?"

"Can you accept the notion you are detached from all other beings, or is there a common thread? Does reality have a question?"

"Well, I'd like to know what it's all about. Where did we come from and where are we going?"

"We want different things and yet the same things."

She wrapped her arms about her knees. "That could be taken as a cynical contradiction."

"Don't you think it's valid?"

"No...well, I mean..." Was this going anywhere, she asked herself?

"I think most people want to hang onto life, immortality, to have power and influence, money. The differences, I think, lie in moral mind-set and material choices."

She stared at his face in the failing light. "Jim, what do you believe in?"

"What do I believe in?"

"Or what do you believe?"

"I regard belief as a luxury. I observe, respond to signals and information and deal with a situation."

She could just make out his silhouette in starlight, one leg drawn up beneath him, braced on one arm and leaning toward her. She could feel her control weakening, had loosed her grasp on the structure of her secure world. She was starting free fall. The pause in their talk was filled with the sounds of tumbling water in an otherwise silent world; and the gyre of night turned overhead. Her words were out before she knew she was speaking, urged by her soul grown weary of the lonliness of parity. "Are you receiving any signals?" She heard herself and wanted to expire.

"Yes, from a handsome young woman who will argue me into a corner if I let her, who knows we are willing to believe according to the commitment each is willing to make." The words softened in her ears, and his voice drew nearer. "...and I believe this gorgeous woman is going to kiss me right now." She did, and her breath at altitude couldn't keep pace with her racing heart. They both were in free fall, falling over and over one another ever faster. She grasped him to her with a force which came from beyond her being, contours discovering to each furtive fingertip. They would be devoured then and there, both consumed by a fire like none they had known nor dreamed possible, the chill banished from the night.

They sat and held each other, not needing voice, for all had been said and understood. He helped her to her feet, and they returned to the hut. On the way, Marna misjudged the path and soaked her warm-ups in the brook. Before turning in, she hung them by the stove, then retrieved her slacks for the morrow and placed them on a bench.

Sleep was a luxury earned. During the night, wind strengthened and orographic clouds formed high on the west slope. Shrieks and moans were abroad in the night as the cold air drove at the little mountain shelter, but no one woke to feed the fire after midnight. It died, leaving Marna's warm-ups damp and icy.

Powdered eggs are a treat generally avoided, but scrambled eggs and sausage from their sealed pouches proved to be a royal delight.

Sun brightened slopes warmed their hopes of crossing the summit to a spectacular vista of the northern ranges. Suppressing a notion she had forgotten something, Marna donned dark blue shorts and hung her warm-ups from outside her pack. She took the lead, breathing deeply of invigorating air and exhaling white clouds.

Any difference between their chosen trail and straight up wasn't worth the argument. At one particularly demanding chimney Jim hung back, and she wondered if he had hurt a foot or was snapping pictures. "You all right?" she called down.

"Marna, the view here is wonderful."

"Wait, I'll be right down."

"No, you'd miss it. You're it."

She glared and could have shot him. As the day lengthened, wind increased from the west, and the sun dimmed through a thickening haze. As soon as they found a spot where both could stand, they discussed the wisdom of continuing the summit route. Their circle of visibility was steadily shrinking toward them. They checked the time and decided to take up a lateral route transiting the mountain at a lower elevation.

When Marna's breath came in less of a pant she broke the train of thought. "You aren't asking me any questions about...you know.."

"This is pleasure, Marna, no business." He put his hand to her arm and helped her to her feet. "Trail forks about two miles farther on, and we want to get over the north col and reach Emerald Springs before this stuff closes in on us."

"Right, oh, master guide."

Progress became sluggish, and Marna didn't experience the same vigor she had felt on the previous day. Climbing and jumping to each succeeding rock exacted mounting effort. The air temperature was dropping. By noon the weather had deteriorated, as ascending moisture laden air built clouds barely above their heads. When a cold drizzle commenced, they halted beside a cairn, the next one ahead already invisible.

To retreat by the way they had come demanded a perilous descent in decreasing visibility. Jim estimated they were nearer their objective than their point of departure that morning and about the same elevation. With the air filled with super cooled droplets, their lungs were hard pressed to meet their bloods' demand for oxygen. Marna's legs were blue from cold. She slung her pack down to retrieve her slacks to pull on over her shorts, but hunt as she would, no slacks. The shivering reality was she had left them at the trail hut and had only her damp warm-ups.

Jim was alarmed at her color and urged her to don the warm-ups, anyway, arguing they needed to get off this ridge and at least the wind would be blocked from her legs. Stepping and balancing on roundish boulders became tenuous in the growing wind, and the cold droplets continued to aggravate breathing. It was all happening too fast, and chill from a white void was penetrating.

"Marna, we can't keep stopping to check the map; we've got to find one of those down trails and find it fast. Emergency procedure from here on in. We've got to get you warm."

"I'll be all right, Jim. Why don't we stop and make some tea, won't that be a good idea? Besides, it's just a little way. You'll see; everything's fine."

"Move, Honey. Here, my hand, you grab it." He knew she wouldn't feel it right away if he squeezed too hard; but he didn't want to interrupt the blood flow to an extremity.

Marna had her particular problems. Her heart, though young, healthy and strong could not any longer simultaneously provide the heating requirements for her body and for locomotion. Repeatedly they strayed from the trail, missing cairns and expending further energy re-establishing their route. Marna was oblivious to the gravity of her situation and stumbled ahead while held firmly by Jim until he knew she could go no farther. They must be near a down trail, but now, he had both their packs and Marna, she cradled in his arms. Below the timberline, he could make a leanto of boughs and get her into her sleeping bag. With luck they would find a shelter.

Now, her extremities were numb, and shivering increased to convulsive shudders. Worse, all her education and lifetime

Echo Horizon

experience came to naught, as judgement was an early casualty in this crisis. Her world compressed to whiteness.

Insinuating on her subconscious, otherworldly sensations constructed for her shadow awareness an alter consciousness in time and space. Her world was marked by a pitching and rolling, and she was having trouble keeping to her feet in a swaying void. Her world was reduced to this. She felt nauseous from mal de mer and stumbled against a great wheel.

A voice in her ear counseled to "Easy up." She stood at the center of a circle of water, huge masts and peaks of sails rising into nothingness.

"Make 'er out, Mr. MacLean?" A massive black form materialized and was as soon vanished in the fog.

"Colors of the Atlantic Squadron, Capt'n." Comfort was on the vessel with her, here on *Archer*. How she loved to hear his voice as it sounded over the vessel.

"Show him the merchant colors of Massachusetts." The order was acknowledged and repeated beyond a wall of white. From afar came a voice compressed into a speaking trumpet.

"Send your gig aboard me the instant," it commanded.

"Gig smashed in norther two days out of Nassau," was the reply from near where she stood, holding her breath.

Suddenly, "Look out for the tops!" The frightened, strangled cry had come from her own throat, and she inhaled aromas of tar and galley smoke. A lift line slapped against a mast in a contrapuntal rhythm with the creak of spars.

"An eye to the tops, Mr. Coleman. Mr. MacLean, ready to jibe." No sooner were the commands spoken than she heard the rattle of musketry. A little form collapsed on the deck before her. Air moved around her paralyzed form. "Jibe!" More gunfire.

"Hard down rudder, Mr. Dighton." She knew the voice to be her father's, and Mr. Dighton at the helm was such a good friend to her and Sister. Sometimes, he let her assist him at the steerage. Now, she could only clutch the edge of the companion in terror, unable to look out on the scene.

"Mr. Coleman, the main tops if you will, Sirrah." The main boom swished past her head with a rattle of lines and blocks and a final THWACK when the huge sail took the breeze on the opposite board.

Immediately, the deck beneath her feet convulsed from a thunderous crash. She gagged on the doer of rotten eggs. Shouting intensified. "Up rudder. Mr. Ruck, double shot the twelve pounders. I want that ship's forem'st. Langrage, Mr. Coleman?"

"Aye, langrage, Cap'n."

"Mr. Ruck, fire as target bears." Before the black hulk could return into the void, both bow guns erupted, and she knew she heard the splintering and crashing of heavy wood.. That ship would not pursue. Then all about was stillness, no running of lines nor swaying. Was that Comfort's voice consoling and urging her to come back, telling her how good it would all be? She was infinitely comforted, but this was not the voice of Comfort MacLean. Of that she was certain.

She recalled the warmth of the water in the big swimming pool at the field house, buoyant, caressing, soothing. She felt a pressure ever so gentle; she was held but not possessed. He was taking her home. She felt warmth on her legs, her breasts, her entire being, caring warmth. She became aware of her heart beating in rising tempo with another. He was with her from her toes to her ears, and she knew his scent, his firmness against her flesh, nerve ends poised to detonate her most tender parts.

"Oh, good God!"

"You're feeling better, I hope."

"Where are we...whats...?" Lightning flared through nerve endings. She was reclining on her side, overcome with desire. Lifting her knees she shuddered at the touch of a hot presence.

"Damn it, don't move!" One knee came against him. "Ohhh, that's...that's.." Of a sudden she knew it was real, She was in a sleeping bag with him, neither with clothes on.. She was no longer cold but burning with sensation, all in tune to his flesh, her every fiber responding hotly. She felt she must glow with electrified need and be compelled by a field of energy to move with him, squirming the while, wetter by the second and helplessly lost to love's passion

"For Christ's love, Marna, I nearly lost you on the trail. Don't God, I didn't mean to…"

"I'm all right, now, really," she gasped. She was near losing it and unable to stop.

"You almost died."

"But I didn't, I'm OK," she breathed. Impatient, her fingers caressed him after a feint of searching. She wanted all of him, a feeling of wholeness.

"Christ!"

"What's wrong?"

"God, your fingers are still icy!" His sudden explosion surprised her.

"God damn it, James Starr, are you going to enter me, or what?" She divested him of all demeanor as she rolled to straddle his legs with a wanton attitude, overcoming his hesitancy. She was certain he was afraid of causing her pain. They met in space, each losing identity and becoming one.

Later, trees filtered the sunlight which flickered through a cracked window pane, and Jim was illuminated while scrambling from their bunk to retrieve his clothes. He added wood to the fire, and smoke drifted past the stove lid into what she could see was the one room of a small cabin. Quick examination convinced her it had been abandoned for some time to the local wood mice. A smoke pipe rambled from the cracked stove to its exit in the roof.

"Throw me something I can slip on," she requested in a subdued voice, wondering why she demurred at this time. She wanted to ask a dozen questions, grabbed the flimsy panties from trajectory, and ducked back into the sleeping bag for the gymnastics of dressing.

"Why were you yelling yesterday on the trail?"

"Yelling what?" came a muffled voice from the bunk.

"Why were...?" Her head appeared, and he lowered his voice. "Why were you yelling so while we were struggling on the trail?"

"You said yesterday?" She ran her hands hard up and down through her hair. "We were struggling?"

"You weren't the easiest thing to carry along with our packs down to the timberline. What was the hollering? You cried out 'look out for the tops''.

"I said that?" She stared at him for a moment. "Oh, it was like a dream, I guess. It's silly. You wouldn't believe me if I told you."

"Try me?"

"It was like I was there, one of the people. Yeah, that's it." A new idea took form in her head. She squirmed from the sleeping bag and leaned her head on one hand. "I wasn't really me. I was someone else, one of the people on a vessel that was fired on." Very quickly she became dead serious. "We were fired on from the fighting tops of a British ship for no reason. I swear I lived through this experience. It was real! Father ordered the guns to return.""

"Your father? You could see him?"

"Father was the captain...the girl's father. That's what's so confusing...the father of the girl I seemed to be, a young girl." Jim sat beside her as she continued. "No, I didn't exactly see him, just heard his voice. But that's the point; everything was as it ought to be. We were returning from Grande-Terre Island."

"When?"

"I'm not sure. The guns were huge, but fired round balls and were muzzle loaded. The ship had no power or anything like that.. My little sister and I were simply there as we were supposed to be. Our father had built the vessel and was its captain."

"Have you had dreams anything like this before?"

"Yeah. I suppose." She turned on her back, covered her face and wept. Jim bent to her and kissed her eyes.

"Are you going to be OK?"

Echo Horizon

"Oh, Jim, Billy was shot. They shot Billy dead!" Her weeping convulsed into sobs. "He was just taking his captain a drink, and…and the stinking bastards shot him, the poor little thing. He fell at my feet." Her voice crescendoed into a wail, and words became muffled and confused between sobs. "And I hope the broken horse shoe nails and musket balls Mr. Coleman fired at their main top killed every goddamn mothers' son of them!"

He placed his hand gently on her forehead and whispered her name, brushed her cheek with his lips. "Billy…who was Billy?"

"A little boy from our town. His brother and father had been drowned while fishing, but his mother still wanted him to have a chance to grow up to the sea."

"You know something of the firing of the great guns, then. Any chance Mr. Coleman was successful? That was a name you uttered."

They carried a barrel of broken horse shoes, flattened musket balls, nails, glass, stones, whatever. Mr. Coleman didn't miss. Jim, doesn't this all sound crazy?"

"No, Marna, and you were in a very bad way yesterday. I should have noticed sooner. It can happen before anyone suspects. You were well along into hypothermia. How do you feel, now?"

She turned her eyes from him. "I feel wonderful."

"Don't kid around, Marna. I can call a taxi if you need it." He withdrew from a pocket a small transceiver. "There's room for a bird to set down here."

"Don't you dare. I can walk. I'll have to share you soon enough. Are you anxious to get back? Are you sorry about…?"

"No and no, I'm not. Are you?" He was still very close to her, and she put her arms around his neck. "Did you put me to bed, or did I…?"

"You couldn't have found your left ear with both hands. You were so cold to my touch by the time I found this old mountaineering hut I thought sure I was going to lose you. No time to heat water for a warm drink. This was the only chance I thought you had."

"Kiss me?"

"Then...then, I was so beat after climbing in with you I fell asleep. I didn't mean...Christ! I didn't intend for it to happen. That wasn't consistent with her desires, and she put her nose against his. "Tell me, Jim.." The field of force grew. "..I want to know what you were going to say." She was doing things to him and helping him do things to her, and he knew it was hopeless to resist, that he was falling and could never go back. She met him in passion, and with what breath he had left, he gave his all.

"Marna, I want to wake up naked with you every morning for the rest of my life."

The day was half gone when he attempted the authority figure again and said, "I want you to have some of this hot soup that will be ready soon. The salt will be good for you. When we get back, you should damn well be checked out at the infirmary. I'm sure glad the worst is over." She replied through the smoky blue of the cabin's interior that he could damn well stop worrying and get a life.

After the long descent during which time Jim behaved toward her like a mother hen, they reached a road and hitched a ride to his car. She was still protesting her complete recovery when he guided her into the college infirmary. As it happened, Doctor Ronen Dayan was filling in for one of the regular staff MDs and responded to Marna's steadfast objections.

"First the medical practitioner before the psychiatrist, is that not so?"

"Really, I'm fine, Roni, fine. This idiot is afraid I'll die from a little chill."

He turned to Jim. "What treatment have you...?" A quick look at Marna's eyes... "Should I even ask?" Then to Jim, "No rubbing of the extremities, I think, just to increase slowly the deep, internal temperature,"

"Standard navy training text, Doctor, if all else fails..."

"Yes, I see." He touched her abdomen. "We don't wish the coldness of blood from the extremities coursing the already wearied heart, but.." He looked from Jim to Marna, both grinning from ear to ear and unable to control themselves. "I think we do a work up on this heart muscle. Nurse! Incredible bedside manner of some people. Commander, get out. We have work to do here. Marna, stop the giggling. I take this blood pressure here."

"Bye, Honey, Doc. See ya soon. Gotta run."

The question hit him before he reached his car. How did Doc Dayan know of his service and rank?

Bert Howe

13

Marna was grading the last of her students' papers in her faculty office. It was one of those dark October evenings with promised rain. If some of her students were even semi-literate, then so much time would not be required in establishing the lack of enlightened content. Some of these freshmen had graduated with honors from highschool. "Whatever gave you the idea you could teach, Marna?" escaped in a sigh.

Jim hadn't called and that bummed her. Alone in the building that housed her classes, she was sensitive to every sound from the heating pipes to the rattle of windows in a rising wind. She moved items on her desk in order to continue the background research for her novel and was looking through a bunch of letters not yet explored. The library tower clock struck the hour of nine. Darkness had prevailed since supper.

Soon strong gusts of wind ripped leaves and small branches from trees along the campus drive. Street lights cast eerie shadows on grounds and adjacent buildings. Something about her office had changed. What was not immediately evident. Small things like a table two inches nearer the window frame or the carpet slightly askew. She considered that someone had been nosing around. But what would anyone want here? She left nothing of material value in her office, only notes and lecture outlines. Her files were fairly empty, nothing of interest. None of the ancient material from home was kept here. What she had now she brought this morning.

Faculty maintained an open door policy; locks were unthinkable. A credit card would open the old latches anyway. She kept no secrets, but someone may think she did. Listening to the moan of the wind, she gazed thoughtfully through her window at dancing shadows. A dozen people could lurk beside trees and not be noticed. She thought of the attack on Roni's office and his helper, Gert. She couldn't recall the last name. A shiver coursed up her spine. She sighed and picked up a few letters from beneath the ship's log. One was remarkably preserved, and it looked official. The writer had addressed it to the General Court. No evidence of a seal could she find, so she thought it could be a copy.

> To the Honorable Council & House of Representatives
> Of the colony of Massachusetts in General Court
> Assembled, July 26, 1775
> Humbly sheweth your petitioner that the frequent
> alarms arising from the restless attempts by our
> Unnatural enemies, to which the easy and extensive
> Seacoast within our bounds peculiarly exposes the
> Inhabitants of this county, especially the eastern
> part of it to visitations of fleets in this harbour who
> make amusing movements and magnify their glory
> By the burning of dwellings and the carrying off of
> Livestock and occasions a great use of ammunition
> from shore. Your petitioner is reduced to great
> distress at the poverty of shipping in said harbour
> and prays your Honors, that as the eastern shores
> of this colony is exposed to the ravages of the Enemy,
> he may be allowed to fit out his schooner Archer of
> an hundred tons for a Privateer and make use of
> Ball and Langrage carried by him for the defense
> of said county from Grande Terre Island, and enlist
> thirty men to serve aboard said vessel for the Defense
> of the Sea Coast in the Eastern part of this colony,
> and your petitioner as in Duty Bound shall ever Pray
> & be allowed 200 pounds powder to be used aboard
> said vessel for the purposes aforesaid.
>
> J^{no} Alport

The master of *Archer*…she liked *Sagittarius*..requested letter of marque. At that moment she knew she would feel at home on that craft should it sail on ghostly waters to her very door and she be spirited away. Whatever image had insinuated on her dreamscape, this sailboat had assumed a life of its own. Surely it existed in the past, but something familiar to her existed, now.

A yawn escaped. It was no easy task bringing to life the ancient text from old parchment. She picked up the log.

> Sunday. Have to get home
> For repair and Provision.
> Taking water. Sea be delivering
> Her timbers in the cove we
> Sail not home this day.

Thumbing back a few pages she came to reference to a chase and a prize. Some pages were blank.

> Gave chase sail hull down,
> Six bells Overhaul snow and
> Fire three rnd. Sampson
> Ritchie, Master. Took parole
> Master & officers. Send Mr.
> Dighton on shore as Prize
> Master. Spec'l mention Mr.
> Ruck for'd battery. English
> Colors odd with't St. Patrick

From accounts through 1776, she concluded hunting had been good if prizes were the measure, *Archer* had been hard on the English. The St. Patrick business left her stymied. Just that afternoon she had discussed flag origins with Nancy. Coincidence.

Light reflections from her window went haywire as the panes vibrated. The building was empty save for her, wasn't it? She stopped breathing. What was her trouble? It was only the building entrance opening, a concatenation of footsteps leading to her door...and stopping. Rain beat on her windows as she waited in icy apprehension and squeaked unintelligibly at the knock on her door. Then she exhaled when she saw Jim lean into the doorway. He was glistening wet from rain but looked awfully good to her.

"Where have you been?"

He was expected to know it only mattered to Marna that he had been away from her. "Lord, Marna, you look like you've seen a ghost. You OK?"

"Yeah, right, but I'm glad you came."

"You're not all right."

"Just a little jumpy is all."

"I thought you might invite me to the Cuddy for a beer and some Mexican.."

"Don't change the subject. You didn't call."

"I've been hot on the trail of investigation."

"I don't believe you've found out a thing. I…Are you really investigating anything?"

"Honest Injun."

"Doesn't it cross your mind that a girl could miss you when you're not around?" She sat back and moved her hands from her knees along her legs. Cuddy? We could go back to my place, and I'll whip you up a dinner you won't forget."

He walked to the back of her chair, leaned down and placed his chin on her shoulder.

"What are you doing? Oh, you're all wet!"

"I'm looking at the papers on your desk. Old, aren't they?"

"You're blowing in my ear."

"I thought you liked it."

"Well, I do if…" Her face turned slightly to his.

"You might invite me to breakfast."

"Bring your toothbrush. Yes, they are old. This is only part of a chest full of old letters and documents I found in my attic. I don't have a clue who put them there or how long ago."

"Your mom and dad, maybe?"

"Dad bought the place..oh..ten years ago. We moved in when I was in high school. From the load of dust on everything in the attic, they were undisturbed for a century. They look like they had to do with a community from long ago. I'd like to locate it. Got a few leads, a few ideas so far."

Jim picked up the letter of petition. "Mind if I have a look?"

"No, look at anything you wish."

"This is a memorial in treat for a letter of marque. Did he get it, do you know?"

"We could assume he did. What blows my mind is the similarity between this vessel and its people and the one I visited last spring, I told you all about. Where did those people learn about the boat we're reading about?" She held up the small leather bound book. "Here's the log. Hunting was real good."

He swapped the letter for the log and soon let out a whistle.

"What?"

"Something odd here. If we go by the dates noted, this was compiled some two hundred ten years ago. Marna, what do you know about English grammar?"

"Get real. Not a hell of a lot. Why?"

"Look at this letter." He pointed to some lines. "Now, the log. That entry, look carefully at the first line... 'have to get home.' Anachronistic, don't you think?"

She studied for a full minute before putting it down. "I think I see what you mean."

" 'We have to... We got home... We've got to get...' That's us speaking. Don't you get the feeling this guy doesn't fit the woodwork?"

Marna gave a visible shudder. "I'm getting that feeling." She could feel the blood leaving her face.

Also, the cross of Saint Patrick, unless I'm sadly mistaken, that isn't generally associated with the British naval ensign until sometime after... What is it Marna, can I get you some water?"

"No, Jim, just hold me." Her voice was reduced to a whisper. "I'm sorry."

"It's all right, honey, for Heaven's sake, let it out. It isn't like we were strangers."

"I'm scared out of my gourd." Her breathing accelerated.

"Of what?"

"That's what's so frightening. I don't know what. These old papers...I think they're haunted. There's more at home. They're leading me, directing my life, dragging me to a conclusion. I don't even think for myself anymore. I know things, see events from the past; but it's all a dream world. I drop off to sleep and like step into a vision, and it's all so real. I could actually be living in another time. Maybe all that's the reality, and this is the dream. I'm all mixed up."

"What past? When does this all take place?"

"I believe I have an alter ego living during the American Revolution, and I'm getting to know her better and more intimately. Jim, don't. Don't look at me like that. I'm not crazy." She burst into tears.

"Marna, Sweetheart, that's the furthest from my thoughts. You're upset, and I can tell you some people in Washington are, too. That old wreck in your cove has a story to tell, and it's trying to tell it."

"Who else knows about it?"

"My admiral, my boss."

"I don't dare ask if you've found out anything about my parents."

"Nothing firm."

"I was afraid."

"No, don't." He stroked her hair. "I have nothing that would stand on legs in court, but I'm building an enormous background. Tell me something."

"What? Oooh, don't stop."

"How much do you know about your dad?"

"What? I've known him twenty-seven years. How long before that?"

"He ever tell you about his life before he was married to your mother?"

"Some, I guess...no more than any kid gets to hear from her dad. He was a navy pilot, flew combat missions in Viet Nam..."

"And?"

"I think he flew from a carrier in the Korean War. Gee, that was quite a while ago."

"Back some. He tell you about his younger days? He tell you he flew in the navy in the Western Pacific Theater during World War II?"

She counted on her fingers. "No, that's impossible, he'd have been too young. He was fourteen when the war was over."

Jim hit a wall of frustration. Pete Rankin hadn't prepared him for that response. Even if he believed the admiral's story, and he didn't, his mind wanted to fit the known parameters around the unknown. What if the captain had been nineteen years old in July of 1945, and what if he'd actually fallen afoul a time warp? Would the aging process cease? Could he in the admiral's scenario come onto the *USS Antietam* still only nineteen years old? The whole thing had to be garbage, but he played 'what if'.

"When did you start having the dreams, Hon.?"

"Actually, right after the experience on the old schooner I told you about."

"And the scenes and experiences seem extra real?"

"Incredible." Jim thought a while.

"If they were like ordinary dreams, you'd never get to where you wanted to be and would never accomplish much."

"That's one of the really weird things. I go directly where I'm headed, and we do…my family and I…a day's work. I can count the flour sacks at the end of the day. There's a saw mill with big up and down saws powered by the wheel, and a sawyer comes regularly. I help him scale the lumber and mark the board feet on a plank. My hands are always chapped when I waken. My muscles ache. How real can it get?" She pushed away from her desk. "Let's get out of here, Jim. Tell you what, we'll stop at the Cuddy for a beer, say hi to the gang and go home to that feast I promised you."

"You're reading my mind, Sweetheart."

The rain had brought a number of folks out of the weather into the Cuddy, some ultimately, to get under it. "Look, Jim, there's Nancy and, I think his name's Erick. I'll tell you about him later. Can we join them?"

"Lead on, Sweet."

"Hi, Nan, these seats taken?"

"Not until now. Join us. Hi there. Ooh, Marna, he's good looking. Is he why I've hardly laid eyes on you for two months?"

"I thought you'd met. Jim Starr, Nancy Marsh and Erick..."

"Lehn, Marna. Happy to meet you, Jim. Hope you're enjoying the area." Greetings past, Marna knew she was blushing but didn't care anymore.

"Well, will you get a load of what's coming!? Who is this vision? asked Erick. Marna's attention was focused on the figure approaching the table and all blossomed out in a silvery gown.

"Katie, it's Katie!" she squealed.

"Katie, whatever in the world? Look at you!"

"You don't suppose Katie's performing tonight, do you?"

"Get real, Erick." Then a flash of sparkle caught Nancy's eye. "Oh, she's gone and done it. Look at that rock."

Katie blushed when she said, "You guys act surprised. It's not as if this were a secret or anything like that."

"Could have fooled me," said Marna. "Who's the very lucky guy?"

"Dave...Dave, come out from behind that beer and come over here." To the four at the table she added, "He's celebrating, he says."

Marna spied Sandy just when Dave got up from his bar stool. "What's she telling you?" Dave demanded.

"Nothing much, Dave, but that's one hell of a beautiful stone. Why don't you tell us? Are congratulations in order?" asked Erick. Erick looked the typical Teuton but possessed a genteel personality which had drawn many to him in friendship.

"Well, you guys know me pretty well, eh, 'cept maybe Mr. Starr here, and I only know him from reputation, eh."

"Deserved, Suh, ah most dearly hope," quipped Jim.

"Oh, damn it, Dave, I'm sorry. This is my friend Jim Starr from Virginia. Jim, Dave Brandon from Prince Edward Island."

Echo Horizon

"Mah pleasure, Suh," said Jim, standing.

At that moment, Marna saw Sandy leave the bar and head their way. He was big as a bear and could be as friendly. Instinctively, she kept her eyes on him, knew he'd been drinking and felt immediately uneasy. Jim returned to his seat, and Dave headed back for the bar. He halted when he saw where Sandy was headed. If he were celebrating the engagement Dave had announced to the group, he had forgotten to shave and don appropriate clothes.

Sandy swaggered to the table. "Marna, I want to talk to you...now."

"Aw-w, not now, Sandy."

"He took her by the arm just below the shoulder. "Yeah, *now*, Marna."

"Old Son, Ah heard the lady say not now." Jim leaned over the table with his elbows spread apart.

Sandy let go his grip on Marna and swung his hand around to point a finger in Jim's face. "I don't want to hear nothin' from you. I thought I told you to take a hike a while back." Sandy was hunched in Jim's direction looking meaner than a scalded bobcat.

"Ah don't know as ah care fiddlesticks what you thought." Jim rose slowly from his seat, eyes directed into Sandy's.

"Sandy, don't you think you've had a little too much to drink?"

"You keep to hell out of this, Marna. Ain't no kinda guy from away gonna cut in on my turf."

Jim never took his eyes from Sandy's eyes three feet away. "Mah granddaddy used to tell me, 'Son, you plant yourse'f a hill o' corn, you wants to know how to shuck it."

Sandy looked away for an instant. The others at the table saw it as the moment Jim would uncork a sledgehammer blow. He didn't. Sandy looked at the table, stepped back, looked at Marna, then sort of shambled off and back to the bar. Exhaling was audible.

Erick spoke first. "Jim, that was a close one. Man, I never saw the likes. You sure handled him."

"Thank you, Erick. No, I don't think it was close, and I didn't really handle him. I just don't think the man is stupid, though sorely vexed, I warrant."

"Jim, Honey, thank you." Marna reached out to put her hand in Jim's after he regained his seat.

"Jim, Honey, thank you?" mimicked Nancy. "Marna, is there something old Nan has missed here, something you haven't told me?" She looked from Marna to Jim. The girls excused themselves and headed for the powder room.

Once inside, Nancy burst forth, "Marna, did you see his eyes? No, Jim's eyes. Well, I did. I couldn't take my eyes from his. I've never seen anything like it in my life, that look in his eyes."

"No, I didn't see it. I guess I was looking at the woodwork or Erick or Katie. Gosh, she's so happy and bubbly tonight."

"I thought Jim was going to pop him."

"No, not Jim, he wouldn't let anything spoil Katie's party."

"Well, Sandy sure came on like he was looking for trouble. He might have hurt Jim."

"I doubt it. Don't worry about Jim, Nancy. Sandy would never have touched him, but he wouldn't be hauling lobster traps for a while either."

"What's with you and that hunk of a man, Marna? I've just got to know. Stop stringing me along, please."

"We're seeing each other."

"Yeah, right. Get real, Marna. You guys *are* serious, aren't you? Oh, wow, the trip to the mountains, right?" Realization dawned and Nancy clapped her hand to her forehead.

Marna could feel the warmth rising about her neck. "OK, you got me...for me, anyway. I think it is for him."

"Is he, I mean, are you...?"

"Is he moving in with me? No, he says he doesn't want to do anything to hurt my standing in the community. Oh, Christ,

Nancy, I want him to so badly. I've argued with him, 'What about our well-being?'"

"Run with it, girl; go along with him. You've got a treasure. I can tell Erick is impressed. You know, if guys like each other, you know you've pretty well struck the jackpot. But, Marna, his confidence, that's what it is...confidence. He doesn't know Sandy for beans. What's with this man of yours?"

"He'd scold me for talking about him, but he was trained in the navy's SEALs. He was in Viet Nam as an enlisted man when he was seventeen. He's a commander." Marna was cut short by a whistle of approval.

"So, Erick, what gives? What do you do?" inquired Jim, now free to openly attempt to draw a previously reticent Erick into a conversation.

"I'm a construction engineer, Jim."

"Bridges, like that?"

"Yeah, bridges, airports, roads, artificial reefs, cargo ports...the list goes on."

"You work for some company in particular?"

"My own."

"All right!"

"I contract. I hire when I take on a job. Course, I have a skeleton crew at all times."

"You go anywhere?"

"Anywhere."

"How about underwater equipment, Erick? Can you find things?"

"Ayuh, if they're there to find."

"How soon could you break away to look for something?"

"Tomorrow. My boats are in Portsmouth, but Sylvanus would let me charter his baby, and I have a couple guys need something to do. Can I ask what we're looking for?"

"Good man, Erick. I like your attitude. Airplane. You're hired."

"Just like that, I'm hired? No discussion of costs? No bid?"

"Just like that, you're hired. You're highly recommended. I'll tell you that much. Ahh, how about we meet in Beal's office at ten tomorrow morning. We can go over locations, and well, what the hell, you can be paid a draft for a retainer."

"Mister Man. You're on. It'll be a pleasure. Digressing, if you'll permit me, that was one piece of work there with Sandy. He can be one ugly customer. No one has ever backed him down that I know of. What...I know I'm prying, what do you do?"

"Erick, old boy, Ah didn't really back the man down. That would be demeanin' foh him and undignifahd foh me. He just knew he had choices, that's all. As for what I do, I'm an investigator with the navy. I was trained as a SEAL.

Erick whistled. "Nancy or Marna may have told you, a bunch of us...oh, all ages...have got together a Continental militia company. We're part of a regiment in the county. Wives get together and help the guys make uniforms. We've mustered veterans going back to Coxie's army, lotta Nam vets, World War II and Korea. We're having a muster for musketry back of the college next Saturday. Love to have you along if you're interested."

"Sounds great. I'll check with Marna. She can come? Here they are back."

Jim drove Marna home and set to work with her on a late repast which they didn't care when they finished.

Sometime in the night her thoughts mingled with sleep but presented a pattern. Her brain told her she was awake and wanted to work on plans for her restoration of the mill and dam, and she imagined herself roaming the walkway on a dam, listening to noises in the sluice. The outfall splashed and gurgled on its way to cove's head. The call of a night bird was on the wind.

She had been walking the brook that afternoon of a shortening day, but now the sky is darkened. She looks at Saturn and Jupiter over Big Candle Island, but why is she sprawled on her stomach on the top of the dam? Voices behind her, no moon,

Echo Horizon

and the night bird calls once more. The stones are cold to her body. She shivers.

She had washed those garments at break of day, and here she is lying in dirt. Sister's soap be death to most corrupting soil, but it bideth not well with her hands; and the dressing of the stones was prelude to finer grist but was no mercy to her hands either. Of that she's reminded at the selecting of flints and cocking her gunlock. Ample time they be for reflection this night, one of many such vigils with raiders doing the devil's work on this coast.

They had murdered two poor souls by their hearth and woulds burn them in their hovel had not armed neighbors run them off. Fear is they must return to burn the mill, wretched vermin in their ketch. Caleb named them 'shaving mill' because they cruise so nigh the shore.

In the stillness she hears Ruth Dawes' breathing. Would the beating of her own heart warn the brigands beyond the ledges? They must not be allowed to serve their four pounder carried on the bow. In the impound the call of a loon. Night air is raw from the sea. Earlier vigils had been even colder, and she had lain chilled to the marrow until the scene swirled and she make not her own way home.

She bends her legs to her and turns to crouch behind a boulder, flat on its top. She dare not loose her long rifle lest it clatter on the ground and give alarm. She can see bright planets, recently risen, in reflections from the quiet cove at flood. A trout ripples the water behind her. If they ride in mischief this night into the cove, she, Ruth and Caleb must end their predations. Mother and Sister tend the loading of the weapons in the doorway of the mill to be passed to the fore on demand.

The sound of a tree toad comes on the breeze. That is Caleb's signal from under a huge tree at the far end of the dam. She smells fish before she makes out the form of a ketch in the starlight. She answers Caleb's call with an owl's hoot. Not close enough yet. Sounds in her ears made by the coursing of her blood mute those of the millrace.

Have a care, no quick movement. Level the rifle. She points in the direction of the big island massed below the planets. How bright are the stars. She must not miss. Take the one nearest the bow, then him at the tiller. These cutthroats can't be expecting a volley from shooters who are able to strike them betwixt the eyes at five chains. Any more light and the ambush must discover.

Stronger is the smell on light sea air. Does anything betray her presence? No time to worry. Father it was told of three planets seen only with the aid of a powerful glass. She sees a figure as a shadowy form at her sighting notch. Squeeze. The night shatters. A flash disturbs her eyes, and the stock slams into her shoulder. With echoes still drumming on her ears she hears a splash as a body hits the water. Herons squawk, wings flap, two more quick shots and the awful smell of powder smoke.

Sister nudges her shoulder and carries away the piece even as she hands another. Level and draw back the hammer. Did she close the pan and strike the stock? Another form at the breaching tackle of the cannon. Squeeze. A flash, and her rifle bolts against her lame shoulder almost at once with the crack of Caleb's rifle. Ruth's shot joins the pounding of the echoes, and the night is confusion with the squeak from the rudder post and the running of the main sheet.

A match glows at the bow, but the ketch falls off its head as the bow erupts in powder flash and thunder bangs off the shore. Langrage scythes through branches away from the dam. She and Ruth are swiftly handed reloaded pieces and each send shot toward the ketch. Two shadows crumble to the deck. Is that the lot? They can barely see the boat in the smoke as it drifts onto the pebbly shore and leans tiredly.

She woke to a world of coaxing smells from the kitchen and found herself served breakfast in bed, knowing she wanted her rose water and glycerin powerfully much.

14

"It happened again."

"What happened again?"

"A crazy dream." She sat up straighter to look at him, nearly spilling her coffee. "Jim, I was there, I swear it. Look at my right shoulder. See how red."

"Mighty pretty shoulder. Yeah, it is red and swollen."

"I've got to put something on my hands. They've never been so uncomfortable."

"You might wash that smooch off your face, too." She came back from the bathroom still scrubbing at her face. "It's some sort of grease, not petroleum, more like tallow."

"Let me look at that shoulder again. Girl, you must have held a shotgun four inches from your shoulder and pulled both triggers. That's swollen."

"No, that all happened to me in the dream...or it wasn't a dream and I *was* there."

"Marna, what on Earth are you talking about? Whoa, OK, this happened on the mountain. I'm gonna back up here and you start all over and tell me."

"It was after I closed my eyes I guess I was concentrating on what the mill and dam will look like when I have them rebuilt.."

"Aww, I thought you were thinking of me."

She punched him softly. "Don't interrupt. I think I saw every stone, but I know I've seen them before, many times. And then I was lying prone on the dam with a rifle."

"Wait a minute. You were in a firing position with a rifle?" She pulled away and sat right up. "I was dreaming. I must have fallen asleep right away. There was Ruth Dawes and my mother and sister...and Caleb Gordon, a neighbor, I think."

"You'll have to tell me about Ruth Dawes and Caleb."

You remember, I had that terrible dream on the mountain, about Billy being killed. Ruth was his mother. We waited in the night for raiders to sail into the cove, and we shot them." She put her hands to her face. "My God. I shot two, maybe three, and I wanted to, wanted them dead. We were so angered by their attacks on defenseless farmsteaders. We called the boats 'shaving mills', 'cause they sailed so near the shore to avoid detection, and…oh, Jim, I killed them."

Jim struggled with a desire, on the one hand, to hold and comfort her in her wild distress, and on the other, to help her get out whatever twisted pictures she had conjured in a bad dream,. so he placed a pillow at her back and started in with careful questioning.

"Honey, have you ever seen or heard of a shaving mill before this?"

"No, never."

"Can you describe the rifles?"

"Father brought back a dozen rifles from a trip to Pennsylvania, up the Delaware River. He said they were made in Lancaster. He had a barrel of flints and some fine rifle powder from the French islands."

"Sounds like you just described the famous Pennsylvania or Kentucky rifles. You know, Daniel Morgan's men were armed with those when they journeyed up the Kennebec River with Arnold in 1775. Have you ever seen one before? Have you ever read about your shaving mills before?"

"No, never. How could I dream about…?"

"Let me see that bump on your shoulder again." He helped her bare her arm. "Good Lord!" Jim's mind was leaping in a search for logic, something tangible from which to continue. He suspected he was already over his head. His heart ached, and he couldn't keep his concern for his lady out of his voice. "Why don't you just tell me all you can remember from your dream?"

"The horrible part was I wanted to do in the raiders. We had waited in ambush night after night. The brigands had murdered two elderly people down the coast. I could hear the sounds of night birds, and the air from the ocean was in my face. Mother and Sister were loading the rifles and ready to pass them to us. I could see a reddish yellow flash and hear the flat slam of the shot. I had to remember to close the pan and hit the stock to make sure the primer pan was filled."

"Can you remember bodily feelings? Were you cold? Do you recall odors? Did you have to go to the bathroom?"

"Yes, the stones were like ice. I had to go so badly I could...well. The smell of the powder smoke was awful, and there was a lot of it. Jim, I was there. I don't care how crazy I sound. I was there. This was all too real."

"Sweetie, I have no argument. If I'd not heard you tell about this experience and seen that red bump on your shoulder, I'd say you had fired a .458 or a twelve gauge shotgun before seating the butt. You have some liniment to rub on your shoulder?"

"Yes, and it sure is uncomfortable. I'll get it. My hands are all red and dry every time I get near that mill."

At that he looked at her before he could respond. "Every time...what mill? Is this the one you plan to rebuild, I guess damn near from scratch?"

"I can recall every detail. I've spent years working in that mill, and I've been on the dam hundreds of times. I fish for trout in the pond."

"Marna, that's one hell of a declaration. I don't have a clue what we're dealing with here, but I've got an idea. Would you talk about this with Dr. Dayan?"

"You think I'm crazy, Jim, don't you?"

"For God's sake, no. You want answers, don't you? Wait, where was your dad in this dream?"

"He was on the *Archer*, fighting the British."

"Hold on. You know that? That's part of the background of the dream?"

"Yes."

"You have a name, is this one of the third person dreams you and I talked about on the mountain?"

"I am Sarah. It was *I* on the dam... killing people."

"Will you talk to Dr. Dayan?"

"If you want."

"I want." Jim knew he had his hands full. He had been told such an account, and yet, he knew nothing. He knew just enough to know they were in perilous waters. Something Jim knew from his soul. He loved this woman, and nothing was going to cause her hurt or harm if it took his life to prevent it. He would get to the bottom of these events to which he had been made privy if it took his dying breath. He considered then and there resignation from the service. He could sell his farm and be financially independent.

Something was not all that clear between him and his boss, the flag officer to whom he had reported for five years. His unease grew. That hadn't just happened. He made up his mind on one issue, and he drew Marna to him. She was breathing heavily, almost pained.

"Marna, my love, I'm not going to leave you. You've got company. If you can stand it, I want to move in here with you." She rolled and pressed herself to him.

Echo Horizon

15

Erick was alone at a table nursing a cup of coffee when Jim stepped through the door to the Cuddy. "Pull up a chair. I'll save Katie a trip and bring the pot over and a cup. Donuts?"

"About a bushel. Make that a barrel of coffee, too. That's a heated discussion the other side of the room."

"Right, I've been noticing them. College brings some strange types into the area. Some of these ragheads are trouble. Take those two. I can pick up a little of what they're saying, a dialect I picked up in the Persian Gulf. They've got it in for the Great Satan, that's us. Wait a minute. Somebody ought to let Beal in on this...not enough Americans have died...something about a sterner lesson..an airplane..perhaps an airplane exploding in the sky...the Zionist dog for certain this time. Man, Jim, if this isn't a case of conspiracy I've never seen one. Course, some of them are so full of shit no one knows when to believe them."

Sure burns me to see these arrogant bastards come into the country on a diplomatic passport, then no one can touch 'em. Although, one of these days..."

"You want breakfast before we talk to Sylvanus, Jim?"

"No, this will do fine."

"Look at that s.o.b. He's treating that poor girl whose trying to wait their table like dirt! Well, that's the way they treat their women in their country. Hey, I've had enough of this. I'm going over there and.."

"I think I see Katie coming. She'll straighten 'em out. Relax, Erick."

The sun made a flash of gold in Erick's hair as they walked in on Beal past his big picture window. Jim put his cell phone back in his pocket after thinking better of a call. And he'd gotten Erick quieted down.

"Whatever you guys have on your minds, you've got perfect weather for it."

Bert Howe

"To get right to the point, Syl, we need your boat for a week," stated Erick. The last time Erick had been in this office, Sylvanus had told him he was crazy as a hooty owl if he expected anyone to believe on face value that new pilings could be driven under the wharf without tearing out or tearing up the restaurant and removing much of the wharf's planking.

Since that time Syl had invested profitably in the 'Lehn Method' of sleeve boring and sectional pouring of concrete pilings, and it saved Beal hundreds of thousands of dollars when Erick rebuilt his wharf.

"Of course you can use the *Charming Sally*. Either of you checked out in gas turbines, or would you like me to throw in Josh, my engineer?"

"We like to have Josh on hand, don't you think, Jim?"

"Works for me. I know there's not a whole lot to the things, but we need someone who knows his way around."

"Done, Gentlemen. What you lookin' for?"

"You never rest, Old Man. I figure nothing gets by you," said Jim. "We're looking for an airplane with the help of Erick's side scan gear."

"Good luck."

"Neither of us thinks any part of the plane's out there, Syl," added Erick.

Doctor Dayan's door was prominently located. Marna knocked and a resonant voice answered with an invitation to enter. Roni, wearing his jogging suit, was leaned back in his chair with his feet on the desk, blue striped running shoes on his writing pad.

"You should come in and sit. Wait, I give you this chair." He sprang to his feet and held the overstuffed seat for her; she gazed at the wall covered with diplomas. Roni flopped on a couch, hands behind his head, fingers locked and knees up.

"I didn't intend for you to give up your desk. Are you sure you'll be comfortable there?"

Nodding, he crossed one leg over the other. "So, to what do I owe this grand visit?"

She knew he was studying her and was glad she'd spent more time with her hair than usual. Where to begin? How should she play this game? Game? Good God, this was a professional visit. "That was a grand day we spent on the clam flats." Pure corn ball.

"I, too, had an enjoyable time in the clam flats. I really think much on coming to America. My mother says..." Marna spied a dish of dried fruit on the table beyond the couch. As if he had eyes in the back of his head he said, "You wish to try the apricots and pineapple? Help yourself."

"Your mother sent them to you?"

"No, she is a terrible woman." Marna stepped to the table and sampled the fruit, biting into a honeyed pineapple slice.

"My family says I am not enough the Jew. In medical school in Haifa I am too much Jewish. In this country everyone wants to know how come I am so American. Right after I have seen the tall buildings in New York City, I tell them I am very Jewish...just enough for me, and I am very much me. I like Israeli people. I like American people, but most of all I enjoy being myself. There are terrible people in Israel, as there are terrible people in America, but mostly there are good people, too."

Marna picked up a notepad and played with a pencil. "You were born in Israel?...What's your trade?...How do you make a living?"

After a few minutes of small talk during which Roni was aware that Marna was ill at ease, he sat up and turned. "You wish to trade the desk for the couch? You have come to my office with heavy heart. So, will you talk to Roni?"

"I'd like to stay as we are, then you can't...you..."

"But you want to talk. OK, I listen. Begin as you will."

She hesitated, then started and stopped. "I don't know where to begin. I really don't, it's so crazy."

"Try the beginning."

"I...you'll think I'm nuts. I don't think I've ever done this."

"Shall we lose such words as crazy and nuts, OK?"

"Well." She sat straighter in her chair. "Have you ever remembered something, something clear and vivid that you couldn't account ever experiencing, so far as locations and travels and what you know you've been doing with your life?"

"Let me think. I was hit once by ground fire. Remember something that shouldn't have happened. Is that it?"

"Sort of, well, take sailing. I've been on Dad's old schooner *Arcturus*...He sold it a few years ago. I have a feeling I've been on sea voyages, traveled on a much larger vessel. It was also a schooner." Marna struggled to employ words which matched her cloudy reminiscence. As the mists thinned, her mind was able to deliver concepts more focused and resolved. As photons fall from eons of travel into the influence of a refracting telescope, impulses from her newly acquired recall were so condensed. She told Roni of the day she was pulled from the Atlantic and the visit on the strange boat. She spread before him from her mind's eye the array of documents she found in her attic.

"You have been reading much from the vessel's log and letters you have found.?"

"More than that, I think. I sense things that are real, but happened a long time ago." The words sounded strange even to her. "But these memories seem to be a part of me." Roni was silent. "Roni, did you hear me?"

"Yes, I hear. Go on. I listen." He stared straight ahead. Again she hesitated.

"Don't you want your notebook?"

"No notebook." The very thought of Roni's clinical audience had upset her, and only slowly was she restored by his reassurances. "What you will tell me I want to hear."

"I know it will seem wild, Roni, weird; but I've never seen it so clearly as I do now, and there's no one else besides you that I..."

"Yes."

"It began when I was on the mountain and got so cold. Well, I've had some unusual dreams since."

"Your internal temperature was dangerously lowered."

Echo Horizon

"I don't suppose anyone told you about the dream I had."
"By anyone, do you mean someone named Jim?"
"Yes, Jim." She shifted in her chair. "I was on a schooner. It was like total recall. No, that's not the way to describe it. I was on the schooner. I was part of the scene, could see and hear my surroundings. I heard things and smelled tar. It was real. I've had dreams since, always aware that I'm someone in a perfectly natural reality but not the person I am now in the environs to which I'm completely adapted. Does that make any sense? I'm somebody else. Even though I know the feeling of being me, I know I am someone else in the dream other than the 'me' who is in this room with you, now. Everyone must have that same feeling of being, but I am always the *same* someone else when I dream. It has to be dreams, but I don't know anything about the 'when'. I just know I've been somewhere and done something. I don't know what's happening to me, Roni." She spoke even faster, and her voice became shrill. "The people in my dreams know me."

Before she could continue, he asked her, "Do you have a name?"

"I'm Sarah." She made no reference to the third person singular.

"What do you think of Sarah?"
"What do you mean?"
"Do people like her? Do you like her?"
"I think so...she's so...I'm so busy keeping alive. I don't think I have time to wonder."
"How will you tell me of Sahr...excuse...Sarah?"
"How will...?"
"Will you say 'I' or 'she'?"
"Oh...I."
"He nodded his head slowly.
"That means I see through Sarah's eyes, and I think as if I am she."
"How much do you feel in your dreams?"
"Ohh-h, everything."

"Soo-oo."

"I think a long time ago something terrible happened. I know we were on the schooner I mentioned, We had been in the tropics...someplace we weren't supposed to go, and we had sailed back to northern waters. It was spring."

"You have said 'we'."

"My sister and my father...we were on his schooner, and it had these big guns on it. I don't think they were supposed to be there either."

"Do we have names?"

"My sister, younger sister, was Mehitabel. Captain Alport was our father. My mother wasn't on that voyage. I mean the one I'm thinking about. She enlarged on the experience on the strange yacht in the spring and the coincidence of names.

"This is the captain, then, who is named in the old vessel's record from which you have read?"

Marna thought he was going to continue with the notion, when he stopped. "That's the weird part. The schooner is named *Archer*. I can't explain, and I know it sounds like I have an overly stimulated imagination; but it's much more than that. Roni, we were overhauled by an English ship, a war ship. I guess we were all English at the time. Sarah's...my father ran up the merchant colors of the colony and spoke to the captain of the other ship..."

"Hold one moment. Can you tell me of sensations, any recall of feelings? Was the sea rough, weather cold?"

"Sort of rolling waves, a little wind. I have no recollection of feeling cold. I smell smoke from the galley stove. Lines were slapping lightly against masts, smells of tar and paint. There was this little cabin boy. He was bringing his captain a drink of something..."

"That was Billy?"

"Billy Dawes. How did you know?"

"Not important...tell you later. Go on."

"Tell me. How did you know his name?"

Echo Horizon

"At the infirmary, you had a relapse for a short time, a period of delirium. You could not remember?"

"It's as if I've always known what happened that day. Funny, in the dream I'm sure I know I have a memory and a life; but after, when I awake, I remember only what took place in the dream."

"What more can you tell me?"

"Sarah is on the boat, and I see through her eyes. There was, suddenly, shooting from the English ship, from the tops. Little Billy was killed and three men wounded."

"Can you describe the sounds?"

"Shouts, orders, and you know the sound a shotgun makes when fired over the water with nothing from which to echo?" Roni nodded. "I hear all these dull thumps and the sounds a one ounce ball makes when it strikes something solid. I can hear voices. The captain ordered Comfort MacLean to ready to jibe. Mr. Dighton was at the helm, and the command came to up helm, and Mr. Coleman..."

"Mr. Coleman."

"He was in charge of the great gun at the stern, an eighteen or twenty-four pounder. I'll never forget the sound of that gun or the feel of the boat shuddering under my feet. Father had every gun fired at the English before they knew what hit them in-spite-of the fog, then sailed away."

"You tell of this like you were there."

"No confusion, everyone knew his task and did it. Roni, I have to have been there. I can smell the gun smoke, rotten eggs, Ugh!"

"Comfort MacLean, was this someone you knew?"

"He was my...he and Sarah were in love."

"How old Sarah?"

"Sixteen or seventeen. Roni, it's like they are still in love, like this thing just happened yesterday. It's all so vivid. He was First officer."

"You cried out on the mountain about the tops. The commander has told of this. Then, again, in the infirmary, you were lucid in your recollection of the little boy who was killed. You don't remember this?"

"I'm aware of knowing I had a dream. I don't recall shouting on the mountain nor the spell in the infirmary."

"What of the English?" Roni asked, rising and walking to the window.

"Mr. Coleman blew most of their foremast away which left them with a lot of weather helm."

"Excuse me?"

"A square rigged ship to sail sweetly is pretty well balanced by the wind striking an even distribution of sail along the length. You remove the heads'ls, the foretops'l and foretopgallant, and it becomes a big weather vane. They had a tired old time steering. Anyway, Sarah's father ordered the schooner about and raked the ship with cannister from the guns at the bow. It was a mess."

"There was war?"

"He said America was at war with England."

"America, not the colonies. Can we know which war of the two?"

"Let's see, they raised the colors of Massachusetts. I'll have to say the Revolution. Roni, what's happening to me? Am I...?

"Nonsense, there appears nothing for being upset. In that pretty head lies a store of information. You are a sensitive person, and I think, one who has a wonderful imagination."

"Roni, don't you...?" She swung to the side of her chair.

"Have you told me something which causes me concern? No."

"But it's so real...the sensations of fear and joy. I even feel it when Sarah has to go...to the bathroom. Only there weren't bathrooms then. Sarah helps her mother in the family mill, grinding grain. I've heard the waters in the race, heard the machinery start when the main belt moves after the sluice gate is opened. Frogs sang and croaked in the pond in spring; and when the men were building the schooner, Roni, you never saw people work so hard. There was this little farmer, Caleb Gordon. He and his ox helped Sarah's father build the dam."

"What of Sarah's parents? Can you tell me of the mother and father?"

Different from other people in the settlement, spoke differently like from another part of the continent. Her mother is Betsey. I notice similarities because that was my mother's name."

"I think here lies much of the influence. You have had strong feelings where your folks are concerned, correct?" She nodded agreement. "Isn't it natural to dream of them since you miss them and there is mystery?"

"How is it I feel the mood of the people in the settlement, can know the struggle just to stay alive, fears, hardships, good times, social restraints? Sarah's father had a way with his neighbors, could laugh and make others laugh. It's all too real."

"Marna, listen to me. Some things I have wondered for a long time. Today, you tell me of these occurrences which are strange for you., and I don't know what to tell you. Who can give a medical opinion on perception or sensitivity? In the scientific community, what is truly known of such things? Can we speak of retrocognition? Who knows? Such is reported to be. You have told me all that you have on your mind?"

"I don't want to be too self centered. Perhaps we should examine your past."

He chuckled. "Too much sand and wind, I think. No, it is time to take a good look at what you have told, see what it is. I do not have lightly what you say. Have we an effect, we must find the cause."

Marna nodded slowly.

"You have a window. It is like a window, but you don't see out. The mind perceives. You see, but you don't see, and all through the energy of someone else. Who is this someone? What? When? Who can say what is the limit of signals from the brain or carried in the genes? For a time you sense, you feel, you possess identity as this someone, Sarah, no?"

She looked at her hands.

"She is your reification. You see part of the world as you think it existed for her."

Marna's face grew tense, and she shook her head. "No, Roni, I see it as it was. I mean, I actually see it as it is. I know it. My God, my five senses, they're all involved…even despair. Roni, I read a letter written to this poor girl by her one and true love. She is cold and exhausted from her labors when the rider delivered it months after it was written. She sobs her heart out, and I feel it right here. She isn't going to see him for another three months. It's winter; and all the while, she and her sister and their mother must keep the mill running. They share their food and firewood with their neighbors, and they must remain alert to defend their home against raiders. Sarah can shoot. They all could. Her father left them with some long Pennsylvania rifles. Sarah knows how to select a flint and can cut a candle at a hundred yards."

"Wait…wait…slow down. What is this Pennsylvania rifle? You said rifle, not musket?"

"It was as long as a man is tall, forty-five caliber, a much smaller bore than some of the old muskets the men in town had. It was patch loaded and made a sharp crack when fired."

"You have recently seen one of these?"

"I…I've never seen one. I've never heard of them except vaguely from reading about Daniel Boone when I was a child."

"But you know, now."

"Yes, they were made in Lancaster, Pennsylvania, quite illegally, for the crown forbade manufacture of firearms in the colonies." She wanted to continue talking, for she realized he was ever more attentive to her words. She recalled the event on the dam waiting for raiders, the quiet cold, the ambush, how the starlight was all they needed, how Jupiter and Saturn hung over Big Candle Island.

"Marna, you agree with a window on another time? Can we say that? But this window is someone else's eyes, and if she gets a speck of dust under a lid, you feel it?"

She nodded vehemently.

"Are you aware of something…something about what you say when you speak of Sarah?"

"No."

"You speak mostly in the present tense…in the past tense or perfect tense for the others."

Her quizzical face lifted to the ceiling.

"Why do you think this is so?"

She shook her head.

"Always, I think a dream can reflect whatever fundamental mood underlies the subject…,but all five senses and a mood of emotion that fits the situation," he demanded with incredulity. "And you tell me the window is showing this. Excuse me…Sarah."

Marna smiled for the first time and continued with a plea in her voice. "Roni, can you make anything at all out of what I've told you?"

"Who is asking, Marna or Sarah?"

"What?" Her voice was just below high "C". "Marna, Silly."

"Always Marna?"

"Always Marna," she confided.

"When did you begin to notice any of this, before or after the discovery of your old documents?"

"That's not easy to answer. I think something happened after meeting Commander Starr."

"Ohh-h?" His intonation caught her off guard.

"Oh Christ, Ronen, you know what I mean." She started to lose it, watching his facial expressions.

"We will do well to make note of anything unusual which overtakes from this time on. You will tell me, Marna…I am serious…if you should have a feeling the window is working the other way."

"Like if Sarah is watching us, or now? What do you mean?"

"You have the idea. One wonders what is meant by "now", as it appears a most subjective concept. As perplexing, perhaps, as solipsism."

"The thought has occurred to me."

"How do you feel at this moment, Marna?"

"Restive."

"You will tell me of anything that happens. I mean if it's 3:00 a.m....always call me."

Something there was, indeed, of which she wished to speak from the beginning. Now, she was afraid...afraid its mention would discredit all she had revealed to him. She was never able to laugh off that foggy day when the schooner had sailed off with her wet clothes. Coincidence, fantasy or whatever, she had fled that morning in panic and had fallen into the surf, nearly to her death. That part had been chillingly real, but she had been rescued by the crew of Captain Alport's *Archer*. How could it be she was reading of this same schooner and a man named Alport in letters and documents over two hundred years old? Roni, who had been pacing the room in deep thought, broke her reverie.

"Tell me what is troubling you. Your face is so pale."

She emptied her soul to him save for the circumstance of the wet clothes. Who were the men on the schooner? No one she spoke with had seen them before or since. Where had they gone? Roni looked at her, and she tried to continue.

"I keep coming back in my thoughts to *the mill*....something about the mill. In my dreams of Sarah's world, the mill and dam seem to be a focal point, a point of view from the mill. I have a notion it is so secure it will last forever; but I don't have a clue where it is. McCobbs Cove...somewhere I know McCobbs Cove, but I've found no town on the coast with that name."

"Perhaps a local reference. We look." He reclined against the edge of his desk and studied the far off look in her eyes.

"So real, Roni...so feeling. She lives at McCobbs Cove, comforts the widows, works the mill, knows everybody in her village. She wants my help with something, Roni, and I can't find her. So long ago..." Her voice trailed off. "So far...so many years..." Tears streamed from her eyes.

"We will find her...such a girl we will find."

Roni stood once more. "Such a girl as our Sarah, and she loves this officer of the *Archer*, Comfort MacLean. What a man

Echo Horizon

he must be, but you have said little of him. Why is this so? What is he like? How does he look?"

She sat still, face set in stone. "Good God, I don't know. I only know Sarah is in love with him." She combed her recall of the man who placed his cloak around her shoulders when she was shivering on deck. "Oh, yes, I do know what he looks like. Jim...Jim could be his twin. What does this all mean?" It required a few minutes to calm herself.

She gazed at the floor, then lifted her eyes to the ceiling and looked into the far corners of the office as if expecting to find fragments of her other worldly experiences. She saw Roni's reflection in the window as he paced by. They were quiet a while. Had everything been said?

"What does it all mean, Marna, indeed? You have told of wondrous things, and I think nothing I say to you, now, will impact on you as much as what you have already experienced." He paced past the window once more and stopped. "Also, it matters little where you are. The experience, the experienced and the experiencer are one. I speak of non-locality. Marna, I think your dreams are every bit as real as you are real, sitting there across the room from me."

"But, Roni..." She sat very straight at his remark.

"Let me finish. All is connected. We are at one with all else, the star, the snowflake, the grain of sand. Hindus, Zen Buddhists, Taoists all have told. Shamans the world over and from all times have devined reality, and a body of thought grows among scientists around the globe. They are just coming to understand the concepts after realizing what the words of the old ones were saying. New theorems arise from the old.

"The void...or as the Hindus name it, Brahman, or if you will, the implicate universe...the void is a realm of thought. Therein no distance nor time exist. These are constructs in the explicate universe, the non-void. All that we see about us...and that includes you and me, time and space, rocks, trees...are interpretations of the brain as part of a universal consciousness.. Or, in other words, what you see about you is an illusion arising from nothing but energy wave fronts and interference patterns of light; that is reality for us. It, however, is a very familiar reality because we have been born into it and have for a long time been accustomed to it."

She stood abruptly and bumped a stack of books which went on the floor, and he waved them off as being of little importance.

"In some fashion, Marna, you may be in tune with energy harmonics in an interconnected field of energy and can tap into other more or less sophisticated levels of reality which, it is said, co-exist. It may be that you are able to use the nonlocality of events as well as the timelessness of the implicate to construct another reality for yourself."

Marna took in deep breaths, eyes wildly searching for solid reference. It was all coming too fast and beyond anything she imagined. "Am I nuts or something? How can this be? I mean, I'm real, you're real...this desk..."

"It is, after all, a theorem, Marna. Science of modern days is not yet ready, I think. We can discuss in more detail sometime. What we have in the pure science is a theorem which can explain all that has occurred; but in any event, it is clear you have a gift. From all that you tell me, I can conclude nothing but that you are seeing events as they have taken place, as well as having taken part in them. How will we explain that without first taking up with a good theorem?"

"But what if I step over and don't come back?"

Roni didn't answer right away but resumed pacing, looking past the window as if anticipating someone's approach.

"Your mind tells you that you are living from time to time as another entity on another time plane. Time is an enigma. In the molecular and atomic levels, subatomic, where is time? The brain perceives its reality from signals which it processes as the senses deliver from the energy input of particulate matter. It relates cell addition, growth and development to regular pulses in the universe, such as orbital motion by the planets. This is regarded as time. Is time, then, the cause of growth and decay, or are the processes of nature related to regular pulses. Your mind tells you time is not a factor of reality and it may make this announcement from another so called time plane. Your mind is able to perceive time as a conglomerate of what the brain perceives as past, present and future. This is shocking conjecture, but we simply must have an hypothesis to argue for the experiences you have been subject to.

"From what I am able to put together, your mind is able to proceed on at least two time planes. Others could emerge without warning. Could our Sarah be wanting you to find something for her or do something for her? That might help explain the intense energy surrounding your 'events'."

Bert Howe

16

"You've got that whine well muffled, Josh. How'd you do that?" asked Erick.

Josh pulled his head in from the side port and stood back a bit from the wheel. "All in the tuning of the exhaust system."

"Doesn't this thing go! What do you think, Jim?"

"Goes like hell. I guess there's power enough at slow speed to tow the gear. But didn't Syl say it cut his cruising time to the fishing grounds from five hours to one? Could help our cause."

"Six thousand horsepower in a constant dead rise hull. I guess," added Josh.

"Take us in, will you, Josh? We got to get over to the firing muster."

"Hold on to your hats, Gents."

"Will you look at that rooster tail!" exclaimed Jim.

Jim followed Erick from the latter's SUV to a group of men examining targets.

"What kep' ya?" inquired Erick's cousin Mike, platoon guidon bearer and acting range officer.

"You'll never believe just thirty minutes ago we were twenty-five miles at sea, Mike," replied Erick while Jim looked on at the musketry.

"Not bloody likely."

"How are we scoring so far, Mike?" asked Erick.

"Not bad, Cuz, 'cept for Al here. He can't hit the ground."

Al, a Viet Nam veteran, did not display amusement. "To hell you say, Mike. Them last two were the sweetest shots you've seen today. Admit it." Al wore a buckskin jacket in lieu of his blue coat with crossed white belts.

"Gauge says you crossed one line and didn't come near the other," Mike observed. The target was a broadly printed "V". The shooter was challenged to place a ball so that it passed through the paper tangent to both legs of the "V". Some were firing at conventional bullseye targets. "I think you're still snapping the trigger, Man. Hell, this ain't no M-16; squeeze that puppy."

Three more shooters reclaimed their targets and approached Erick. The taller of the three stopped by Mike who inquired, "You still pullin' to the left, Bob?" Bob studied his target seriously. "Nuthin's wrong with your groupings, old Buddy. Let's try this. You remember how your M-1 had quite a bit of trigger take up before firing? Well, you've got damn near a hair trigger with your "Kaintuck" here. Next time, feel your heart beat, squeeze light, and try to discharge between heart beats."

Bob was a survivor of the Twenty-Eighth Division and remembered the Battle of the Bulge. A lot of his buddies didn't make it home.

Erick greeted the three and offered, "You guys take Gunny's advice'n you'll do all right." Mike smiled at the mention of his old nickname. "Yah, Len, what's up?"

"Could be the sights, could be me."

Erick examined the target. The gauge wasn't required. "Gotta be you, Len. If it was the sights, you'd still have a grouping. You're all over the paper. Don't get me wrong. I wouldn't care to be anywhere down range of you. Work on your breathing."

Len *had* been working on his breathing since Chang Gin where he had lost a lung and Mike had earned a second leaf on his Silver Star. They both were in the First Marine Division.

Jim turned in time to see Nancy pull into a parking space. "Way she pulled into that slot, Erick, I'm willing to bet she's got coffee in a huge top heavy urn and donuts and bagels for an army." Both laughed. "I had no idea what an operation you have going. Your people take this whole thing refreshingly serious."

Erick called a ribald greeting to Nancy and ran to help her as she opened the rear door of Erick's van. Over his shoulder he responded, "Yes, they do." After lugging the urn to a table by the range master's position, he continued, "Jim, this is one of the only situations I've experienced where the younger guys are

Echo Horizon

truly attentive to the advice of the older members. You need to be with it a while to really appreciate it." To Nancy who was the first into the donuts, "You shooting today, Hon?"

"Hi, Jim. Excuse my stuffed face. You bet I am. I'll show you turkeys some trick and fancy shooting. Where's my Hawken?"

"Aw, no you don't, no cap and ball. Jim, she can shoot the wings off a gnat with her big fifty. Nan, be nice. This is flintlock time."

"You big sissy. You can't stand to have a woman shoot your ears off, now, admit it." She gazed off over the range and noticed, with the lull in shooting, the last of the black powder smoke drifting away from the direction of the buildings.

"Maybe Jim will join us in a shoot-out after muster."

"You're on, Ladies and Gentlemen...what the...? Hold on. What in hell is that noise? Can't be...it's automatic weapons fire!"

"Right, I hear it. Nan, get down!"

Roni Dayan came back from the window. "One more question, I think, Marna. Can you describe the flag you have mentioned, the English flag?"

"I think so. I'm still reeling from all you have told me," she replied, mind elsewhere. "I know what it looks like, now, but thinking back I believe the naval ensign was missing the diagonal red stripes as they fit presently with the cross of Saint Andrew. I think the cross of Saint Patrick was added to the naval ensign, maybe twenty-five years later. I'm sure it wasn't part of the color scheme of the flag on the ship which fired on us."

"Had to have been the American War for Independence." Roni barely uttered the words before one whole window crashed into the room. They remained stunned by a noisy, staccato rattle. Quickly, Roni leaped to bring Marna to the floor as bits of pictures and bric-a-brac flew in all directions across the floor. As he flew over his desk, he dragged her purse to the floor with them. Shouting was heard outside. "Allah is God. Allah u

Achbar!" A crash resounded in the corridor outside the door and shouts of, "Find the Zionist! Death to the infidel!"

"Good mother of God, Roni, what's happening?" More firing. Fortunately, the bullets didn't penetrate the brick exterior of the stout old building.

"Kalashnikovs, Marna, the sons of Islam want me. I think I locked the door."

Marna strained to sit up. "I don't think it will do much good the way they're battering it. I hope...oh, Christ, I hope they haven't killed anyone."

"They do not care, nor for themselves, so long as they will reside forever in paradise."

The door splintered as they spoke, and Marna saw and lunged for her pocketbook, tore it open and palmed her .380.

Roni, no longer feeling like a trapped animal, exclaimed. "You're armed!"

"Damn right I am. If those crazy bastards think they're breaking in that door without a fight..." She fairly shrieked through a dry mouth. Her first shot punctuated her declaration and elicited a cry. A figure with a scarf about his face came into view, and she fired three more times. Two nine millimeter slugs found their mark, one opening the carotid artery on the assassin's left side. A second killer pushed the shattered door farther open and took three slugs from Marna's little sidearm for his pains. He discharged the remainder of his magazine into the ceiling as he fell on top his comrade.

Her clip was empty; she wondered if she had a second. Her time frame had expanded from the first blast through the window. For her, action was slowed. She felt a dreamlike slow motion and took careful aim with each shot. In reality, she was reacting and responding to crisis with lightning speed.

The college was under attack. Erick and Jim had no doubts, and Nancy was sure she had heard screams though the action was a good hundred yards off. The ground sloped up from the range to the main campus and came to a ridge some thirty yards from the campus drive. This meant cover for most of the way to the action, and Erick wasted no time.

"We a militia, men?"

"Hell, yes." Was the reply.

"We going to sit on our thumbs while our people are getting killed?"

"Cut the talk, Cap'n, and let's haul ass!"

Nancy tugged at Erick's sleeve. "What in the name of Jesus do you think you're going to do with flintlocks against machineguns?"

"Nan, we're the only force of armed citizens for fifty miles. We're going to do exactly what you know we must." She ran to the van. "load your pieces, muskets with double oh, grab your shot pouches and powder horns and bear on me. Nancy, put that Christless shotgun down and take cover!"

"In your dreams, Lover. You gonna lead this charge or what?" He knew it was hopeless. Jim drew his 1911A Colt from under his jacket and shouted, "Count me in. Marna's up there somewhere."

"Form a line of skirmish. Close primer pans. Let's go!" The sight of thirty or so men from age twenty to seventy-three and a comely blonde lady running on open ground while slapping the weapons' stocks to send powder from the breech into the primer pan probably hadn't been seen in this country since Hannah's Cow Pens or Eutaw Springs, but it carried with it the declaration of clear and present danger.

"What are we up against with flintlocks, Old Son?"

"AK-47s, my guess, Jim. You keep your head down. I don't know how I'd tell Marna."

"I hope to God we can tell her anything," Jim replied.

"We stop below the top, then have a look, then use what there is of a slope to our advantage. They ducked to a crawl as Erick continued, "Look at that, right out in the open. Oh, Jesus, some people down. I count six. Some aren't moving. Pick a target, guys, have at 'em."

A flat slam echoed off the building and was followed by a half dozen shots in the next seconds. Windows on one side of a van were swept out; a limo gushed steam from its radiator. Suddenly the terrorists were aware of the assault on their flank and directed their fire toward the threat. One clutched his chest and thrust his head against a tree as he went down after a one ounce ball smashed several ribs.

"Gunny, we got to break up this outrage or a lot more people are gonna get hurt!"

"You got it, Cuz. Red, Max, Carty, load them muskets again with double oh on the double. Len, Bob, Mitch, Jansen, we're going over. Get primed and keep low. Muskets, give us cover!"

Flintlock muskets and rifles were up against suicidal fanatics who had already killed or wounded a half dozen bystanders with indiscriminate fire from seven point sixty-two millimeter machineguns. Their rate of fire was about to be tested by a distracting hail of buckshot and the deadly accuracy of Kentucky rifles.

"We ready? Go...go...go!" The riflemen ran in a crouch, heads low while emitting a rolling, howling shriek which would have done A.P. Hill's butternut shirted troops proud at Second Manassas.

A terrorist fumbled with a clip and raised his AK-47 but fired over the heads of the advancing squad. A puff of smoke spewed from the pan of Len's rifle followed by a THWACK as a slug struck the assassin in the head. The smooth bores had created havoc with buckshot, but the advancing men had to reload and were without cover. They must raise themselves dangerously to complete the loading, and two were nicked by the enemy.

A sharp crack emanated from across campus, followed swiftly by two more. Two assassins went down hard. The remainder flung themselves wildly about in search of another attack. Two more shots and another withered to the turf. The little squad of continentals took full advantage of the distraction, though God knew from whence it came. With the few remaining terrorists badly confused, they cut them down with dispatch. Three sons of Islam raced for the remaining van, and two were hit by fire from the unknown allies before they reached the doors. A fiery, smoky blast from muskets sent a shower of buckshot against the van. A third threw his arms up and fell. Two more blasts and smoke, and a fourth who had already gotten into the van died with the van in a shower of glass and two deflated tires.

In-spite-of the confusion, Jim saw a man enter the building where Marna was. He raced toward the west end not knowing how many more shooters were still active. He jumped for a windowsill and climbed like an ape up the side of the building using every cornice and decoration the turn of the century masons had provided for such capers. On reaching the rail of a balcony, he pulled himself over. With his .45 in hand he kicked in a French door and ducked inside to a reading room of sorts. He heard muffled voices and some frightened cries as he darted from door to stair rail, keeping himself as small a target as possible and making random moves.

He eased himself around and down one stair, then another. The Bedouin at the door to Roni's office had noticed the sprawled legs of his fallen comrades. The stairs creaked, he fired and tore up the staircase. He couldn't have seen Jim. He fired another burst, and the firing terminated with a click which told Jim the clip was empty. Jim charged the startled assassin as he scrambled for a clip. The .45 barked at the end of Jim's up swing and gave the voyager to Paradise a new mouth. What remained of the head was slammed against the wall.

Jim grabbed the leg of one of Marna's targets and yanked the carcass out of his way, then rushed to Marna who was slumped behind the desk, ashen white.

Roni appeared from under the table. "Never so glad to see anyone in my life."

Outside, Mike crawled back to speak to Len. "Stay put Tiger; get your breath. I'm going to need your piece. Let me have the shot and powder. Dale, you and Jason give me cover.

Len, someone's bought it back there. Whyn't you see what you can do for him?" He raised himself to see over the top of the rise. Two rag heads were firing wildly at someone off to his left. He heard the crack of a rifle, turned and saw Nancy start to reload. He guessed she had been giving their adversaries some serious problems. They rose simultaneously at regular intervals and fired at Nancy's position.

Mike timed carefully his enemy's firing, then suddenly swung his rifle over the rise and fired. He heard a scream and ducked back to reload. That process can be done under ideal conditions three times a minute. Mike did it at the rate of four. He crawled, belly slide, a few yards along the slope, then rose and fired again. Another hit. A little sporadic fire came from farther along the campus. A siren moaned as the musket men let go another blast into what was left of the vehicles. A squad car from the Sheriff's Department screamed into the area with blue lights flashing. The deputy on the passenger side burst out and fired without taking stock of the situation. Erick yelled to get down, but the deputy was put out of action almost immediately.

The driver fired indiscriminately toward the militia, sending a bullet into Erick's side. Erick went to his knees amid loud hollering. A burst of automatic weapon fire cut that deputy in two. From across the campus rang three shots. One rag head fell from a huge tree, the other died beside the main steps to the building. It was hard to be sure, but it didn't appear that any adversaries were left to confront.

Erick, still ambulatory, took every measure to account for his men. Nancy ran to him and eased his weight off his left leg. Both were soaked with perspiration. Carty and Red were limping. Al caught one in the shoulder, but most of the blood shed by the militia was from superficial wounds. Erick's was the more serious and from friendly fire, at that.

It took days to sort out all that took place that afternoon. Nancy drove Erick to the hospital, then home. He was on his feet that evening when a clatter was mounted at his front door. Television news scavengers were on hand with floodlights and video cams aimed at a talking head, then at him. Erick responded with a crisp "No comment". The talking head started to push her way in the door but ran into a bristling Nancy Marsh.

"My man has been through enough and he's hurt. Now get the hell out of here!"

The head continued to push and demand until Nancy planted a set of attention-seizing knuckles on her mouth and slammed the door. The eleven o' clock news proceeded to put the whole event before the viewers with no regard for fact. The account of the fracas on campus was further twisted by self-serving spin doctors. The media were divided as to who did the provoking...who were the good guys and who were the bad guys.

The militia was, for the time in the limelight, and the lockstep bleating of the gun control enthusiasts demanded muzzle loaders be added to the lexicon. No mention was made of the helpful fire from across campus, nor were the shooters ever identified nor seen after everything died down. Some passersby remembered seeing three men dressed more or less like seafaring men walking toward the campus that day carrying very long guns. The assumption generally was they were joining the muster.

Bert Howe

17

"Good morning, Jerome. Yes, Dayan here. How is everything in the Department of Astronomy? I wonder...What? Yes, it was dreadful, Jerome. No, not a scratch. Fine. Do you think you...? Brave, very brave. I think none seriously. Yes, the commander, most timely. Who, my associate, Marna Gantry? Uncommonly cool under stress. Yes, you could say she saved my bacon. Only you, Jerome. No, I'm not aware of the cowgirl to whom you refer. Look, could you do me a...? The police? The first two on the scene I know were unfortunate casualties. Yes, the militia...well, hardly a full fledged combat arm, flintlocks ranged against automatic weapons. Of course I'm aware they're heroes, Jerome, not to be overlooked, the heroine, Nancy Marsh. They saved the day and took from the field of international terrorism some of the best that could be deployed. What next? Who knows? True, only in America could such a debate rage. Not a mention in the major rags of Americans defending their own against foreign aggression. Yes, I have read in the New York rag the urging for reparations for the victims' families overseas. Yes, I have read of the schmucks who demand the banning of all muzzle loading firearms...

"So, Jerome...no...listen, I have little time, as I know you, too, are far from enabled by the constraints of time to dabble in light gossip. The positions of two planets, Jupiter and Saturn, approximately summer or late spring of 1776. You could call me back? You have on the computer? This is well. No, Jupiter and Saturn."

Ron held on while he leaned back in his chair and surveyed the wreckage of his office, as yet not put to rights. The assault was short but brutal. Had Marna not been armed and known what she was about, they both would have perished. The intrepid commander had arrived subsequently in most timely manner and changed the mind of yet another assassin.

"Yes, good, Jerome. What's that? In May and June, rising before the sunset. During the umbra, the pair floating each like the Star of David in the eastern sky. You have been most helpful. I owe you.

That same morning, Marna and Jim were taking their time at breakfast, he urging her to stay away from the college for a few days.

"It'll take some time before this town settles down. Some innocent folks were killed, and a community stood up to international terrorists in magnificent fashion. But a lot of people won't be thinking, bound to be trouble."

"God, what now? Look at that bunch swarming into the yard."

Sit tight, Marna, and keep the coffee hot. I'll attend to them."

A television news van had pulled onto the grass, off the drive, and a man with a camcorder on his shoulder was followed by one with a camera. A young woman carried a microphone; all trailed wires. When Jim opened the door, they started to push past him with shouts and commands.

"Get a good angle on the female shooter. Ted, bring that lighting closer."

"Just a god damn minute," Jim shouted. "Hold it!" His hand was on the shoulder of the one with the camcorder.

"Who in hell are you?"

"Someone who's about to knock you on your ass if you take another step this way. You're trespassing."

"That's ridiculous," replied the woman with the mike. "You can't stop us from reporting the news."

A voice sounded off from the van. "Any trouble up there?"

"Nothing we can't handle," shouted the man with the still camera.

Jim was clearly annoyed. His stance should have left no doubt. "Off this property! *Now*!! You with the camera, you snap that picture, and I'll feed it to you." The flash blazed in Jim's face, and he shoved the camera into the man's mouth, removing some teeth. A burly type ran from the truck and up the steps to be met by a foot in his stomach. Jim grabbed the camcorder and threw it at the van, took the bearer by his ear and the woman by her earphones and started them in that general direction.

"Now, if there isn't someone among you able to drive, I'll call for an escort. And believe this, any of you come back here to bother my girl won't be able to walk much less drive!"

Back in the house a moment later, Marna draped her arms on his shoulders. "Gosh, Sweetie, I'd have come out to help you, but you did a marvelous job all by yourself. Come over here. Why don't you sit still while I make another pot of coffee? You sure know how to get everyone stirred up."

When after a time the phone rang, Jim was relieved it was Roni on the line. "Don't get too comfortable, Hon. Roni says he has something we should deal with now."

"Thank you, Roni, I think."

Half an hour later, Roni closed the door behind himself and took a seat across the coffee table from Jim and Marna. He declined refreshment. "So good of you both to drop whatever it was you were doing."

"You'll never know, Roni," sighed Marna.

"There can be no peace…news hounds, the investigations."

"Who's coming at you, Ron?"

"So, Commander, it seems your U.S. Attorney, the District Counsel, Attorney General are all taking different sides. Where will it end?"

"Get used to injunctions and subpoenas, Roni. You weren't even an armed combatant, so that makes you an undefined entity to the politicians, a real threat. They can't pigeon hole you."

"They what, Commander? Oh, yes, the pigeon hole; but let us take up something of true importance. Need I remind you both that we take the same side in matters personal as well as political?"

"Take us where we're going, Roni," exhorted Marna.

"It is well, then, I have spoken with Jerome Levi, who chairs the Department of Astronomy. He has remarkable astronomic records and the means to call them up." He turned to Marna. "I am at liberty to discuss that which you have confided in me?"

"Roni, this hulk and I have no secrets from one another, I think." She poked Jim in his ribs. "Well-l-l, do we?"

Jim straightened. "Oh, hell, no."

"It is good. Marna, you have told to me all of the instances or events to which you have been party?" She nodded. "Each is significant as it relates what could be described as a whole scene, earlier ones setting up a background for action. All seem to fit together. Marna views these scenes as through the perception of another girl, hears herself addressed by another name. She not only views, but is a part of the scene and its activity, knows herself to be a distinct individual. Am I correct so far, Marna?"

"I would add that my five senses are involved. The detail is so intense I'm convinced I am in another place."

"Another place, where?"

"I don't know, Roni, somewhere on this coast."

"You are convinced, when... during the dream or after?"

"Oh, after. During the dream there is no question of being convinced. It's simply happening."

"What do you make of it so far, Roni?" Jim was anxious to push the subject along.

"I came to see you this morning because I have encountered information which moves Marna's experiences from the area of conjecture to the point where you Americans say, 'Hang on. We gotta deal with this'."

"Roni, what in particular...?"

"Marna, in any discipline that is recognized with which I am familiar, nothing can explain what you have told me. We look on new ground. Commander, may I be presumptive to the point of asking you if you have left anything out in your conversations with Marna? No, don't demur. What we have here is too serious for games."

"You told me about my father...what the admiral told you?"

"You have it all, Sweetheart. I've pulled no punches. You know what I know."

"We have, then, the even start. Marna, you have an identity in the here and now. That's all any of us can be sure of, our identities. But you take a vacation from the here and now, and it is with another identity. I am correct so far?"

Marna nodded.

"Commander, your initial concern has been sorting out the disappearance of Marna's parents. Your admiral, I think, has other concerns."

Roni continued, and Jim's mask cracked to reveal a puzzled expression. Who had discussed any of this with Ronen Dayan? "Your admiral discovered, no, uncovered something so bizarre as to defy explanation within a Newton/desCartes universe. Is this not so? Can we begin with your first meeting with Marna in the summer? So much has happened."

"Roni, while we're letting our hair down, I can see why those birds were after you, and they *were* after you, no mistake."

"For us to play games, Commander, serves no one. I have duties beyond flying and medicine."

"Your squadron identification comes to mind, Ron, something like Ariot-Meofefime."

Roni's face brightened perceptibly.

Jim continued. "I recall reading about Osiris and a classic pre-emptive strike."

Roni smiled and said nothing further about himself. "Back to Marna. We have an incident which has been reported and which has no explanation. Marna, you are comfortable with what you know of your family history?"

"I've handled it, Roni. Sometimes I wake up and feel that someone is stomping on my grave, but, yeah, I can live with it."

"Jim, can we say we three have assumed a level?"

"I've stopped unraveling, Ron. I was assigned a case. She's sitting right here beside me. Since I am very fond of the lady and she is no longer 'a case', I can live with what we've read and been told. I'll toss protocol out the window and tell you I've wondered some about Admiral Rankin's real agenda."

"Marna, Jim, what do we know of time dislocation? I have been given a piece of information this morning which throws a new light on Marna's perplexing exploits."

"And that is?"

"Commander, Professor Levi, our campus astronomer, has checked the altitudes and azimuths of the two planets Marna remembered from a recent dream event. They were actually located as she saw them in her dream, and that dream scene took place over two hundred years ago."

A sound of exhalation ensued. Then Marna got out of her seat and asked if she could get drinks for anyone.

"No, thank you."

"Not for me, Hon."

"It all seemed to me to be so matter of fact, so natural. Sure we were all very tense waiting for the marauders night after night, but everything was as it should have been. I certainly wasn't concerned with who I really might have been."

"Marna, my good friend, how could you know of Jupiter and Saturn in their places unless you were there? This is the...how do you say...paradox."

"For weeks I've been baffled by what amounts to two identities, but it seems so natural. For some reason I know I'm dreaming and will wake from the experience."

"What if someday you don't recognize you're dreaming and don't wake from the experience, Honey?"

"I think I'll get myself a drink, a good single malt."

"This is speculation. What we know of the power of the mind is zilch. Her knowledge of the planets defies science, but it also predates science and may be the origination of science."

"That may be so, Ron, but Marna brought back smears of flour in her hair. The last time she had gun grease on her arm and head."

"All we know for certain is that it was an animal fat. The two substances occur commonly in most households, though I take your point, Commander. We have enough of substance with Marna's mind constructing arenas of activity with detailed knowledge beyond imagination. We also observe a tendency for these episodes to involve increasingly greater violence. This concerns me."

"Well, Roni, I think it safe to say none of us accepts outright time travel as viable, but I think you have touched on something with mental constructs."

"Guys," Marna broke in. "Maybe there is no explanation and none needed. Who knows that this isn't the norm and that an uneventful sojourn in a macroscopic universe is the unusual?" She looked back as they stared at her. "Look, Nancy is writing a story, historic conjecture and all. I haven't read any of it, but she's briefed me some. Where does she get her ideas? She *imagines* events. I dream I'm *experiencing* an event in history."

"I'll need to think on that," mused Jim. "I can only relate what was going on with my own life in Virginia. My granddad introduced me to dousing for water. It worked for me right off the bat. We used sticks...pieces of wire. I don't know what *won't* work. People ask me, do I believe in dousing, and I tell 'em no, I don't...nor do I disbelieve. It works. I ask them to explain gravity to me and ask if they believe in it."

"Most pragmatic, Commander, and from this kluge surrounding Marna you are trying to make sense."

"As much sense as one can make out of machinegun bullets in two hundred year old oak timbers."

Marna pulled away from him. "The worm holes, you didn't tell me anything about machinegun bullets. What else don't I know?"

"I'm sorry. My apology. I thought I had, honest."

"Wait...wait...too fast. I catch up. Machine gun bullets in the wood we found in the mud?" asked Roni.

"I want to know what other little secrets Hawkshaw Fanshaw, the detective, didn't tell me," she chided.

"Hey, wait just a damn minute. The file is right there on the table, Love. It's all there. I'm not holding back secrets. We're on the same side, remember,?"

"You'll be required to prove it to me," she sniffed.

"OK, by God, I'm going to Washington next week, and I'll hand in my resignation." Silence followed.

Finally. "That's rather sudden, isn't it? We haven't discussed it, even. What will you do?"

"Keep very close track of you."

"Can the domestic scene wait? Among the unexplained is Marna's acute knowledge of flintlock rifles prototypical to those used in defense of the campus. What is strange, also, is her dream adventure predating the recent fracas, so there could not have been the power of suggestion."

"Shall I tell Roni of the gold coins I found?"

"You mean, you haven't?"

"I haven't told anyone but you."

"Treasure, also from the old wreck?"

"Beautiful and old," she replied.

"Roni," Jim piped up. "They shouldn't even exist. Elizabeth the First supposedly called them all back to be reminted. Marna's find beats all."

"You will make a date and show me?"

"Whenever."

"This gives credibility to an ulterior agenda of the admiral," said Ron.

"You got it, Ron, the admiral has had a couple of bozos nosing about. Some of the local guys gave 'em a bath one night. I think they were the ones who attacked Marna the day she fell in the ocean. Yeah, they were looking for something, but the admiral promised to call off his helpers."

"And you believed him?" Marna teased.

"No."

"Then we can all agree your boss certainly has ulterior motives."

"I'm afraid so."

"In that case neither Marna nor you is safe."

I regret this file was ever uncovered, except that I would never have met the woman of my dreams."

"I thank you both for seeing me, and I laud the fulfilling lives you pursue in spite of this enigma. If we come up with explanations, who is ready to believe? Who is ready to tear up three hundred years of struggle to understand the universe and existence? Marna gives us a glimpse, perhaps, on another plane. She may be functioning as an instrument calibrated beyond our senses. Certainly, she gives us a look through a window onto what we deem the past. Who is looking our way?"

"You allude to danger, Ron. I think I can handle any that has its genesis in the twentieth century. You're suggesting harm could come to Marna in her dreams?"

"Christ, Jim, what a suggestion!" exploded Marna.

"Both of you, let's sum up. Jim, you were participant in what we shall name as the first in a series of dream events. You remember that day on the mountain?"

"Who could forget?"

"The trend to greater violence disturbs me. Marna has described a small farm which includes a grist mill. She dreams of every day life, complete with sounds, smells, sensations. She has described timber by timber the construction of a fairly large schooner-rigged vessel and taking the cider jug to the men. She told of the craft's launching and a voyage during which an English warship fired on them, and a little life was taken. Jim, every line and gaff, the square topsails...Marna's eyes and mind were there for the accounting.

"Marna, you have told of lying in ambush for Tory raiders, of killing the force and capturing the vessel. Women protecting hearth and home is the theme of your tale. You described the weapons." Roni put his hand to his head. "And in real life you are the lioness of the pride."

"Dreams, Roni," said Jim.

"Marna described the sky from the top of the mill dam on which Sarah and her comrades waited for the raiders, cold stones beneath them. She faced east and Jupiter and Saturn were there before her. Just this morning, as I have told, Jerome Levi, his head in the charts of the Heavens, verified the positions of those same orbs in the spring of 1776. Just dreams, Jim?"

Looking at Marna he continued. "You recently find yourself in the unexplained presence of men whom you suppose to be pursuing their fascination with history on a vintage appearing sailing vessel. They recovered you from certain death in icy waters by their timely intervention. You recall names, only no one else has ever seen or heard of those men.

"The preserved log of the schooner *Archer* comes into her possession," he pointed out to Jim. "The journal is unmistakably aged but contains twentieth century syntax. She experiences such events as we have discussed, remembers names and finds written reference to these names. The personality Sarah describes Marna's parents. Ah, I realize this might be explained more conventionally. Marna, your safety is all important, and must take precedence."

"Roni, you don't really believe..."

"I do, Marna. Your description of Comfort MacLean, the object of Sarah's undying affection, would do Jim total justice except for the beard. Comfort is bearded. Jim, would you know if your own beard, were there such an amendment, would show red highlights in sunlight?"

Jim looked very surprised.

"No, perhaps you wouldn't. Whatever is driving Marna's dream world is taking her more and more into harm's way. In her dreams she is playing...no, not the word...working with dangerous situations, more shooting. Song of the prophet, we must take into account the hellish day she was called upon by the fates to kill in order to protect her life and mine. How can we know the degree to which these events, real and perceived, are related?"

"And now, we have reached the edge of reason. Stay with me on this," said Jim as he reached and drew Marna, now willingly, toward him. "Several months ago I was sent here to talk with a young lady about an aviation tragedy which claimed the lives of her parents. I'm all right with that. But I don't mind telling you I have fallen hard for that same young lady." He squeezed and got a smile in return. "My life has changed, and I hope hers has. She is everything and the only thing to me. However, until I can officially put in for retirement, I am still under orders, and the scope of the investigation has increased astronomically."

"Erick Lehn, bless him, with a hole in his side is out there on the water every day searching for wreckage of a blue Piper Navajo. To date, goose egg. Oh, plenty anchors and junk, couple boats...no Navajo. I'm at a wall. Now, you tell me Marna is in danger from her dreams?"

"Exactly so."

"Did I come down with yesterday's rain?"

"Mental constructs, who knows their energy? What has taken place is all of a piece. Nothing in life is disconnected."

"Are you suggesting this lady could dream her own...?"

"Hey, guys, come off it!"

"Would you bet the life of the woman you love that this could *not* take place?"

"Whew!"

Roni stood and stepped toward Marna, reached and touched her shoulder. "Marna, through the eyes of the influence named Sarah, you have described Comfort MacLean, and he could be Jim. I believe this Sarah wraith wants you to do something or find something for her."

"But what?" demanded Jim.

"That information could resolve the dreams. But whatever, I believe Marna can be depended upon to deliver. When this will have been accomplished, I think Sarah will be less prominent. I believe nothing innately malevolent exists in the influence, so I am unable to assess the real nature of the peril. However, I see the risk as too severe. Sarah longs to be with her lover. It is war time, and she will stop at nothing, in my estimation, to be with him. This is where you come in, Jim, a very large counter influence."

"I intend to hang on to him," said Marna.

"All are agreed Captain Gantry's airplane was brought down by a bomb; but no wreckage has been found by several legitimate agencies. Hypothesis: A bomb carried by the aircraft exploded, but not until fractions of a second after the craft and its occupants were transferred to another time plane."

"Honey, I think I'll have that drink."

18

Marna was wakened early by her telephone. She shot up out of bed and reached to answer it. Her heart jumped because she missed him and wanted him to make as early a return as possible.

"When can I expect you?" Alone in her house she curled around the phone as if she were in the middle of a party.

"…Just one more stop and I'm on my way. You still haven't heard any take on the identities of the guys that came to our aid at the college, have you?"

"No one knows anything more than we heard…three men looking like they'd come off a boat and carrying very long guns. One woman said she assumed they were headed for the muster. Funny how they attracted so little attention. Nothing since."

"Well, I'm hittin' zero here. We don't have a secure line so…what the hell, no sign of the admiral either. I mean, he might as well never have existed."

"I don't understand, Jim."

"Neither do I. No office at the air station…even the building's been removed. No one knows a thing about Naval Special Accounts. This is weird. I'm out of a job. I went to the Bureau of Personnel. Thank God, they have my records, so I got paid. They processed my retirement, and I have six months of paid leave coming…"

"Am I to believe you never went on leave?"

"Never had that good a reason 'til I met you. Marna, I'll drive straight through. Ought to be there about eight tonight. How about a date?" His cell was breaking up and he blurted, "Miss me?"

"Right on, you got it. Your signal's weak."

"OK, that's it." Jim made a detour to Fredericksburg and a small jewelry shop where he spent a little time. The proprietor, whom he knew, helped him pick out a whopping diamond in a simple mount. He paid cash.

He loved the soft sounds of the Porsche, and didn't push it beyond the pace of the general traffic which was always at least ten miles above the posted speed limit. Hours later he was beginning to feel the grind when he crossed the bridge into Maine and was truly ready for R&R when he reached what he affectionately called home at eight thirty. It had been dark a long time, and he was disturbed that no lights shone from the house. That hit him. The second shock was finding Marna's car parked in the turn-around.

He bounded the steps to the porch, unlocked and raced through the door and put on every light downstairs.

Earlier that same afternoon Marna had returned to her office, finding the mood on campus subdued as she had expected. She felt the tension in students and faculty who, she knew, were itching to ask her about her encounter with the assassins.. It was increasingly obvious her image on campus had changed. Len Fenster, the department chairman, was almost forced to acknowledge she was alive.

On her way home in the late afternoon she stopped at the Cuddy and watched the light fade on the Harbor. Nancy came and sat at the table with her. They each made their one drink last through their conversation, though all had been said over and over. Recollection of the fight at the college was still uppermost in their minds. Immense aid had come from the still unknown "troopers" who had descended on the scene from veritably nowhere. Nancy was obsessed with the thought that their timely intervention had provided the distraction that had saved her and Erick. But no help was forthcoming from the community as to their whereabouts.

Nancy's research was dead in the water for the time being, and Marna admitted her book was on hold. Both despaired of supporting information for their thesis.

Marna wanted to be at home when Jim arrived, wanted the fire going and candles lit. Making a home for Jim and herself

Echo Horizon

was foremost in her thoughts....wherever he was would be home. He had expressed more than passing interest in her restoration project, though the old farmstead was no longer an obsession with her.

Enough light lingered when she returned home so that she gave in to temptation to follow a newly cut path to the old foundations. She knew clouds were thickening and might pour forth rain at any time. When she reached the stones, wind had increased, and a strange yellow pervaded the sky. She thought she heard thunder, though it was late in the season.

She sat on a stone and looked in the direction of the well. It had been a simple matter to fetch water in the long ago. Close to the well had stood a tree trunk with a deep, wide notch cut into the top of it. Fitting loosely in the notch pivoted another smaller pole with its heavier, longer end resting on the ground away from the well. From the end of the pole over the well hung a plunging staff with a slim, long "J" cut into the lower end, and it was here that the person drawing water placed the bail of the wooden bucket. A push down filled the bucket; then due to the counter balance of the long end of the "seesaw" like pole, it took little effort to raise the filled pail. Quite ingenious, really. Marna thought she would go all out and equip the new well with a well sweep.

Indeed, it *was* thunder, and rain was nigh. It would be so nice if the old house were really here and she could duck in out of the weather. Imagination took her that far, and whatever had passed for reality that day dissolved as she became drowsily conscious of the moan of wind in the eaves.

Sounds of thunder attenuated in the softness of night, and threads of dreamscape parted to allow fragments of thought to begin to pilot her being. Her universe was a gyre in slow rotation. No great wind was there to disturb the timbers beyond a whisper, but she was nagged by doubts this was her bed. Had a creaking of the bed ropes awakened her, or was another influence abroad in the night? Again a rumbling not strange to her ear.

She sat up in bed and saw from her casement window the vault of night streaked by pale moonlight which bathed the sea. Streams of fog made fluid the solid shorescape of ledge and firs. Evergreen tops cast stunted shadows on gray drifts which spread over the scene, silent save for sea waves washing kelpy reefs.

Jupiter and Saturn arrived at their pre-dawn altitudes, and a sea turn spilled a milky swath of fog into McCobbs Cove to hide the lowest branches of spruce and all but hide the mill and dam at its head. Misty billows softened roof lines of the manse, and shadows followed the way of the breeze. One shadow moved. Curtains at her dormer window swayed, and she tugged at her coverlet, her rope bed protesting her turning, then starting to shake.

The slam of cannon displaced the quiet, and love's dream was lost. One. Two. Three. In all, seven in the concatenation of a broadside. Fully awake, she determined a king's ship pierced for eighteen. Patiently, she awaited response from the twelve pounders in Captain MacAlister's battery and released her breath at the four answering bursts of thunder, number three rising in shattering response above the others. So, Gabrielle, a long French great gun, was yet in voice.

Where was Little Bess? She must soon join the argument. The English would stand at long balls for their nines, but Little Bess would find them all the same. With an even greater impatience did her window rattle at the very next clap of heavy bombardment, fulsome even at a league and a half. She guessed the English had made acquaintance with a twenty-four pound round shot a moment after hearing the gun.

Another sound did visit upon her, the lowing of cattle. As in wars past, even now in the third year of rebellion, women were left behind to care for hearth and farm and all that needs doing. The kine desired her to their milking and must soon bellow and stamp the shed down were she late in attendance. She gathered herself at the edge of her bed, and with a toe nudged the chamber pot from harm's way. As she fumbled for flint and striker, her previous day of labor in the mowing field was suddenly remembered by each muscle.

Once her taper came alight, she worked her brush through chestnut tresses., then grasped and dove up into a skirt of green muslin. Waist and apron followed and did twist, eliciting a harsh word. With satisfaction she noticed her fullness in the glass.

Even at nineteen she preferred to go about barefoot in the summer and feel newly mown stubble on the bottoms of her feet; but *such* clothing in the heat of the day, especially when cleaning the mill. She was certain Mehitabel was permitted to show more ankle than she *ever* was. If only she could be first at hearth this morning. Was there a chance? She'd show Mistress Goodiemaid.

Mehitabel at sixteen was a practical homemaker and preferred cleaning, stitching and meal preparation to farm chores. But she was such a scold! Mehitabel gave her no peace about being bounden for spinsterhood. She studied her hands in the light of the taper. A glance told of need for Sister's lambs' grease. She must turn the hay today and rake.

With a quick toss of her head her long hair settled behind her shoulders, and she started down the narrow stairs. Bacon's own aroma and that of hot cakes greeted her as well as a cheery "Good morrow, Sister, did you and your bedstead become as one this night?" Then that laugh. She glanced in vain for table to lay, kettle to put to heat; but Mehitabel was already pouring tea, that which was named Indian brew.

Mehitabel seemed to wear a smile permanently etched on her face beneath brown eyes and blonde hair braided and neatly pinned around her head. She replaced the kettle on its crane and returned to her porridge, stirring with one hand while holding her indigo from the embers with the other, kitchen alight from hearth and sconce. Summer mornings by the sea made heat from their hearth bide well.

"Where's Mama, Mehitabel?"

"Gone to attend a stirring about, an animal which lurks to set upon the fowl, I misdoubt. She has taken down the rifle." A shot caused the girl to loose her apron as she jerked her head around.

An answering shot sounded close by the door, and Mehitabel grasped the mantel above her head. "Sarah, that is no animal. Oh, what of Mama?" She called her Sarah. It seemed strange to her ears, and she was certain she knew another name. She saw her wainscoated kitchen as if for the first time, and all about appeared as if in dream consciousness. Had her mother been fired upon? As in a dream she moved toward the door, waded against a flow of current, and yet, she was her own self. She was no other. Why was she in this dream? All seemed so real. This was her home. These people were her family.

The door opened before she could reach it, and Betsey Alport stepped inside. She slung her cloak to a waiting peg and replaced the long rifle on a row of pegs over the mantel. "Clean and load after we eat. Sarah, if you please, fetch that berry pie. I have a great hunger."

"Mama, what…are you unharmed? Whatever has happened?" Had she not known her mother all her life to this moment?…yet she wondered what to say next.

"Sneaking villain, I winged him. He was nigh to the battery your father labored so long to erect. I warrant he was misguided and was want to spike the guns. We'll give the alarm to Caleb, come he by this morning to finish mowing."

Mehitabel twisted her apron and looked downcast. Sarah spoke for both. "You gave us a fright, Mama. I wonder shall Sister be able to eat."

Betsey picked a slender clay pipe from a dish on the table, took from a crock some dark shreds and tamped them into the bowl. She sat as she tipped a taper to light.

"No harm comes by. The intruder, once found out, took fright and couldn't hit the inside of the barn with its doors shut with that club of a pistol he carried. How the sound carries on such a night."

"Dawn comes on us soon." She was indeed Sarah and always took note of the sounds of weapons. She reflected on the echo from the far side of the cove.

Echo Horizon

"Oh, the guns...the shooting," cried Mehitabel. "Will it never cease? The gunnery from the Saxton battery, I doubt I slept a turning of the glass. I hate it, Mother."

She was aware of her sister's feelings and pictured for a moment her own love lying on the shattered deck of her father's privateer. "The English, Sister, I warrant a sixth rate or a brig, perhaps, sought to magnify their glory by terrifying the townsfolk, burning hay and stealing livestock. Captain MacAlister's battery may have inspired them to seek society elsewhere."

Girls, our stock desire attention. Eat, then." Betsey released a wreath of smoke and glanced toward the parlor. "See, the light of dawn be upon us. We dally while invitations to industry go unanswered."

"Yes, Mother, but I hate this war," grumbled Mehitabel. "Thrice have we been attacked by Tories, and we wait these three months for Father. Oh, I shall wed a rich merchant and keep his manse, and he shall hire captains and sailing masters to ply his ships in trade. You, my Mother, risk all to guard the artillery Father has left in our care. What can three women manage with such monstrous guns?"

She wanted to reply to her sister's question that they three should load and fire, but she hesitated.

Sister went on, "I shall entertain my husband's associates and not cower by my hearthside as some spinsters I could mention, waiting for their sailors. My husband will bide with me each night at home." The flounce...

She wanted to shriek but merely winced and nearly choked on her porridge. The arrogance of this baggage. Could she bear another instant? Suddenly, she lashed out. "My baby sister was a suckling and remembers not the vexatious writs of assistance, currency, stamp, quartering and Townsend Acts. She knows naught of the tea act and the coercive acts. Would you live with Tories who have plied their shaving mills the length of our coast, pillaging farms and murdering innocent folk? Would you dine with fops and bend to a tyrant's will?" Breathless she submitted to her mother's calming voice. Her face hot, she could feel without touching with her hands. She looked out from subjective eyes and thought of her father whose image resided in her younger sister. He was probably this day homeward bound with a cargo of powder and shot. She thought tenderly of Comfort, his first officer, who one day must hold her trembling body close to his. This thought softened fury to tolerance.

"This hue and cry is wrong," snapped Mehitabel. "We do not drink tea. Cutting mercers despair of aught but bare shelves. Hardly a fair made implement can be purchased, and this killing so a few wealthy freebooters need pay no tax…"

"Mama, hear you this outrage? My own sister speaks with the tongue of a loyalist. Is there no shame?"

Betsey drew impatiently at her pipe, clearly favoring that they be at labors.

"Pshaw, it is so. The killing is horrid. Look what took place at Fort Washington, and poor Mr. Greene a Quaker…"

"General Greene, Moppet!"

"Girls, girls, I would I might say 'Ladies'."

"Well, Mr. Franklin said these words himself…"

She knew that she as Sarah put her head in her hands in frustration and angst. "Spare us, Sister."

"He said he never knew a good war nor a bad peace."

"Mercy!"

"Girls, we have this day no other of which we may be certain. We have this day in which to conduct our duties. Far from home sail your father and *your* good man, Sarah. I beg you be at peace and hold your tongues."

"I beg your forgiveness, Mother." Mehitabel reached for the kettle to pour water again for the spice tea. It was flavored with lemon brought home from the French islands. "I still hope I have the good fortune to wed a rich merchant."

"Would that I possessed the power to grant your wish, Child."

Echo Horizon

The sea amplified the sunrise and sent rose-hued light streaming through a freshly scrubbed front window into the parlor as from an inner luminescence.

"We meet duty e'er the day be done and ready the mill for the grist. Attend the flax and herbs, Mehitabel. If Captain MacAlister send for the cannon, you know where the extra powder be stored. Your father offered it all to him."

"Indeed, Mother, and good riddance."

"I have meant to speak sooner. Be ever mindful to whom you speak, and of whom. It is said a spy lurks in the village, and the English know the disposition of the battery. Worse, Tory informers know which farms are weakest. They select their targets for plunder with good fortune."

Sarah's mind the while was on Comfort. With his and her father's assistance she had gained an uncommon understanding of military and political aspects of the rebellion against the Crown. She was ever drawn to contemplation of future fortunes for her land, at times dreaming of enormous power and brilliance. Her interest in all things natural was keen.

From a peg she grasped her mobcap which she fastened with two pearlescent pins, and tied her apron while following her mother out the door and to the mill. Sun broke over the trees to illumine McCobbs Cove, The shoreline was ledge and huge trees grew to the shore on the far side.

A path led along the north side to the dam. Firs greened the water in flood in the growing brightness. A cicada crackled in the sunlight through the resinous aroma of balsams. A raft of sea ducks gave rapid way as an osprey hit the water and rose with a fat fish. Songbirds abounded. Sarah was confident she and her mother would be cooled later in the day by a sea turn.

"Sarah, let us hasten that we finish the sooner." Her mother stood on the walkway on the dam, sun burnishing highlights in her auburn hair. "You are vexed by your sister. Recall when you were sixteen and dwelled in a world of your own."

"But she is unfeeling save for her own thoughts in her little world."

"She prides a neat house, and we need not." Betsey winked at her nineteen year old.

"But she gloats of it and bespeaks me a spinster."

"Nonsense, despair not. I know these to be wearying times, but we must bear up."

"She is so disturbed by the sound of gunfire. What if the militia mounted no cannon nor possessed powder? What injury must the English put us to, then?"

"Poor chance of injury whilst the English stand at long balls, even so, I doubt the west battery could hit the water if they stood knee deep, and I would with Mehitabel see the whole fracas end."

"I warrant no killing at Saxtons." She heard herself chuckle and she knew through the being of Sarah, she was able to bring humor to the fore. "…Lest the match boy burn the powder monkey and number two man drop a nine pound shot on his toe."

They busied themselves, putting to flight dirt and corruption after cattle had been milked and fed.

Land heated beneath summer sun, and sounds were heard of water gurgling from the sluice but none of wind. A trout broke the mirrored surface of the mill impound, a cicada sang, and water splashed under the great wheel as it stole past the dam on its way to meet the tide.

She stood alone on the dam, leaning on the rail, tresses tied back under her mobcap in deference to her labors. This was her home, yet she felt detachment, as if at any time she might vanish from the scene. Grease provided a comfort to her reddened hands, but what could soothe her heart from the strains of love, as she was long separated from her man by the tides of war?

She and her mother sacked the last of their bran and flour, but the nether stone lacked dressing e'er they continued enterprise with the harvest of corn. They would speak of this with Caleb due by this day.

Smoke from the huge chimney of the house found no ascendancy and made murk of the interval. While Sister minded her bread, Betsey joined Sarah on the dam and wiped a floury hand across her head. She knew well of the melancholy in her daughter's heart.

"A fevered day, this, Sarah. The devil knew of our plans to right disorder in our mill. I would have word of your father, gone these months of trial. We know not how fare our fortunes in battle. We inquire of Caleb come he by. Surely, he has heard news squeezed past the English squadron. Would I also find a breath from the sea, Sarah girl. What think you on that?"

"A storm must come of this swelter, as Father would tell. I warrant a wind from the sea and the hour be twain." Her mother strode to the end of the walk attracted by a grown clamor. Sarah ran past her mother and onto the trace to see Caleb speaking vigorous encouragements to his red ox, Herschel. She could believe the animal rolled his eyes in detachment.

"Morning, Mistress," Caleb greeted her, "Be right to the mill with the burden I favor this beast's attention."

"Will you cart the chains to the gunnery, Master Gordon, at the foreside?" asked Betsey. "And, Master Gordon, as soon as you prize the moment, the nether stone lacks your pride and skill and the corn must make demand."

Herschel slowly leaned forward, and with much clucking from his master, moved the cart toward the rocky headland. The two returned to their labors, probed into corners of the building and raised a pall of dust which plagued for an hour or more until, finally, faint from so long a spell since breakfast, they paused to dip water from the sluice to cool themselves.

To the house they returned to linger with Mehitabel over hot biscuits and molasses, a space of time far too short. Through the windows was a view of the sea more gray as wind freshened from the southeast. This change in air must allow a determined effort in the mill until sundown. High sun made sparkle on the waves, but a more leaden surface prevailed under darkening sky to the north and northwest.

Afternoon aged, and rumblings of thunder were heard as breezes, brisk from the ocean, flung curls of smoke from the chimney.

"What of the storm's path, Sarah?"

"Father has spoken of the pointing of the anvil. I think it passes us by to the north." With that she saw despair in her mother's eyes even as she walked up onto the dam to look longingly to sea. Sun still glinted from highlights in her mother's hair. Patches of wind ripples raced across the cove, darkening the waters. She turned the windlass to raise the gate on the sluice, thus turning the wheel on its creaking axle enough to move the nether stone.

"The storm brings wind off the water, Mama. Hear the roll of thunder."

"And the wheel hangs near lifeless in its race since we lack a downpour to fill the pond on quickened waters."

A sound came on the wind which was not thunder, but as loud. One followed quickly by two, short and punctuated. "Look, Sister runs to us from the manse, Sarah. What possesses that girl to flee so over the ground?"

Mehitabel held her skirt aloft with both hands and made short space of the distance to the mill. Sarah started toward her.

"She points wildly toward the sea…oh, it's Father. Have a care, Sister, what is amiss?"

The youngster gasped as she halted before them, flour and dough on her apron. "Quickly, Mother, Sarah…Father's vessel…here and under attack…Oh, only hurry! He is damaged." She started to sob and bent over while trying to regain her breath.

"Slowly, Sister, slowly. Who attacks?"

"An English ship pursues Father. Go we now to the guns to give aid?"

"Heavens preserve us, yes. Flint and steel, Sarah. Come, girls, we'll get your father safely home this day."

Months of separation and fate brings their loved ones to their very door. Locating stone and striker, Sarah took them up and raced from the mill. She flung an arm up before her face and fled through savins, brush, past patches of ox-eyed daisies. Blueberry fronds swayed with the traffic as they three ran to the rocky bluff whereon waited two long thirty-two pounders on carriages, pointing toward a growing sea with crests of white and biding their time. Sarah paused and stared at the spectacle drawn before her. On waters gray beneath a sun now veiled moved a vessel, an image more vital to her than home itself. Spray spread skyward from breakers whitening ledge and reef, and islands dotted the seascape. Leaning on a reach with what canvas was left to her filled, the familiar schooner had found home and required shelter in the cove.

Its tall, raked masts normally carried a skyfull of sail, but now, two jibs, foretops'l and fore topgallant were shot away with the fore topmast. To maintain balance, her mains'l was down, and she sailed under fore stays'l, fores'l, main top and topgallant to haven.

Archer, the sleek, black hull of her childhood, had come home at last; but Sarah gasped when she saw the pursuing vessel pass to leeward of Big Candle Island and felt her heart skip a beat at sight of smoke streaming off her bows even before she heard and felt the slam of the bow chasers. Two geysers erupted short of the schooner which continued to labor on its board to pass beyond the reefs, loose sail kiting.

Sarah grasped hopefully at the thought of the English ship faltering under the lee of the island. "She'll sail like an applebutter kettle at the time Father wears off on entry to the cove and must present *Archer* broad on to the foe. To the guns, and we speak the Englishman a letter of metal to cause him distress!"

The turn of the sea air visited their nostrils, and lightning glittered off to northward through dark, towering clouds. The sounds of wings scattering to the air competed with running surf, and another cloud of smoke was swept from the Englishman. Another spout of water short of the first reef spoke carronades lacking final elevation. Came the slam, then another, then rolling, echoing thunder. White spray from the rounds was carried by winds which still favored the enemy.

If only they could recall all that Father had instructed them, for the huge guns must be served this day without the aid of menfolk. Each stood monstrously heavy. Father had erected range cairns on the reefs and made marks on the guns' cascabels. Mother warned of scarce time for the pursued to tack into the protection of the cove before the enemy ship overcame the range and destroyed the schooner.

"Sarah, powder...smart and lively!" Betsey pulled her hair, glinting in the shrouded sunlight, from the sides of her face and reached under a carriage to draw forth sponge, rammer and funnel. A dozen solid shot for each gun reposed beneath sailcloth with kegs of powder, all protected by close fitting flat rocks. Sarah hefted a round against the cold metal of a gun barrel, a ball of bog iron barely seven inches in diameter. It slipped and caught her finger, evoking a squeal and a curse. She and Sister pushed, but to no avail. Even with tackle they were barely able to move the ordnance. They must load from outside the embrasure. Each breath seemed a turning of the glass, and nearer ran the English.

"Good, Sarah girl, in it goes...about three of these measures, near a third the weight of the ball. Ohh, don't spill. Mehitabel, cast your eyes away from the powder. You know how you fare with combustibles. Damn, maybe a mite more. Did your father instruct to stuff some of this caulking in the barrel, or is it breech?"

Already puffing with effort, Sarah managed to reply, "Bore, do you mean?" She stood the funnel against the rocks.

"Now, the shot. Give it here. Uuumph, ohhh Lord, it's heavy. In it goes. Drive it firmly against the charge. Ready on the next. Hurry. That bar. Give way. We'll point...allow a lead...so-oo."

Frantic labors by the three translated to half a point inroad to the ship's track. Once more they heaved, the strain setting spots to swim before Sarah's eyes.

"Screw, lever, the coigns, we adjust elevation. That hand spike on the carriage. Oh, child, let me see. Did you pinch your finger?"

Her finger throbbed, and she raised her voice in excitement. The English fired again, and the schooner was at the second reef. "Mama, let the finger be. Have you the flint I carried?"

"Yes, Sarah." Her mother pointed to the igniter hole. "Here, nearly forgot...powder right here."

"Mama, be calm and we do just simply fine. Let me have the flint." She reached over the igniter hole and struck once, twice, then a small flash and smoke, and she was near to being thrown from her shoes by the ensuing concussion. Clouds of sea birds rose with raucous squalling. The gun leaped against its breeching tackle, and a concatenation of echoes crashed from shore to island. Acrid smoke obscured their view and assaulted their noses. Sarah heard her mother complain of deafness. They had forgotten to open wide their mouths as Father had cautioned.

Sarah moved to the second gun, as Mehitabel choked and chewed on smoke, but shook her mother's arm the while and pointed. The pall had cleared enough that they saw a creamy pile of water settle at the enemy bow. They had his attention. Mehitabel was jumping up and down when the next shattering explosion sent them reeling. The great gun bolted on its restraints and hurled the rough, cast iron ball close over the vessel to splash near aboard. It spoiled some rigging on its way over.

"Sponge the barrels and we reload." Sister had mounted the breastwork and poked the long sponge handle into a bore. The smell of burned powder lingered in Sarah's nose as she climbed out and sat astride a gun, working the sponge inside. She rose, not for leverage, but the metal was cold against her legs. More rounds would change the temperature. Her mouth was dry.

"What, Mama, two rounds...these with thumbscrew? Chain, yes, I see it, that which Caleb has brought us, all in short lengths. A havoc we'll wreak." She worked an end link into the slot and tightened the screw, same with a second shot. "Double the powder? It would follow, but do we repose trust a fiery fury not hurl us to the far end of the mill impound?"

They loaded and rammed, working well together. Betsey turned the coigns to depress the range, changed the pointing. At the flint's dictate, both guns convulsed in turn, one upon the other in cataclysmic declaration, sorely damaging the vessel. Its foretops'l flapped in the wind. Much rigging and some yards were violently scythed from the ship; and the foretopm'st and royal came crashing down in a tangle depended from the crosstree of the foremast with its clewed up fore course.

She heard herself scream with excitement as she watched the main topgallant stays'ls and heads'ls join the sorry midden of cordage, wood and canvas. As headway fell off below steerage, the issue was in doubt for the English

"Could he, God willing, be Mowatt?"

"Too many guns, Mama." Comfort MacLean had taught Sarah the sails and lines of a man-o'-war, and before her, the enemy was hacking about everything she could name of useless rigging and employing the vigor of an entire watch while struggling to avoid irons on a lee and hostile shore. Ravenous fury from shore had taken from them the name of pursuer.

"Once more, my girls, fire and pound them into the surf an' we geld the haughty spirit of yonder roosters. Oh, look you, what action your father takes to him the nonce!" Even numb from concussions, they loosed yet another salvo on their foe, for he lost helm and spanker and was reduced to a drifting hulk.

Mother, Sarah, see," Mehitabel croaked, "The schooner presses the attack!" Foretops'ls and heads'ls juried, it had turned and was beating toward the stranded Englishman.

"God's blood, children, what will he not do next?"

"He fain make kindling wood of the host, Mama, if he fail to strike his colors. Or he will tow or send in as prize. Oh, let it be Comfort. Let Comfort bring it in under my eyes."

"Well done, Ladies, now to house. Your father will want food and drink for all. Hustle, there may be wounded to attend."

Twilight cast its spell on a reunion of kinship and the telling of adventures. Cider flowed, and meats and pies diminished with appetites honed by months of shipboard fare; and Betsey saw to be profligate in numbers of tapers set alight in kitchen and parlor.

Mehitabel stood illuminated, and perversity danced its mischief in her eyes. "Desire Comfort speak of maids in far ports to whom he has given eye."

"Silly baggage, enough of your impudence. Mama..."

"Girls, see to our folk they lack naught."

In time Comfort MacLean was able to break away and move beside Sarah, and they slipped from the manse when she thought her sister unmindful. Mehitabel watched her sister and went to speak to her mother. Sarah and Comfort clung to one another, desire a firestorm consuming her, and she ached to give of her stored up love to him.

She spoke near tremble. "And you brought in the prize."

"Aye, *Seadragon*, *Cowperthwaite*, eighteen. We would stand at the nether end to the bargain had it not been for our three heroines of the gunnery. How could you command such iron to move and point as you did?"

"The frenzy of the moment, I would have you safe on shore with me once more. You are gone too long from my side."

"Have you my letter which I penned from afar?"

"I sleep with it 'neath my pillow."

"You have missed me?" They stood far down the path, faces close.

"How speak you so? Missed you? I've been distraught with worry!"

"Come, we go aboard. They will hardly know we are gone. We have much to say." Comfort reached in a pocket and pulled forth a ring, and Sarah gasped at the brilliance and beauty of the stone in the last of the day's light. "I give you my troth, Sarah, and I ask that we publish our bans. Squire has offered me the *Coral Empress* when this war shall be finished, and I shall be master. Will you sail with me as my wife?"

"Oh, yes...but you must ask Father. I cannot wear your ring until you have Father's consent. Only, don't wait, Comfort, I cannot remain like this, not betrothed to you, another day." He took her in his arms when a light shown from the door to the manse.

"There you are, Sarah, and the bucket empty. We lack water. Would you mind and I not trouble you the night?"

"Yes, right soon, Mama. Forgive me, Comfort, dearest. Go to the vessel. I'll follow in a trice. We apart for so long...another instant."

"It is best I see to the vessel before you step ont."

Sarah entered the buttery and grasped the bail of a wooden bucket and started for the well at the side of the manse away from the barn. Fog climbed from the cove at the setting of the sun and made soft the ledges and drifted across lower branches of firs. Months of longing were to soon be satisfied.

Now, the only sound to reach her ears was that of droplets striking leaves. Light from windows lanced only short paths into fog drifting past corners of house and barn. Something there was that hindered her progress, and she couldn't find the plunging staff for her bucket. She pushed aside wet branches and decided she had made a wrong choice of paths in anticipation of reuniting in love. Darkness yielded and trees took form. Trees, but where? She gazed on a backdrop of foliage shrouded in mist but could no longer discern light from her windows; neither was there the sound of revelers.

Only thirty paces to the well, how many hundred times had she walked there? Where is it? She stepped forward once more only to fall flat when her toe caught up against a stone. Angrily, she thrashed to gain footing and looked down on a ring of stones in the weeds where the well curb should be.

What had happened to her? This couldn't be it. She looked back in the direction of the manse for reorientation and found only gloom where only moments before merriment had reigned. Here was dampness and silence save for fog horns. She heard no sounds of laughter and was filled with anxiety. Above all things

Echo Horizon

in life she wanted to be with Comfort on board *Archer*, and he must be frantic at her prolonged absence.

No light from the manse…as if it had passed into a void. She turned and glanced in all directions, consumed, now, by unleashed panic, for no explanation was there to answer her confusion. She called and called, shivering in the mist. A glow like light at first break of day confused her even more, and fields were gone over to a thick growth of trees and brush.

"Mama, I am lost in a tangle of weeds. The well is lost. Mama, bring a lantern to assist. Only three mugs of cider, and I am lost."

No echo. Where had her fields gone? No lights where her manse should be. She had let go the bucket when she stumbled. That was gone.

Run!

Run with all her might…run for the cove and find the schooner. Branches tore her clothes and slapped her face. The light of dawn was on her, and the cove lay breamed over with light fog. So still. So empty. No schooner stood at the quay. Longing overcame her, for she knew he waited. But where? Must they know separation again so soon? Her mother desired her to fetch water. So many questions for Father. Again she cried out with pleading voice.

She clawed her way through underbrush and froze in terror at what appeared suddenly before her. Stark and forbidding rose a house where no house should be. Electric brilliance burst from windows and sent shafts of light far into lingering mists.

Her throat was dry, and she could hardly gasp as she watched a door open and saw him walk toward her. She was totally confused. How could he walk from this strange house when she and he were to meet on the schooner?

His arms were held out to her and he called her name. But it wasn't her name. How could he not know she was Sarah, not of a name which sounded from his tongue something like "Marna"? How could he not know? There was nowhere for her to run, nothing left for her but to fall into his arms, and she felt herself quickly borne up off her feet and carried inside the house.

Nothing else in all the world mattered now.

19

November skies offered a prelude to winter but weren't the sole source of chill. Choreographed by the IRS came a message of terror which continued the process whereby Marna was slowly retreating into herself. She barely understood the vague threats casting about on the page, but they were couched in announcement of audit, grim suggestions of under reporting of income and irregularities concerning acquisition of real property in the town of Saxtons Harbor ME, all addressed to the Estate of John Gantry, Captain, USN, Ret.

Heirs, assignees, receivers and trustees were constrained from any action involving estate and all accounts.

"What, Marna?"

A shriek was all he received in reply plus her declaration to place the entire mess in her attorney's hands, this while several heavy objects became airborne and crashed against a wall. Jim remained in the house as she stormed through the door, reflecting the while on this animated return of Marna's connection to her current surroundings.

For days since her latest event an air of detachment prevailed, she being nearly unreachable. Jim's impression was that she languished between two worlds unsure of her identity. The results were calamitous for a relationship, and Jim felt a mounting restlessness. On the coffee table sat Marna's penned notes for her story, and for want of diversion, he lifted a page and glanced. Then, he looked closer, read a paragraph.

What he discovered startled him, for the syntax was written as it might have been by Walter Scott...long relative clauses with maximum use of adverb and adjective. It was so out of place with the character of Marna that he wasn't dealing with it well. Jim's ordered mind took a severe hit.

Marna's visit with her attorney was brief and unpromising. As he explained, the IRS could make any claim they wished and terrorize a citizen with impunity. They had the power of taxation to defeat any defense a citizen might mount. She knew from that moment she was in an unenviable position. Her next stop was the Cuddy, and she was white mad.

Hopes and aspirations with the property had vaporized, but she intended to reside in her home until someone forcibly put her out, and then there would be a fight. Six steps along the wharf from her car she was approached by a familiar figure in the person of Gamewell Jannett.

The Jannett brothers, Ross and Gamewell, were well known personalities along the waterfront. If a boat had sunk at its mooring, it was probably the property of the Jannett brothers. If a boat caught on fire in the Harbor, Jannetts. If an outboard motor refused to run, a Jannett was at the laniard. The Jannetts had reported radar echoes on certain foggy mornings indicating a sizeable boat that no one else noticed.

"Hi, Marna, long time. Hey, been wantin' ta say something. You know that shootin' business back at the school. Well, me and Ross seen these three fellers in a long rowboat justa' steamin' into the harbor that same day. Didn't think much on it at the time, but they looked some tough old customers. I think they were headed for the dock. Don't think I've seen 'em around here before."

She thanked the brother and knew Jim and Erick would be interested in the information. As for herself, she went weak in the knees whenever she thought of that awful day on campus, was sick of the notoriety, hearings and the looks cast her way at the college. She glanced once more toward the ragged truck onto which the Jannetts were loading lobster traps, some of the last wooden traps in the wave of changeover to wire mesh.

She cooled down to her normal temperate level in the comfort of two large, cool beers, exchanged a few cautious words with Katie and started out the door. She stopped short in her tracks when she saw the two in dark suits and narrow ties hovering around her car. Her temperature commenced to rise

Echo Horizon

once more as she plowed ahead to take position behind the wheel.

"Not so fast", was the command.

"I beg your pardon. This is my car and you're in my way."

"Marna Gantry?" She turned and nodded before thinking.

"You are going no where with this vehicle!"

"What is this, a hold up? I have no cash on me. Oh..no..you're car jackers. How about if I scream?"

"Treasury, Ms Gantry, Internal Revenue Service...get out of the car!" He started to produce his ID. No one noticed the two mariners ambling up the cat walk from the float, looking like ordinary lobster fishermen...except slightly different.

The argument continued, but an element of fright overtook Marna as she realized she was in a situation she couldn't handle. She was confronted by men who were robbing her in broad daylight while claiming to be government officials. No difference was obvious to Marna. She started to exit her Blazer just as the two seamen moved to either side of her tormentors.

"Ye'll no be botherin' the lass, mon. Mount your carriage, Mistress." The one started for his sidearm but slumped when a belaying pin thumped him on the side of his head. His companion was constrained so neatly in an arm lock he never had time to respond except to call down the wrath of the whole United States Government. "Ye'll have time to think on that, hearty."

Marna was backing away from the scene as two customers came through the door and were greeted with the promise of quick removal of a pair of troublesome drunks. "The lads ha' spent a wee bit too much time in the society of the ale bench. Come along, maties." The two government men were frog marched to a waiting long boat.

"Where do you think you're taking us? You'll be hunted down and arrested!"

"Not bloody likely. McNab, advise the blokes where they're going."

"Ye'll fetch us ten Spanish dollars for each o' ye, and ye'll serve before the mast on an Indiaman with as gentle a captain and mates as ye'll find on the seas."

"You can't do this..." The belaying pin punctuated the utterance and little attention was drawn to the departure of the two seamen in their long boat with their companions.

Marna's pulse rate slowed, finally, to cruise as she started to round the turn onto Mast Road, but backed up traffic made it obvious she would make slow progress with the few shopping errands she had in mind. It was an Indian summer day with a surprising amount of traffic for so late in the season, as if the summer visitors had not yet departed for away.

The Jannetts had passed this way a few minutes earlier in their old truck sagging under its burden of waterlogged lobster traps, pot warp and buoys. Ross drove, and Gamewell scanned the load. The truck emitted a range of sounds as Ross had sprung from the stop sign and turned to head up Mast Road. A trap fell off and was immediately customized by a Pontiac whose driver was forced to wrench his vehicle to the side in front of blaring horns and face the dilemma of removing the crushed trap from beneath his oil pan.

Traffic was heavy, and drivers searching for parking spaces were clearly irritated. It all came to a stop when an Olds swung out to go around the Pontiac and plowed into a Ford coming the other way. Immediately following the CLANG and shower of glass, a ring of spectators gathered to watch the two fat drivers rolling on the ground pummeling each other, each proclaiming the guilt of the other.

The Jannetts were luckier at Front Street and continued across. Luck was also with those drivers who were able to make an orderly stop and avoid two more traps. Ross did so well at Front, he simply barreled through Commercial Street, leaving a half dozen traps on the road and a Suburu on the sidewalk. Relaxed and considerate out-of-state drivers leaned on their horns as drivers picked their way through the additional

Echo Horizon

wreckage. Temperature registered at eighty on the clock outside Mariners' Federal Savings and Loan.

In cooler times with the benefit of hindsight, two schools of thought emerged as to what went wrong, subsequently, with the Jannett vehicle. Either a universal joint broke, or the clutch burned out. Brake failure elicited no contest. The truck reversed its progress up the hill and gathered speed in its plunge down Mast Road and picked up speed. The driver of a blue Ford chose destruction by way of a fire plug to burial under a pile of lobster traps. Ross held to the road but required both lanes. Gamewell kept his head out the window and hollered a lot.

A green Pontiac LeMans parted from most of its paint on one side before hurtling into the pumps at Villier's Service Station. Two Japanese cars found a lawn across the way, but a third was struck, careened around ninety degrees and jammed against a utility pole, its driver's head bobbing to and fro. Most of the traps were on the road, nails causing serial deflation of tires, and two more fights erupted.

When the scourge reached Front Street, Marna had appeared from the north and intended to turn right onto Mast Road. She completed her turn via the sidewalk, having seen the truck coming in the nick of time. She floored the Blazer and shot across into Heidi's Sidewalk Café, a red table, chairs and umbrella disintegrating under her car.

Sirens screamed as fire trucks responded to the alarm from Villier's before the fuel ignited. Halted and damaged cars took another round of hits as Saxtons Harbor pumper, Engine Two and Chemical Five made four wheel drifts onto Mast Road. They missed by inches a white Porsche already in execution of a one eighty degree skid to avoid the Jannetts. The Porsche skidded into Heidi's stern first and came to rest beside the Blazer, placing the drivers' doors adjacent.

"Get in, Sweetheart, and let's go home."

"Sweety, I must be losing it. I just don't know where I fit anymore. I may be losing my home for God knows why….but the weirdest thing just happened…"

"I know. Look out there. Your car will be here for a while."

"No, stranger than this. I was accosted by two IRS agents who were virtually car jacking me. These two guys came up the ramp from their boat, slugged the agents and lugged them off."

"Who were they?"

"I don't know, but I think the Treasury Department's personnel list is going to show a couple agents gone missing, and, Jim, I have the most awful feeling they're no longer in this world."

"You don't suppose there's any connection with...?"

"I just remembered...Gamewell Jannett told me this morning he and his brother saw three seamen in a long boat come ashore the day of the attack at the college. That the connection you're looking for?" Jim had picked his way with the Porsche out of the wreckage zone, and they were headed for home.

"Honey, I have the strangest feeling those weren't IRS men trying to impound your car. In fact, they could be the clowns who accosted you on the trail last spring. The admiral smells gold, and he wants you scared out of town. If I'm right, this is getting serious. He's got the juice to get a threatening letter out of the IRS like you received."

The scream had been a long time building, and Marna put some lung to it. "Aaaaaaaaaagh!!!! Shit!!! I'm me, goddammit, Marna Gantry! I'm a real person, living in a real world in a real twentieth century!!" She was going over the edge emotionally, and he stopped the car and put an arm around her, said nothing.

She felt the earth move. The arch of the firmament flickered within her perception.

"Those two guys from the long boat. They pulled me out of the ocean and took me to what seemed like a real vessel...but it never was. They weren't real...so, where was I?..and here they turn up again, and I don't think those feds are ever going to be seen. The one called McNab...he was one of the ones I told you about...he told'em they were going to serve before the mast on an Indiaman. What in hell does that mean?!"

Jim drove on to house by the sea. Where they found Roni's old Plymouth in the yard. "What do you suppose brought Roni around here?" He, then, appeared by the side of the porch and waved a greeting. Inside, Jim set water to heating for coffee.

"I have come, my friends for the sad goodbyes."

"What's come up, Roni?"

"Ahh, Marna, Commander, my friends, the clouds of war gather over the desert, and I am needed in the homeland."

"You're packed up, then, and ready to head for the airfield..well, come in and have some lunch with us, you have time for that, surely."

"It is a pleasure. Yes, there is time."

"I think Marna would like to run something by you, Doctor, just this one more time, would you, Hon? I'll fix us some lunch."

"Please, Marna, I will listen to what it is you wish to tell."

She stood transfixed a moment, viewing the present moment as no more real than sponging the bore of a muzzle loading thirty-two pounder. She wanted to start at the beginning and spoke of her return from classes at the end of the day and walking to the old foundations, the threat of rain, of wishing she could just go inside shelter out of the rain and her imaginings of a manse and barn. The next thing she knew she was awakened by thunder which became gunfire a league or more away from her bedroom. She described the ensuing scene and events as though she had to have been there.

"I searched for her most of the night, called Erick and Nancy for help. It never occurred to us she might be sitting on the old rocks where the old farmstead stood. The venue of her dreams…she had to be right here all the time."

"I was. The flat stones on the shore…they're the same ones where the guns were. My dreams have been centered right here. This is McCobb's Cove!" She related the entire story to Roni; and, then, they moved to Jim's lunch of juice, cranberry muffins, navy coffee and omelet. Roni had some questions.

"Your account of the activity with the cannon, your description is so vivid the mind of the listener is thrown off balance, no? I am increasingly aware of your vast technical knowledge, historic as well as current. It is spoken of in town as well as with the students. Marna can fix about anything and start any motor, no matter how cranky. But the emotion, your elation at the return of your love. Excuse. Sarah's love returns, but all is through Sarah's perception as we have agreed. To have him close and then to lose him, you have recounted this emotional rollercoaster with detail beyond anything I have seen in practice. Now, you feel within your heart of hearts all is resolved. You have found him again or never lost him, for you respond to him every bit as exquisitely as Sarah's response to Comfort McLean. Yes, indeed, Jim and the first officer could be as one."

"What are you saying, Roni?"

"Just this, my most fortunate fellow. The shade that lurks in Marna's psyche is still searching for Comfort McLean, as I live and breathe. The trend of Marna's events continues violent, now to the extreme. Her dream partner has asked her hand in marriage and has announced he has been offered command of the merchant trader *Coral Empress* after the war…"

"How would the squire know which side would be victorious", asked Jim.

"I don't think it mattered much to Squire Skimpe, Hon."

"We know hostilities ceased here along the coast in 1783, long after the Treaty of Paris. When first I met Marna and was brought here to her home for pizza, I had opportunity to glance through ancient books among those on her shelves. One was a revelation in that it compiled accounts of wrecks on the seas from the 1780s to 1840 when it was published. The *Empress* was listed as lost with all souls in 1783. Not only has Marna, in relating her story, stated she and Comfort were to spend an extended honeymoon of a year or more sailing to the Orient and back, she has related from her dreamscape an actual historically accounted for vessel and throwing our conjecture into greater turmoil."

"You mean you think if I marry Comfort after the war and sail with him something really bad will happen?"

"That is my fear...if you dream Sarah marries Comfort. How can we know? We test uncharted ground. I search. I peal the mind. No precedent exists for this. The shade wishes you to do something. Oh, good that is Earth and Heaven, I meddle. Can it be that you two can unite in marriage, tie the knot? I only pray that you can and will soon. I believe that will lock out the peril." One could hear a pin drop.

"Are your intentions honorable? Do you intend to make me an honest woman?"

"Have you got a surprise coming, my dearest. What the hell, Roni, you may as well bear witness for us. Wait here a moment." Jim repaired to the kitchen and retrieved a small package from a high shelf. When he returned, "Hell, probably couldn't hide anything from her, anyway." He opened the box and took from it the magnificent ring he had bought. He reached for her left hand, and already her eyes were like saucers. "Will you marry me?" The firelight and lamplight glittered magically from the diamond. He was careful not to hurt her finger. "She says she got that pinched between a gun and a round shot."

"That is real enough. What was the size of the shot, Marna?"

"About seven inches diameter, near as I can remember."

"Just like that, an answer."

"The powder load, Hon?"

"More questions...a third the weight of the ball...anyone knows that." Marna flung herself into Jim's arms and began to eat him alive.

"When will be the day of feasting and vows?"

"Tomorrow if she'll do it, Ron."

"A grand beginning to a life of belonging. I am so pleased for the two friends who have welcomed me to their country. I gather, Marna, you do not reject the suitor?"

"Get real!"

"I should leave you doves to your devotions, but I would ask if you would accompany me to the field and return this compliant junk pile to the university parking. It is a loaner."

"If you're ready now, let's go."

As Roni pulled in at the Meadows Air Field, Marna recognized Benjie at the controls of his parked "J" with the canopy slid back. The engine was turning over and putting out a lot of smoke. "Stop here, Ron, let me out. Someone needs to be at that fire extinguisher. Benjie's over primed his crate again."

She ran to the aircraft and stood back from the whirling prop and listened to a very rough run up. She moved to the side and caught Benjie's attention and drew a finger across her throat. The roughness ceased and the prop jerked to a halt.

"What, Marna?"

"Awful rough, Ben. I think number one or two cylinder's exhaust push rod is sticky."

"Beautiful, just beautiful; I needed to pull the engine today. I'll do 'er."

"If I'm right, will you let me take it up later?"

"You checked out?"

"My dad, remember? You signed off on the FAA form."

"You got it."

Roni's Cessna was being preflighted by a young man and woman in blue jumpsuits. The steps were down, and he headed for the plane after giving the keys to the car to Jim. "I do not like the good byes. So, you two, have a life." He reached in his flight bag. "Marna, our notes, all in this little book. You keep. I wish I could know the outcome, but it would be difficult to reach me." He touched her face. "Shalom, my friend. Shalom, Jim. Love one another." With that he was in the plane and taking his seat at the left pilot's station. In another moment he was turning into his take off roll.

20

On a day such as the one on which they saw Roni off, Marna was checking Jim out in the rear seat of the SNJ prior to taking her own place. Benjie had the fire extinguisher. The engine started and ran smooth as a watch. She got her altimeter setting from the tower, not wanting to think later she was under water. Benjie was still stinging a little that a girl should know more about airplane engines than he.

Before giving her the signal to taxi, the tower advised her of an approaching front.

"Nan-niner-niner-niner-whiskey acknowledging." Benjie pulled the chocks, and she rolled toward the runway. Marna slid the canopy forward. "You hear me OK, Jim?"

"No problem." The plane gracefully left the ground, and its gear was up before tree top level.

"Where do you want to go?"

"How about a good view of the bay and the islands?" The hollow voices sounded as if they were in each other's heads.

"You got it." She turned and banked toward the sea.

"Jim, somewhat tense, was starting to enjoy the vista of seascape dotted with spruce covered islands. Rich blues of the deep gave way to browns and greens as the waters shoaled up to the islands. He had no way of judging the size of the waves except to remember the runs he had made with Erick on *Charming Sally*.

Suddenly the ocean swapped places with the sky, islands with clouds, as Marna executed a slow roll followed by an eight pointer. "Hey, I enjoyed my lunch much better straight and level."

"Excuse, please."

"I thought you intended to go up with Benjie."

"Not on your life, and leave you with two cuties working in the grille?" She flew a series of square patterns, the most energetic maneuver being some lazy eights. An hour went by before the radio crackled to life. It was the tower at the Meadows.

"Nan-niner-niner-niner-whiskey, weather update for region of your flight plan. Surface winds have picked up to thirty knots, gusts to forty-five. I repeat." He went on. "Barometer has fallen steadily last hour to 29.62 inches. Return to Meadows not advised. We have a disabled aircraft on runway with collapsed landing gear. Find alternate aviation facility. Repeat."

"Not good news, Jim. Look down there. Isn't there a lot of white on the surface? That wind sure is making up. We gotta find us a field."

"Can you make one more swing around that island off your left wingtip?"

"Right, something you want to see?"

"Looks like a good sized sail boat down there. Yeah, that's what it is, a big black boat under shortened sail. Bring it lower, Hon, please."

"Jim, that's a fog bank behind it, and good God, look, it's reached the island while we've been talking. We better get down out of here."

"Can you see that boat? She's a beauty."

"Wing's in the way. I'll make a steep turn so I can see." The engine sound reached a higher note as Marna made a complete circle around the vessel. "I'd say it's pitching, wouldn't you?"

"I would. Look at the rake of the masts."

"The what?"

"Both masts are raked back. Looks like a Baltimore Clipper."

"Jim, what did you call it?"

"I said it looks like a Baltimore Clipper. Chesapeake Bay saw a lot of 'em back in the early eighteen hundreds. They could run like the wind, nothing faster on the water then." He suddenly yanked the phones from his head when he heard an ear piercing scream. The plane took on some erratic behavior as Marna

Echo Horizon

gestured wildly. He brought the phones slowly closer and heard her exclaim, "*Archer...Archer.*"

He yelled into the mike, "Are you OK? What's the matter?"

"That boat...that's the one I've been telling you about. I was on it in the spring. I watched her being built. I'd know it anywhere..."

"Are you serious, Honey? Then it *does* exist. *Somebody* pulled you out of the water. You're certain that's the bunch you've been wanting to thank?"

"No question. Hey, where did it go? You see it anywhere, Jim?"

"No, must have been overtaken by the fog. We better get back. We've got the makings of a bad one coming on. Look at that stuff make in below us. Honey, make a one-eighty. We're going to be above that stuff all the way and maybe through it. Where we going to land."

"Only spot comes to mind is the drill field."

"The what?"

"Where Erick and the militia muster for drill...plenty of room to land. Take off? I don't know. Hold tight. I gotta get some sky out from under us. I'm letting down right over Saxtons Harbor."

"Wait 'til I get on the ground. I'll hold you tight."

Fog formed in mid air far in advance of the well-established bank moving on shore ahead of the front. Sun was already low on the horizon as she raced the few miles to the drill field and made a small field approach under power right down between the branches of two giant oak trees, flared and made a three point landing. It was rough, but they rolled to a stop on their wheels.

She slid back the canopy. "Don't think I can get it off and outta here."

"Not to worry, my dear." Jim had his radio out and was giving directions to a helicopter sky hook crew. "Meadows...Meadows. Christ, it's gotta be on your field list, ten miles north of Saxtons Harbor. A cream and blue SNJ will be tied down against the coming blow in a hay field three miles southeast of the Meadows. Yeah, after the storm. This thing is an heirloom."

"We got to haul outta here. Let's get these wings tied down. How we getting home?"

"Looks like we hitchhike. Look at these leg straps. Don't you think they're rather loose?"

"Oh God, Jim, if you'd ever jumped with that chute that way. Can't take you anywhere."

They piled out from the vintage pick up on the wharf, grabbed their chutes and waltzed into the Cuddy. "Oh-oh, somebody run tell Sylvanus the people who riled half the shingles off the Cuddy roof just arrived", announced Katie. "Well, look at you two. Oh-hh, Marna, what in hell? Look at that rock!! You been doing something you oughtn't?" Friends gathered from around the room with congratulations. Even Syl wandered out of his office. Jim took him aside. Syl wanted to know why they didn't just reach down on their way over and pick up a sandwich.

"Any sign of a big schooner, clipper bow, regular Baltimore Clipper? I'll say a hundred feet minimum."

"Not to my knowledge." That was good enough for Jim, but where was it heading? Where was it, now?

They were offered a ride home, and soon lights blazed. The wind had picked up considerable since landing. Mercifully, it had let up about the time of the small field approach. Now, it was howling. November could throw some wicked storms at the coast, and this November was commencing to do just that. Already, boat owners who hadn't gotten the message in the daylight were abroad in the harbor securing boats, adding lines here and there. This promised to be a bad one.

Jim started a fire on the hearth, and Marna threw some goodies together they could eat as finger food. Soft music flowed through the living room, and light glinted off wine glasses. Soon the rains hit, and the wind was a persistent moan in the eaves.

Jim thought Marna seemed well grounded in the present and felt an ease in his being that hadn't been there in a while. They were able to focus on plans for the future. He was certain her attorney would uncover the sham of the threat from IRS and disclose its source as Admiral Rankin, who now must be considered absent from duty without authorization. He wouldn't let up, Jim knew.

Rain hammered the windows. Heaven help a small vessel abroad on the seas this night.

Somewhere in the vault of night which was now far longer than the daylight hours, Marna was aware of an awakening. She consciously donned her night robe and descended the stairs to the fireplace, recovered her treasure and opened the small door. A presence was in the room with her, and she knew only the need to escape. A flashlight appeared in her hand, and she slowly picked her way down the precipitous stone steps to a vaulted tunnel. Her left hand rubbed against a vast and smooth surface for several feet, and she dismissed her light's revelation that it looked like the wing of an aircraft. Footfalls sounded behind her; she dared not look back, then nearly tripped over a metal box with the lid partially off. She stopped to look inside and recoiled at the sight of a mass of gold coins, whereupon her own she deposited along with the new found riches.

Foot falls had ceased, but she knew someone had been there; she could smell tobacco smoke. She stood frozen a few moments but began to move back. Whoever was or had been there knew she was by the light from her torch.

No one.

She wakened again, stirred, felt a breath on her ear, alert and conscious only of the warmth of the human form entwined with hers. She yielded to the firmness of his entry and was carried on gusts of passion to heights undreamed of.

On yet another wakening she felt the house shake in the fury of the wind and heard it shriek around cornices and eaves. Not only did rain lash the windows, ocean spume and spray washed over all. Waves pounding the ledges seemed to concuss the Earth to its very core.

Breakfast was leisurely, and they watched with awe as the sea tried repeatedly to claim the land. They could see that quite a number of trees were down. Brief snatches of news on FM spoke of boats smashed on shore, wharfs torn away and some houses floated off...nothing lass than a November hurricane, the track of its center just inside the Gulf Stream. If they lost power as much of the area had, they would not be without water, as Marna's father had contracted a shallow well blasted in the rock beside the house and equipped with a pitcher pump.

The rain continued with lessening wind during the day, but visibility across the cove was limited. On the next day winds from the northwest had cleared much of the area, and blue sky was on the increase just after sunrise.

Marna wandered about the downstairs contemplating an early breakfast and complaining of a slight attack of cabin fever because of the duration of the storm. When she looked out onto the cove she froze, nor could she utter a word. It was as if her breath was stuck. Jim noticed the squealing sounds and came around to where she stood rigid.

"Good God, its here. That's the boat we saw from the air. It must have sheltered here through the storm. Marna continued to stare at the sight of the vessel under main, heads'ls and stays'l gliding past the house and passing to the mouth of the waterway.

Suddenly, she uncoiled and bolted for the door, ran across the porch and across the drenched lawn to wave and shout at the schooner. Jim was sure he saw the man at the helm wave back.

"They must have run lines up to trees on the shore and just weathered out the storm." Jim watched with her as the vessel glided past the mouth of the cove and passed seaward of the big island. Neither could say much as they prepared breakfast together.

Marna sensed again the light of the firmament flicker slightly. Then, strange to her eyes, the kitchen table dimmed and, like a digitized picture, fragmentized into particles which began to fall away. She turned aside, stunned, and when she looked again, all was normal.

Breakfast finished and cleared away, they started a walk to survey the damage done by the huge blow to the surrounding countryside. It was enormous. In all directions, views hitherto blocked by trees and foliage were open vistas. They were more than two hours climbing through wrecked tree tops half way to the head of the cove.

Having enough of confrontation with the jungle, they returned and drove into town. The chaos was a thing not experienced in half a century, streets flooded and closed, wharves smashed and boats stove up and sprawled on Water Street. Marna began a repeat of the event in her kitchen, except, now, whole structures dematerialized before her eyes but were restored to view after she turned aside.

The Cuddy was undamaged and appeared the sensible retreat from the confused state of the town, and they continued breakfast. Marna steadfastly gazed beyond the windows for a chance view of the schooner *Archer*.

Bert Howe

21

In the fastness of night, she experienced an awakening and set a taper alight in a living room window facing seaward as to attract an ocean traveler. The horns of an aging moon shed dim light on the sea, not quite delineating the horizon but reflecting off the advance faces of small wave trains.

She knew she wished to lie abed but descended, instead, into the tunnel and came again past that thing which she knew to be a wing plane but chose to make no issue. Again the foot falls, the smell of a cigarette. She was being followed, and she knew she was hearing voices, fragments of angry discourse, then silence.

She woke, conscious and alert, though strangely unsure where she was. Protesting bed ropes she heard as she threw aside her coverlet and swung her feet over the side. Her ceiling was bare wood and sloped, and she noticed as if in review her bedroom surroundings as she swiftly dressed, then started down a turning, narrow flight of steps. She knew she had a purpose and let herself into the cellar after securing a candle.

An archway led into a passageway which she entered as if in a dream. Slowly her candle flame became two, then four and continued to become multitudes of small beacons. Walls of the tunnel disintegrated into fragments and fell away revealing broad daylight and a vista unknown to her. She tossed her head and reached to tidy her hair, grasping, instead of hair, a pillow.

She had been dreaming again, another of those nonsense dreams of confused images and moments of consternation upon awakening. Her knees were drawn up in the tiny berth, and the dim light of the moon, a few days beyond full and wearing a wreath of clouds, sent a dim light into her tiny quarters.

How many nights had she slept on this unforgiving shelf? *Archer* was short handed, and she and her mother had agreed to fill in on this cruise. She was aware of great moving about above her on deck..her mother's voice. "Search where you will, Cook, but in the name of God, find something fit to eat for this crew. Our hard money is better than any script, but steal if you must. We go to sea not an hour with sour beef and wooden vegetables. Take MacNab and two men with you, and scour the area! Where be my daughter Sarah she not be on deck?"

So, she was Sarah. Her conscious mind knew another name, but this pre-dawn air and moonlight was reality, and she knew she was on her father's privateer. They had sailed into Newburyport on the Merrimac River two days past to replenish supplies, and so far it was precious little they had replenished. The chandler had refused to sell them powder, claiming the committee had forbad it. Betsey knew this was balderdash. He was saving it for his friends. He would let them have all the ball they wished, but no powder, so she took the matter into her hands.

She told off three men to loosen the starboard spring line and brest the vessel so the starbord twelve pounder bore on the chandlery. Next she flounced down the wharf and into the haughty shopkeeper's establishment with a time piece in her hand and announced the hapless merchant had three minutes to start carting a dozen kegs of large grain powder onto her vessel from his magazine or she would send a ball through his digs.

Mr. Coleman was at her heels, dumfounded, but anxious she not forget a keg of musket powder which he preferred for priming charge. He also scooped up an armful of powder bags. On their return to the vessel, Mr Ruck was overseeing the loading of the last pipe of rum.

"Where be the capt'n, Mr. Ruck? I've not laid eyes on him a turning of the glass.

"He gave orders to say he had ventured toward Essex to view a stunning innovation in chronometers, Mum."

"Now, here is a six hooped pot...oh there you are, Sarah. You slept snugly, did you? Do ye break fast yet? Not enough your man must return to Virginia to be by the side of his ailing da and leaving us lacking a first officer, now, our captain must go atrinketting in Essex. Two hours have we to a dropping tide, and the murderer of your uncle sails the sea unchallenged for his deed of perfidy."

Betsey's brother, Nathaniel Thatcher, was skipper of *Lydia*, a fast brig and letter of marque. He was overhauled by a British cruiser and taken prisoner. His officers were paroled, but he was forced to remain day and night on the quarterdeck where he finally blasphemed the king and was shot down in cold blood by the English master. Sarah's family had sailed into these waters to find the offending vessel and settle with it.

"Do tell me, daughter, how we find your uncle's executioner, knowing not the vessel's name nor its description. First, for land's sake, let us eat. Cook has not that is fit to be called food. I'll try."

"Mama, take some deep breaths. Ye must relax." Sarah knew herself not to be a little girl and could speak thus to her mother. All was so real, but she must wake soon as another girl. She was so sure of that.

"Yes, Mr Ruck....."

"They be men in the tasting room at the distillery claims to be paroled officers of the *Lydia*. One Robert Lane was spoke to be first officer and knows the vessel by sight who took them...*Sea Damsel* 12, Carnody, Master."

"Thank you, Mr. Ruck. Desire Mr. Robert Lane to wait on me at his earliest. Have you seen Mr. Dighton?"

"He be swayed up to the fore truck inspecting the topmast stay and the upper peak halyard. I'll hail…"

"No, kindly wait, Mr. Ruck, that he finish and not need to ascend twice." Betsey finished with her eggs. "Daughter, I truly must get after your father and put an end to his dawdle that we stand out of this bottle and be at sea."

"Mama, does that mean that I..?"

"You are in command when I leave the vessel. I shouldn't be long."

"The men are anxious to close on that Englishman, Mama. Tide turns at noon, and a noon tide means a lot of water is going out to sea down this river."

"We should make this tide..you are right." With that she was off to the livery stable to hire a rig. The sun was bright on the water, and the sparkling day was the type she knew would produce heavy weather as the season approached the equinox.

It wasn't long before Mr. Ruck appeared with a gangling fellow in tow who proved to be Robert Lane. She heard Ruck's voice and chose to meet them on deck. It was her call. Introductions done, he told her of the chase and engagement. She had little doubt who chased whom. *Lydia* was outgunned if not quite outsailed, but the rest was inexcusable in her mind. Her mother and father wanted revenge.

"Mr. Lane, I have no doubt you have served as an able officer. Would you take berth on *Archer* as sailing master?" He would and dearly wanted another chance to get to sea in-spite-of his parole. "Then, there is an end to it. You have but to collect your effects and come aboard. I will have a copy of the articles and your commission in the captain's quarters, and you can sign them at your first comfort...Oh, there you are, Mr. Dighton; I didn't see you come up; but I have urgent matters to discuss with you.." The girl they all knew from her childhood as Sarah was getting into matters. She marveled to herself at her feelings of ease as she went about the immediate business of getting this vessel and its crew ready for a punitive voyage. They stood victualled, and the last of the water barrels were being topped off. She could see in the distance Boatswain MacNab, Cook and two assistants, one drawing a ramshackle cart, the others grasping flapping and squawking fowl and driving two porkers before them.

"Mr. Dighton, you are a master fine seaman, navigator and I don't know what not. You have a way of drawing men to your way of thinking without expressing your own opinion. You are well respected. Will you sign the articles as first officer for this voyage?" Mr. Dighton had a shock of white hair and eyes as black as bullet holes. Usually he stood bent slightly. He stood now, erect

"Whew, allow me to collect my breath, Mistress. This is your family's wish?"

"The command is mine, Mr. Dighton, while my father and mother are absent. I know their minds and they would approve. Would you be reluctant if you knew you might have need to sail under my command?"

"Not in this lifetime, Mistress."

"It is good. We have signed a sailing master, one who was officer on my uncle's brig and knows the ship we seek." She had barely finished the words when a clattering of hooves went from the packed gravel of the post road to the quay's planking. The rider was spreading an alarm. He leapt from his horse and went up to Mr. Dighton."

"Cap...Capt'n! From Salem I've come. A man o' war sails nigh the coast and has scattered shipping. All the cruisers from Thatcher's to Marblehead have sailed south."

"She be our captain..."

"Stay, Mr. Dighton. Sir, my first officer will report to me all the details. Kindly continue." She met the boatswain at the gangplank. "Well done, Boats, fresh meat and, Good Lord, look at the vegetables. Spare me the details. Stow it quickly and have the horn sounded. We are going to sea. An English raider terrorizes all in this neighborhood. Three powder kegs didn't make it to the magazine. Will you have them secured? Oh, and, Boats, you are second mate. What say you to McNaughton as boatswain port watch?"

"Master fine choice, Mistress, Oi'l send him to you."

"No time, pass the word."

"Mr. Dighton, anyone not aboard this vessel in five minutes swims or stays ashore. Then, take us to sea. Here you be, Mr. Lane. Earn your keep, we're going after an Englishman."

All hands were reported accounted for. Sarah was about to leave her family ashore and take her vessel in pursuit of an enemy. Mr. Dighton ordered the loosing of lines and sail to be made. Mr. Lane saw to the raising of the mains'l and forestays'l. *Archer* was lying along the quay pointed upstream. The stays'l was backed, and Mr. Dighton himself took the helm to work the rudder with the current and saw the big schooner swing away from dock and turn smoothly to head downstream.

They picked up speed, exceeding the rate of the current for steerage, and the two jibs were raised. Men hauled on the fors'l lifts and brought the gaff to a peak. Jib tops'l and main and fore tops'ls were followed by the main stays'l, truly a cloud of sail.

Archer felt the sea as they passed the Plum. She entered the rollers with a smooth shouldering of the sea aside with no pounding. She settled into her element with grace and comfort with a northwest breeze treating her to a beam reach and a brisk passage.

Mr. Dighton stayed at the helm to oversee the men who would stand their hitches at the helm. A double watch was posted, and Sarah made her tactical decision known to her first officer. "A square search, Mr. Dighton, ever expanding in length on a side. If hunting were good for Master Carnody, little need would there be for him to move on far."

As the day wore into afternoon, she noticed the gradual turn of the sea shade to a skimmed milk color and knew the cirrocumulus clouds to be drawing over the sun. She knew she couldn't communicate that term to her crew.

"A square search, Mum, and I've not heard of that maneuver."

"Just something I thought we should try." She took him into the chart room and explained with sketches what she was about and how she adjusted the courses depending on the wind, as a windward course would be far from into the eye of the wind.

At eight bells, the starboard watch was fed while the port watch held the duty, and she stood on the quarterdeck. Wind had veered easterly a half hour before. She gazed forward, hoping to hear from a lookout that a sail had been sighted. She knew that soon she must waken. As real as all this was, she must wake.

The deck was large with no breaks. A deck house was positioned aft the foremast and one aft the mainmast. The forward house could still serve as hatch for the hold, but had been converted to accommodate a larger crew during hostilities to handle the guns and serve as prize crew. Access below was provided by companionways. She watched McNaughton move about the deck inspecting every line, checking downhauls and lifts, sheets and braces for the square tops'ls. They were served down the masts with blocks to be out of the way of the big sails. He changed the positions of some belayed lines at each pinrail. She knew he must know the order to shorten sail would come soon.

Already the sea was growing in front of the strengthening east wind. The lower deadeyes were in the water and lee scuppers awash. Anyone in the way of water coming over the weather bows was getting ducked. She knew that forward motion was being lost. The vessel was so heeled on a reach the wind slid right up and over the big sails. She moved to Mr. Dighton and asked his opinion. He was of the same opinion; and since the season was advanced with night coming on, he wanted to shorten sail, clew up the tops'l send down the jib tops'l to ready for sailing off and on through the night while visibility was not their ally. No light would be shown at the stern.

Where was Master Carnody, and where would he be spending the night? Sarah saw that all the crew were fed, then entered the galley to nourish herself. That done, she asked Mr. Dighton if he agreed to a rum ration for the men. He did. She couldn't get used to the change that had come over the man. An excellent seaman was turning into a fine officer. She noticed Robert Lane kept much to himself. Maybe he would feel more at home later.

Bert Howe

22

Wind dropped in the night. Dawn broke on a calming sea. Mr. Lane had the watch, and she asked him to have all sail set, for if they were to find their quarry, their best defense lay in the magnificent speed of the schooner. It was built for speed, a design which would not be seen generally on the seas for twenty-five to thirty years more. Mr. Lane passed the order to John Pope, ship's carpenter whom Sarah had promoted to boatswain of the starboard watch.

The big main stays'l slowed and gentled the boat in any roll; and in full daylight she called ship's company to muster. She had to talk to these men once and for all. Well, it was the Sabbath, so she would read a few words first. That done, she launched into it.

"In saner times we would have followed wise counsel to remain in port until Captain Alport returned to his vessel. My mother has taken up the challenge to find him and return him by the ears if necessary." She warmed to a hearty chuckling. "Meanwhile, word of a skulking Englishman has put fright to many an American heart. Our plan is to take as prize a certain English villain who has seen fit to summarily execute a young privateer captain from the port of Newbury. Lying there we denied ourselves the joy of coins sliding between our fingers from the condemnation of our prize. I have counseled with two of your chosen officers who have agreed with me..." Her mouth was drying at the very moment she realized she had every man jack of them with her and ready to do battle and injury to the enemy. "Are you ready and willing to accept me as your captain and sail into probable battle without Captain Alport?"

John Pope, one of the most popular of all the crew stepped forward. "Mistress, we know you as a lass who kep' us in drink while this vessel was still on its stocks. Ye be a hellion with great guns, that we know an' our lives to bear wit. And nerves of flint, so I am told, during a cold night more than once in vigil against un shaving mills. And as for drawing a double angle on the bow and staying off a lee shore, you shine wi' the best of men. I, for one, will sail with our young captain to the lintels of Hades and back." The cheering was cacophonous. "Say it, lads, let me hear you." Shouts of agreement rattled the rigging.

"Mr. Lane...as you were..I think me I'll take my glass and go to the fore cross tree. Please keep the deck. We can all boast of our new sailing master. We were full and by yesterday on the way from harbor. I saw you see to the stretching of sail from luff to leach until all was trim. The vessel has a fine tune to it this day. Well done. Have a care." With that she ascended the shrouds to a dizzying height, but she didn't know what else to do. These men were competent. They didn't need her in their way.

The night of wind had fetched them to the west she had no doubt, but no rain. Sky and sea were of so near a shade they were difficult to distinguish and would need a higher sun to delineate. She hoped for clearing sufficient to allow a good noon altitude.

Some day, and they would not dream it in their wildest dreams, women would take their place in their world and nothing would be beyond their doing and done well. As dreams went, she found this rather enjoyable, and since she knew she was dreaming, she knew she would wake out, and there would be Jim beside her. But she didn't, and just the faintest notion ascended in her consciousness she wouldn't.

Mr. Dighton had posted a man in the chains with a lead line, and she heard him call out fair water. She saw no sail all points. There. She knew she had read that somewhere in a log. Why wasn't she waking?

Did she really have an Uncle Nathaniel? Certainly not in the twentieth century. Then, he would be an ancestor. This was ludicrous, because she was dreaming all this anyway. That meant she was making it up in her sleep. No, she wasn't, she corrected herself. She wasn't thinking ahead to events. They were flowing through her conscious awareness, and she didn't know what was coming.

Three days they searched in the Gulf of Maine and had spotted whales but no English. She was still perplexed at sailing without her mother and father. She had taken stoic action in the face of severely adverse circumstances, and her crew supported her; still, she was not at her ease. She worked over charts, such as they were, she lamented, made entries in the log and checked the barometer, all things a good commander would do. But she knew she was not necessary to the running of the schooner. It was well manned. Perhaps they indulged her. She didn't need to be humored. Men!

Never-the-less, she kept to her duties and consulted with the mates. They were good with the men and well respected, no bully tactics here. This was a new nation, she mused, not the tyrannical arena with rule by fear that was England. She knew she warmed to the notion of new nations throwing off the yoke of oppression. She wanted to see more…that is if she lived.. That note met with derision in her mind.. After all, this was a dream. Sarah didn't know it, but Marna did. Marna. What was Marna all about? For one thing she knew she was a creature of lights and warmth and devices that would blow these peoples' minds. Now, Marna was on a wooden vessel with little creature comfort for men, not to say women. How will Sarah behave? What does she want? She didn't hear Mr. Coleman knock the first time. She did the second.

"Begging pardon, Mistress, a sail to the northeast. We think hostile. We would have your orders."

"Thank you, Mr. Coleman. We repair to the deck with haste." She was being deferred to. This was a man's vessel in a man's world, and they wanted her to direct them. She took in a sweeping glance at the deck as she emerged…not a line out of place, no luff in a sail, all drawing full. No gear obstructed the boom travelers. This crew was ready for action. *Archer* settled into sea swells and surged forward with a minimum of disturbance to the waters.

She knew she was shaking when she took the glass and made it a short way up the port shrouds of the main mast. It was

English, still hull down. She saw it to be a brig and guessed it was fast. So, *Archer* was fast. She was designed to be fast and built rugged. God, yes, she viewed her vessel in the female gender. Why not? The English had seen *Archer* and would know it by its raked masts. No other like it existed on the Atlantic.

She knew the host took a course to intercept. Wind was southwest; the Englishman was beating to the windward. *Archer* possessed the advantage. The foe would mount, what, nine pounders at best, but eighteen or twenty of them. Bad for Archer. She would have short carronades on the bow. Good for *Archer*. The foe was beating into the breeze. That meant a lot of work for her crew. *Archer* could change course with a minimum of fuss. She could hold her position relative to the enemy, or sail off and on in a series of reaches and at a brisk pace. That would mean a lot of work for the English if they intended to do battle and *Archer* remained upwind. What did her father call it, weather gauge? No matter. What mattered was to keep every advantage she could and literally wear the Brits out.

She shinned down and took her officers into counsel, probably the first time in history a vessel was conned by committee. This wasn't funny, she scolded herself. Come on, time to wake up. She voiced her ideas for the first phase of engagement.

"Would you, then, move in and away for quick shots at the English rigging?" asked Mr. Coleman.

"As long as we maintain the wind advantage, we should do him as much harm as possible. I submit my estimate that our ordnance has the range."

"Aye, that should be the case. First the bow guns, Mr. Ruck, then Big Molly at the stern. What say you?" asked Mr. Dighton. I would place the initiative to fire in the hands of our gunners, Capt'n, and sail the schooner to provide every advantage." Mr. MacNab urged the point taken, and she wanted to say they were all big boys but didn't. She gave the nod of approval.

For the ensuing hour she stood the deck beside the wheel and heard John Pope urge his men with the sheets as they changed board after board, now leaning in toward the foe, now playing over the waves away. They kept the English hull up, and she saw the yards turn and men scramble, could almost feel the vexation of the captain who wanted mightily to grapple alongside and smash *Archer*.

The Brit was clairvoyant or had seen *Archer* close aboard. He appeared not to want its stern in his direction...rather only the broadside guns. Could he know of Big Molly? She took him on wider and ever wider excursions to either side of the wind. The English crew had to be tired.

"Ready with Molly, Mr. Coleman. I will drop back just out of range." How did she know what the range of a nine pounder was, or that the gun weighed a ton and a half, and one gun breaking loose could cause the brig to list so that it might lose control and broach?

The Brit made his first mistake. He did not clew up his fore course to slow his progress and prepare for gunnery. Sarah watched her advantage increase., then gave the order for a change in course which placed the stern right on the Englishman. She knew Big Molly's crew had now trained on the target. The eighteen was below her feet in what was now her cabin.

"Mr. Coleman is to fire on opportunity," she called to the boatswain. Words were no sooner spoken than her deck shook, and the target was obscured by powder smoke. "Can you see him hit?"

"Aye", called the lookout, "The ball has taken the railing port side by the fo'c'sl and a great cloud of splinters there was."

"We have his attention. Helm, bring the bow to bear smartly. Mr. Ruck, do not await my order. Fire on opportunity. I would have splinters, a mast, or some rigging."

Archer was spry in answer to her helm. Sails were close hauled, and she wore to bear and belched smoke and flame on the wind. One ball drove up a creamy geyser close aboard, and the English crew would no longer need to clew up the fore course, fore course yard having crashed to the deck.

"Bear off and we stay out of range of his chasers. If he present his broadside, we lay a ball into his magazine."

The Englishman lumbered onward when, suddenly, he went wide of the wind onto a larboard tack. His port broadside erupted in a series of detonations leaving a wall of gray white smoke sweeping back over the brig. *Archer* had been swift in taking the wind over its port side, and the rounds fell short and behind.

"He'll be slower until he can replace his parrel and set another yard, Mr. Dighton. Mr. Lane, kindly see that Mr. Coleman continues to fire at his discretion at every opportunity. I want that vessel pounded. Same message to Mr. Ruck. I depend on you to give either that opportunity. Smart sailing so far. Keep it up and good luck." She knew she did not sound like any commander these men had ever known, but they trusted her, of that she was sure.

Coolly, in the throes of battle she stood her quarterdeck and watched the scene forward when not seeing the foe through her glass. Mr. Ruck, thick black mane, himself built like a tree gave the impression he could serve a twelve pounder by himself; but he had a crew of four at each gun. Mr. Lane stayed by the helm and conned the tactical maneuvers of the schooner.

The day continued with high clouds between the sun and land for much of the time with the result that the southwest wind became unsteady. The strange and oddly matched duel continued. Cook brought the men food and drink while *Archer* fired a round, then bolted. The English return fire fell short. Through the afternoon *Archer's* guns holed a lot of canvas and hit the hull above the water-line several times, but did not do serious hurt to the brig's rigging.

With the sun lowering on the horizon, *Archer* had fired its bow twelves from just beyond range of the nines aboard the brig and had turned back to weather when the wind dropped to a zephyr. The color of the water near the English showed dark where it still enjoyed wind, and the foe pressed the advantage by sailing up toward the stranded schooner. The brig's captain spoke a broadside of metal toward *Archer*, most falling short; but

Sarah felt her deck shudder, and suddenly the wheel spun wildly. Mr. Dighton and McNaughton overhauled the wheel but had no control of the rudder. The first officer ordered a long boat over the side to take the bow in tow and swing the stern to bear and lost not a moment in seeing it carried out. Almost as soon, the English bore off, apparently not the slightest bit interested in inviting the pounding they could anticipate from Big Molly.

The result of the loss of rudder control was the same as a weather helm. The schooner came up into what remained of the breeze, and Mr. Dighton ordered the main and fore sails lowered. It was still the season of short twilight, and for some reason the brig did not close for a fight to the death. Sarah conferred with her officers, and the opinion was made that splinters had accounted for too many casualties for the British captain to risk boarding. Also, enough air remained for the schooner to be turned to bear with its tops'ls. The eighteen pounder was a constant threat to the Brit, and with dark, he would also hesitate to close with his nines, not knowing when the big gun bore on him.

Thus were the opinions of all, but they were in a fix, no one doubted. "Can we repair the damage to our steering?" she asked. At that moment Mr. Pope joined them with the report that a lucky shot had smashed the rudder post which protruded externally above water-line on the stern, its top just below the row of windows at the captain's quarters.

"Mr. Pope, can the rudder post be repaired?" Pope removed a clay pipe from his teeth, one which had not produced smoke in days. He was short and wiry of build.

"We parse a right smart spar end up alongside the damage, wind the cable to 'er, we can sister it simply fine. I find four stout lads ain't afeared the water and has cat's eyes, they do 'er smartly."

"We dare not show a light to give the English an aiming point plus a gauge on the bearing of our guns," responded Sarah. She feared an attempt at boarding from small boats after dark and the resulting loss of life, even if one managed to come alongside, having missed annihilation from the six pounders. It was clear the British were doing nothing while daylight lasted, for presently they had no wind.

Work on the timber to be sistered to the splintered rudderpost was begun at once and continued after dark under shrouded lanterns. Finally, John Pope called out, "Who will see himself fit to swim wi' the mermaids and brast the timber to the rudderpost? You'll work by starlight at the most, and we run a line from each man to the deck we don't lose a lusty lad."

Though most on board had never thought of swimming under any circumstance, there were more than enough volunteers. "Then, William Wiggin, is it and Lion Ashe. Do I see Dowdy Flint there and Joseph Lark? Cook will lace you with extra rum before the bath, and we have fellows stand by one of you gets the shivers in the water." Pope walked briskly to Mr. Dighton. "The lads be ready and need most of the night, but we'll do 'er."

It did require most of the night. Marna, now Sarah Alport, captain of *Archer*, pinched herself and appealed to the universe to know why she did not waken. As Marna, she was ready to go home where she ought to be right now beside her love. Enough of dreams. If this one continued, someone was going to get hurt. A very frustrated British captain must be pondering what he will do when appear the first breath of air and light by which to maneuver.

Well, what was she going to do to frustrate him further? From whence would come the morning wind? Most probably from northwest or north as a land breeze because of the cooling of the ground through the night, As the sun warmed, wind would back to the southwest and south-southwest as a sea breeze. Air would rise over the land. She would still have the wind advantage, could sail three points closer to the wind than could the brig. What she didn't know was how long the repaired post would last under the strain of combat. They could ghost out of here now and go home, but she wouldn't suggest it.

Echo Horizon

She walked her deck in the knowledge she could count on her lookouts. Stars still granted enough illumination that she didn't trip, but she was seeing the bow of her vessel in the first light of dawn. She saw something else which tightened the muscles around her stomach. A long boat and two gigs were towing the brig into what would soon be long ball range for her nines. If he had way sufficient to swing his vessel to present a broadside, *Archer* was in for a wild daybreak. The eastern horizon began to glow with the faintest rose hue.

It was now or never, and she sent one of the watch below to wake the officers. Her face felt a rising zephyr. She must see to swinging the bow to lessen the target outline and bring their two twelves to bear. She was not concerned presently with the thought of the Brits crossing her bow in a "T" shot.

"Aye, Mistress. Yo, back the heads'ls and the topgallants, lads. Let 'er off the breeze easy." John Pope was indefatigable, up all night, now here to meet the challenge. Mr. Ruck was starting the gun crews at the twelves. "Take the long boat, lads." A shot blasted out, its powder ring illuminating the water in an instant of yellow light. Another blast. "Reload and run out. We have their attention." Both guns erupted as one, and three men died in the bow of the long boat, oars splintered and flung about. "They'll tow no farther, and they will not board. Take the near gig. Ahh, good lads, they've cast off and are lining it back to the brig.

Elation was short, for a rolling broadside crashed down the starboard side of the brig, bright flashes allowing quick glimpses of the vessel. The main topgallant was holed, forestays'l parted and a ball banged off the side of the schooner. Several geysers spouted up dreadfully near.

In one frightening moment she knew the Englishman had more wind than did she, nearly becalmed. She watched with a feeling of helplessness as the brig wore, its bow turning away from *Archer*, apparently to avoid a sluggish passage through irons with the chance of being dismasted all at once by the twelve pounders aimed at it. Ruck fired the bow guns at the stern of the brig, and a shower of splinters flew up from the ornate poop. The main topgallant yard swayed down, broken in half, but still he wore and didn't pause when the port battery bore. He had the range. Deliberately, smoke billows enveloped the brig stern to bow, and *Archer* shuddered, two men down, pierced with splinters. One man was taken over the side by a ball through the mid-section. Two more taken down…She felt the horror and revulsion of death. Number one gun on the port side was shattered off its carriage, and *Archer* was hulled in several spots above the water-line.

Her bow guns erupted again, and one of the English nines would not fire again. A ball went through the English fo'c'sl. The two gigs had not reached the mother vessel, and the long boat foundered. *Archer* was wounded and could not take much more punishment, not nearly as much as could the brig, she knew. To strike her colors was unthinkable, but more of her people would die.

Unnoticed so far, a staccato roar was building in the distance. Indeed, the very sound pattern had not yet ever been heard on Earth. It grew in intensity with a definite whine under the roar, finally starting questioning glances from the mates. The eastern sky was red with the promise of the sun parting the horizon. The sound came from west, and whatever created it was not far off and approaching fast. On top of that the accompanying detonations struck dumb the crew of *Archer* as they stared across the water and saw a juried foreroyal, stays'l, royal mast, topgallant yard parrel and yard crash to the deck of the brig. Clews, sheets, braces, lifts and downhauls, shrouds and buntlines fell in a mounting tangle. Men died in the boats, some hurled into the water by an angry force beyond ken. Splinters flew from the rails, and more men fell.

Mere seconds after the men of *Archer* first heard the noise, a form passed swiftly, barely above the mast trucks and disappeared in the sunrise. Men would recall the resemblance of the apparition to a giant bird. The final sounds to be remembered

Echo Horizon

were a growl and whine dropping in pitch as the thing passed beyond the schooner.

Cook tended the wounded, making them as comfortable as he could below, and missed all but the roar. He came on deck in time to hear Mr. Coleman say to his captain, "Not of Earth for certain. Is it a messenger from Heaven or from Hell?"

"Hand of God, Mr. Coleman, hand of God," was all she could think to reply. A shout issued from forward; someone saw the British colors struck in the confusion.

Mr. Dighton was immediately at her side. "In God's name what shade has sent a letter of death and destruction? Minutes might we have had left to us only to strike. Will I have a boat away to take her?"

Her face was deathly pale as she responded, and a boat was lowered, manned with an armed complement and quickly away. Too taken up in the excitement of victory upon near defeat, Marna was absorbed by the responsibilities borne by Sarah and was the more in character. She commanded a damaged vessel with wounded men on board and a crew which had viewed a spectacle that only she understood. Eighteenth century Sarah knew it couldn't happen, but so did twentieth century Marna.

Now, she needed to take her vessel and prize to shore if it would float, as well as injured men to port. She calculated her best chance at Haven was the port of Townsend, though the Halifax squadron was always a factor. She gave Robert Lane command of the prize and the pine tree flag of her county to fly from the brig's spanker gaff.

She would have no need to raise the subject of repairs, much less speak the order. Mr. Ruck, John Pope and Mr. Coleman went about quietly conferring with the men. The smashed cannon went promptly over the side, damaged rigging was cut loose and men were lowered over the side to patch hull damage.

She watched the boarding crew through her glass and saw no sign of treachery from the enemy. Work proceeded for the next hour when she noticed a succession of canvas shrouded bundles being slid over the side of the English vessel. Her dead would await a proper service when all was again tranquil.

How many could be alive on the brig? Surely, someone had lowered the colors. Presently she was aware of repairs proceeding across the water, and the hull of the English brig had not settled noticeably. Damn tough, those English craft. Her vessel was built for speed, and it was never intended by her father that it would stand in wait for a message of metal from a broadside. Eight angry guns at a time did have at her, though.

What should she do, now? The men had earned a ration of rum. Better to wait, she decided until one of her officers suggested it. Sun was well into its transit toward noon when she realized how hungry she was, but she wouldn't disturb Cook from his attention to the wounded men in his care. She gave a heave in an effort to relieve the muscles which had been knotted in her for hours. That's what she could do, feed her men. She would make one hell of a martingale stew and finish the fixings off with pie. What she needed was to wind the charcoal to her soapstone fireplace and oven. The galley was well victualled.

Wanting something to wear on her head she repaired to her quarters. Her mother, having been aboard for a spell might have left a mobcap behind. She looked in pigeon holes, cubbyholes and drawers when her attention was drawn to a fair-size box she took for a vanity case. She opened it and drew in a sharp breath. Inside reposed a gold bracelet with zodiac charms attached all about. One was missing she figured to be Sagittarius, but the significance of the find escaped her. She found no cap but returned to the galley and produced a feast of which she was justly proud. She received a smile from Cook when she made inquiry of his needs in sickbay. He admitted to being tormented by the aromas.

She called Mr. Dighton to sample the fare, but before he could summon the crew, a cry from the lookout. "Boat heaving away from the Brit this way." Four men rowed *Archer's* boat back against a freshening breeze. The schooner steadied under stays'ls, but she was certain both vessels had drifted considerably since sunrise.

All three of the brig's boats had been made sieves and were down to the gunwales amid drifting death, grim evidence of the cosmic intervention at sunrise. The boat's company shipped oars with Bunker Woods, a husky lad, first aboard.

"Mr. Lane bid me give this to Captain Alport."

Sarah heard her name and went on deck to take from the lad a heavy leather pouch with the royal crest engraved on its face. She excused herself from her crew and went below, thrusting her head around and inviting anyone who was hungry and not on watch to eat. "Don't let it get cold."

In her cabin, she opened the pouch to a sheaf of papers all headed with a crest. She read and looked up, turned pages and read on. Strangely, she knew what she was holding, for as much as Sarah experienced the reality of the eighteenth century, Marna's recall remained intact, a memory with its genesis in the twentieth century. Somewhere a connection in Marna's recall heard a young woman with blonde hair discussing something....frighteningly like that which she viewed now. She held in her hands orders from the Council of War. Inescapably, the hand of Lord North was seen to be involved. Orders mandated the taking aboard of a vast quantity of specie, source not stated. The bearer, supposedly the captain, was to proceed to New York where a great initiative was to fan out among the Tory population and bribe top Continental officials, some named, to quit the rebellion. Some names on the list caused her to reel. Those who could not be turned were to be assassinated. The entire Continental Congress was so specified.

A vast quantity of specie, that meant the brig was holding a treasure as she read. God, such a prize! She grew faint with the realization she desired to sink the enemy. Not smart. On deck she went straight to Seaman Woods.

"Mr. Woods, has Mr. Lane examined the holds?"

"Not completely, Captain. He's been on a bit of a run burying the dead, and they are mostly dead, not an officer left alive. The gunner's mate cut the ensign halyard. Two men, no men of the sea, these, Ma'm were found skulking in the captain's cabin. Mr. Lane ventured questions, but they refused to answer."

"Well, now, we'll see about that. Mr. Dighton, can we move, and have we full steerage?"

"Aye, Mistress."

"Will you make ready to move along side the prize and have a derrick rigged?"

"A what, Mu'm?"

"Oh, rig as heavy a spar as we have and a tackle likewise as strong."

"It is done, Miss. 'Boats' will parse 'er up we make across to the brig. Aye."

Once lashed along side, Captain Alport ordered the two landsmen brought to her cabin. This action was accompanied by marathon blasphemy and demands for gentle treatment for officers of the crown, followed by dire threats for "damned pirates". The more vociferous of the two was tall and hawk nosed, dark britches meeting nether stocks, the body wrapped in a greatcoat. The quieter of the two had plainly spent most of his life in dining halls and ale houses attested to by the bulbous red nose and rotund form adorned by cape and beaver.

"Thank you, Mr. MacNab, show the gentlemen this way to the captain's quarters…"

"We would have your captain wait upon us on deck, Wench! See to it the instant."

That issuance brought fury to the fore that was Marna's, and the ensuing blast caused Mr. MacNab, with generations of Highland gristle in his fiber, to blanch.

"Mr. Pope, have a suitable gibbet prepared at once that our guests can dance the hornpipe above the waves!" The words were shock to the two English fops, but the scurry of men with spars and rope precipitated a slump both in their posture and in their arrogance. "Now, if you two peacocks are ready to divulge to me the reason for your presence in civilian attire on an armed man o' war which has attacked me, we will retire to my cabin."

They were escorted below and offered seats. She asked Mr. MacNab to remain.

"Your names, gentlemen?" The taller of the two, in wig and long accustomed to ignoring lesser beings, confounding contemporaries and confusing superiors, demurred.

"Fortunes of war, Mistress, and we say nothing except we protest your demeaning action and demand to be taken to your captain be he still living aboard this bum boat."

"You arrogant ass! You contemptible kiss up! Your buddy a toad, or can he speak up for himself?"

"Enough of outrage, strumpet, we won't be treated in this manner!" She lost it, and Marna, rather than Sarah reeled back and let him have it across his chops with an open hand. The man rocked off his chair and looked up in surprise from the floor through brightening crimson from his neck piece to his hair roots.

"You incredible fop! I am commander of this warship; and I have just read over your Orders in Council for sabotage, assassination, intrigue, and I goddamn don't know what not! You were found on an armed brig of His Majesty's Navy in mufti. I can have you executed as spies at my pleasure. I may see you hanged this very day, and I can order you flogged in the bargain, and your soft backs will really smart, guys. Have it your way. In the meantime, you don't talk, you don't eat. Neither shall you drink" It bothered her just a little to realize she was enjoying their squirming. She, then, ordered Mr. MacNab to escort the two prisoners to the most uncomfortable part of the schooner he could find and there secure the spies.

She placed Mr. Dighton in command and stepped past the rail onto the brig. Repairs to *Archer* continued to smarten.

"Mr. Lane, you have made quick progress with a hard mess. Can we look carefully at the captain's quarters?"

"This way, Captain." They entered the stateroom. "You received the dispatch pouch we sent across?"

"I have read it and am distressed beyond words. The foe should be carrying a vast treasure. Not here, I venture. Can you spare two men to search the holds?"

"Done. Mr. Dow, tell of two of your men. The others may rest a spell. We go below." At that very moment, one of the surviving English crew, face showing hesitancy as well as fear, approached Mr. Lane and swore on all that was holy he and two others were Americans from a small Machias merchantman pressed into service. The young man identified himself as Emmett Fall. He looked with disbelief at the woman who was addressed as "Captain" but looked her in the eyes when she told him he and his mates could consider themselves mustered to articles on her privateer rather than prisoners. He also knew the English were carrying something special and thought it was located in the shot locker.

When, indeed, a number of boxes were located where Fall had said, Marna, in Sarah's character, ordered that he and his comrades go on board *Archer* for some American food. Several iron boxes displaying the royal crest were visible above a pile of shot, much of which had been fired at her during the conflict. Some boxes were still buried, and it was a labored and time consuming task to remove all that could be found, thirteen in all, to an easier arena of examination, they being monstrously heavy.

"Who can find tools? Let's have a look inside one of these", she urged. Nothing was where her crew would have stowed it, near at hand. Then it was she became aware that Mr. MacNab was the only man of her regular crew on board the brig; but, at last, a hammer and bar were discovered and put to work. Then followed a chorus of whoops and shouts when the contents were revealed.

Gold offers a soft yellowish metallic appearance....pretty and soul satisfying for men who have fought and bled for such reward. The box was a monster of weight, estimated at a quarter ton. She ordered the coins contained therein distributed among the men according to the stipulations in the Articles of Service maintained by *Archer*.

Little notice was given the designs on the coins as they were counted out. Families of men who had died would receive their men's shares. The remainder of the treasure she contemplated having moved to *Archer* for deliberation until her father, mother and Comfort should be joined once more with her. However, the work involved stayed her judgment. Better to remove the mass once when they should reach shore. No one would be denied his rightful share.

She retired to her cabin and gazed once again at the demonic orders which, if implemented, would drastically alter history as Marna was to know it in the twentieth century; the energy to contemplate simply was not present. She was physically and mentally used up. Continuing to think and function more as Sarah, she continued the withdrawal from her nineteen hundreds indoctrination and reasoned within the parameters of the reality which was Sarah's. Of one thing she was aware. She felt good to be addressed as Captain Alport. Although she had participated in victory in a sea battle which had significance in changing the outcome of America's rebellion, the rationale which was Marna's supported the notion no one would notice. More and more she resigned herself to not waking again in the world into which she was born. Conjunction neared completion as Marna became less Marna and more Sarah. For Captain Alport the task of taking two badly damaged vessels homeward without components of the Halifax Squadron pouncing on them posed the most important work of her lifetime.

She wanted once more to try reaching her two captives and hearing some sort of explanation which would play in a civilized world and decided to have one brought to her quarters, the one who had nothing to say earlier.

He had little to say in this second session until she advised him how unlikely a future he could look forward to if he failed to disclose all. The climate thawed when he begged to be told what limb of Beelzebub she had set loose against His Majesty's Brig *Apollyon.* She had not inquired in the aftermath of battle as to the name of the vanquished vessel, as no one had formally surrendered the brig. She knew its armament and paused to write quickly in her log under the date, "Taken this day Apollyon, eighteen..." Turning to her unwilling guest who was wiping his brow, "What was the master's name? Quickly, damn you!"

"Whipleigh...Charles Whipleigh, Lieutenant."

She completed the entry....Whipleigh, Master". She could add detail on the voyage home. "Now, Sirrah, you have made inquiry as to the nature of weaponry employed against your vessel. This is the same, along with others of its kind, which will take down every vessel of your king's navy sent against my country and sweep the seas of English influence. If you do just as I shall instruct you, you may be the emissary to return with this news to your country, as well as news of the failure of your obscene mission. If you will not, by God in Heaven, Sir, you shall hang."

The man squirmed and choked and gave ample evidence he believed her, for in due time she learned the names of these two civilians and those of their superiors. She had details of the Council of War and matters which would be of the utmost value to her state's general court as well as to General Washington. The man, Maynard Hunt, was allowed rations and limited freedom of the schooner.

Captain Alport spoke hastily to her prize master, Robert Lane, and bid him stay in sight and God speed. The three liberated Americans from Machias remained on the brig. She was entrusting an armed brig with a fortune in gold specie to him and realized she had passed on her judgement as quickly as she would pick a market day. What matter? She should be waking any moment from this deranged world.

A day and a night brought them to within sight of land. On the morning she signalled the brig to lay along side, which it did, main and fores'l clewed, spanker gaff down and maneuvering under tops'ls and topgallants, guns run out and manned. None other than Robert Lane stood the quarter deck of the prize; and she heard the command to fire...nothing. Not a gun fired, though she could see the sputtering light of the primer loads. When her heart had settled from her throat she bolted to her cabin and re-emerged with three long rifles, two of which she tossed to Mr. Coleman and Mr. Ruck. The third she shouldered and fired on her late sailing master, Robert Lane. A look of astonishment didn't dissolve from his face as he reeled back and hit the deck hard. Smoke had barely begun to drift over the scene when her officers fired at the two Englishmen who had stood nearest Lane.

With the swiftness of cats, Emmett Fall and his two cohorts, who had apparently spiked the guns deep in their igniter holes, moved down the deck with belaying pins and put the wood to the skulls of selected individuals whom they summarily hurled into the sea. This treachery from a man she had trusted came as a surprise and shock. She had paid no heed to Lane's selection of new men from Newbury for his prize crew, nor was she aware he had released a chosen few of the surviving members of the English crew with promises of Norumbegua if they went along in the piracy.

Since she could spare no more men to a prize crew, she elected to take the brig in tow the remaining miles to Saxtons Harbor, a long and arduous journey with a vessel to drag through the water. The task took another day and night including the time to make the trip to an island far off shore where she marooned the remaining offenders with victuals for two days.

They sailed all night with the brig in tow, and in the earliest light of day turned inside the great crescent of an island into McCobbs Cove where the brig was cut loose to run aground as near the dam as possible, to be floated farther in shore with the coming flood tide. The late fall morning offered cold tidings of the winter yet to come when *Archer* was brought to the little quay and moored securely. Litters had been fashioned for the wounded who were carried ashore to the manse.

A discussion concerning the gold specie was held among all the loyal crew and the three liberated colonials. The decision was made to sequester the remaining boxes of coin since their sheer weight would make transportation impossible without attracting unwanted attention. The shares already distributed would keep some in rum for the remainder of their lives and for others, provide the means to starting a farm or trading enterprise. It was further agreed that no additional distribution would go forward until Captain John Alport and his lady and Comfort MacLean should be reunited with *Archer*. The crew was then released from articles and the close-mouthed officers proceeded to unload the treasure.

Employing the main yardarm, the tons of treasure were removed from the careened brig, now beached close by the dam. Seeing her duties as captain coming to an end, Sarah placed the orders, which without her intervention could have changed history, into their pouch and into an emptied iron container. For safe keeping she also tucked in her mother's bracelet. This, then, was placed with her belongings to go ashore while the gold laden boxes were stowed at the end of the dam in a cave that was then sealed with heavy rocks.

All had retired for the night from the vessels save a watch on *Archer*, and the manse and barns served as refuge for seamen who had not slept ashore in months. The flooding tide bumped the brig against the shore as it buoyed anew the foreign fighting craft. The ebbing tide with the near full moon setting toward dawn, left the hull askew and toppling a lighted lantern which had thoughtlessly been left behind. The resulting fire kindled unfortunately close to the powder magazine; and the resulting explosion sundered the hull and hurled bits and pieces of the vessel back into the cove. The dismembered hull had been lifted clear of the water before decks, floors, guns and all but one half hull section settled near the dam. One side with some floor timbers floated free about midway in the cove before succumbing to water, mass and mud.

The explosion was as thunder and lightening and brought the resting seamen to their feet for an early start on the new day.

23

Jim was on his feet in the early light. He looked back and saw his companion's eyes follow him as he searched out his apparel. He admired the contour of her hip beneath the sheets, a venue he had considering revisiting. Now, his agenda included breakfast and a wider tour of damage done by the windstorm.

"You're leaving again." It was a statement made by a not too enthusiastic sounding voice. "Oh, my God, the wounded…my men must be fed and I lie abed. Where away? Oh, my dearest, you have been returned by the fates. I know not what has overtaken you or my father and mother. I pray no one is displeased with our progress…the battle..the wounded. Where in hell am I!?"

"No, sleepy head, I'm not leaving..not without you. Wait a minute. You've been dreaming again, but you are here, and you look good. Why don't I get some breakfast started? I'll bring you some juice. You can tell me about it only if you feel like it…like where this time?"

"I'm OK with it. I can talk about it. Oh-hh God, this one was the winner!" She chose to join him in the kitchen, was none the worse for the ordeal she knew she had been through. Much of the dream was piecing together in the fore of her recall., and she focused on one thought. "Jim, we've got to look closely at the site of the dam."

The hike after the meal was more an expedition and required shoving through branches of overturned trees. "It was hard to fathom before this devastation that all the shore was open field once upon a time," she stated standing by the old foundation. "I was sitting on that rock when I felt the Earth turn beneath me."

"You were fighting your way through all this brush which was bad enough when it was standing."

"That feeling of reunion, Jim. Father's schooner had come home, and we women made it possible with the help of the cannon...then the contrasting sense of loss and grief. That I'll never forget. Then, when I found you, or you found me, I was all right again. Weird."

"Where were you this time?"

I don't know how I'll ever relate all that's happened. Simply, I was commander of the privateer, did battle with an English brig...ohh-hh, Jim, you can't ever imagine the grim detail. It was frightening. I think something quite significant happened. I'll have to tell Nancy right away after I tell you. I'm getting it together. Let's go where that huge tree has been uprooted, something I want to look for. There isn't a chance in a million, but..."

"Take a look, Marna, down in the depression. Someone has moved some stones....signs of digging, fresh, too. What do you think anyone expects to find down there?"

"I don't know. Think we should get the tools and dig, ourselves?"

"Not if I can help it."

"Let's continue, that is if you think you can," she taunted.

"If you were any smarter, you'd have to tell someone."

Farther on toward the cove's head, some stands of spruce escaped the wind's fury; others were jackstraws. They arrived at what had been the reservoir of the mill, an expanse of alders growing in the silt and untouched by the wind. In their midst were the upper branches of an enormous ash tree, and they followed the trunk to a root ball torn from the side of a slope and fully twenty feet in diameter.

"What a hellish force!"

"I don't think I paid any attention to that tree, how it looked when it was standing. It was so huge it was all above my world. Strange, though, I have the feeling I was very much acquainted with it in my dim past," she mused.

"Do you think you could have...?"

"Yes, that's it. I was here. The tree was here that night...of course, I dreamed all that. He was hidden, waiting by the tree when he made the sound of a night bird calling as a warning."

"Who?"

"Caleb."

"Oh."

"You remember; I told you all about that night on the dam. Oh, hell, I'm running on as if it was all real. I don't think I know real from dream any more. Anyway, that was the dream that had Roni so worried. Sure wish he were here to hear this latest one.

Jim started up the rise out of which the tree had grown. "Can't believe the size of that root ball, and look at the square cut stones caught up in it. There's your dam. One of those comes down on us, it's going to spoil the morning. By the way, what's got you spooked about this tree, anyway?"

"I think there's a cave here, and I think I know what's in it; and if it is, then I'm still dreaming and will be forever."

"I think I'm kinda real. I'm no dream. This is real, Marna." Jim turned aside and worked his way in under the roots of the tree which had been wrenched from a clay hillside, taking with them cut granite and limestone blocks cribbed into an anchor for a dam many years ago. Those remaining were twisted about and tipped, no longer where they had been placed by old time masons.

"Looks like it was dynamited out of the ground, doesn't it?"

"I can't believe the force of the wind…yet the house stands. Oh, look there, isn't that an empty place beyond that sort of upright stone?" She pointed to a place under a three foot overhang of large stones.

"Sure is. I'll bet we could crawl in there. I'll have a look."

"Jim, be careful. I don't want those rocks coming down on you."

"Seems secure enough. Hey, I can get in here. You got a light? Ouch! Jesus!"

"Shame on you."

"I did a number on a shin. This place is deep, goes way back in under the hill. Wish we had a light. I don't know what banged my shin."

"Here..here's a penlight."

"Yo, good. Oh, my Lordy, it's an iron box. There's more…"

"*WHAT!!?*

"Marna, want to go back to the house and get a bigger light and a hammer and wrecking bar? No, wait, I'll go with you. I need another cup of coffee before we see what's inside."

"Like hell!. Get a rock. I know what's inside. I helped move them here. I…" She sagged against him, dropping the flashlight. Oh Christ, Jim, when are the dreams going to stop.?"

"You say you know what's inside the boxes? Want to tell me? Maybe you weren't dreaming. Let's get some tools and light so we don't spoil anything." Two cups of coffee later and two flashlights, a propane lantern and fifty pounds of tools, they returned.

The boxes carried a great deal of rust but were remarkably preserved, testament to the iron workers from bygone years who had a knack with turning iron into durable material where the elements were involved.

"We've gotta get some timbers in here before we start moving much of anything. Hey, this one's lighter. I'll see if I can knock the cover free. Look at that rampant lion on the box." The lid yielded, and both peered in. Looks like a pouch with some parchment.."

"Later..don't risk crumbling it. I'll tell you what it is."

"You'll what?"

"Listen, after the battle…oh, I gotta tell you the whole of my dream adventure after we get done here. Well, I was captain of Dad's privateer. We were in a sea fight which we won. All this stuff was on the English ship. The papers will fall apart, but they're orders for nasty stuff to break the back of the rebellion. All these boxes are filled with gold coins, tons of them…Jim, speak to me. I know I sound crazy. I think I am, but I was there. I fought the ship. What a hell of a story! I've got to tell Nancy. Oh sure. 'Hi, Nan, just wanted to tell you I brought in an English man o' war with a bunch of gold. I think our theory was right on. Right!'"

She tried to move a box using every last bit of effort she could muster. "I can't budge it. Can you get this lid off without breaking it?"

"We'll have a go at it, but first we have to put some support under these rocks. Won't take long to cut some posts and wedge 'em in here." When this was done and the gas lantern was lit, he helped her inside the cave with him. If you'll trust me, I'd like you to hold the bar while I try to enlarge the crack I've found below the lid. This thing is well made…lid slides over the rim of the box; but it's going to need some persuasion. We've got to strike around the whole thing and work this poor rusted lid free. Good. Hold it still." He checked a swing with a two pound hammer. "Hold it still. I won't hit you."

"I know, but…"

"There." The sound of iron on iron rang. She winced. "Now, that wasn't so bad. Move an inch." Another strike. "We've got to go all the way around. It'll take some time."

"It hasn't moved a bit. Couldn't we use a cutting torch?"

"Sure, if you don't care what's inside." Marna moved the bar an inch at a time while Jim swung the hammer. They worked, momentarily hearing the hiss of the gas lantern. Jim paused, took the flashlight and examined the face of the box to determine any progress. There was. The cover had moved. Not only that, small slots were uncovered at opposite ends of the box under the lid. He inserted the bar and pried each end in turn until Marna let out a shriek. The cover moved and was tipped, yielding finally to one last prod.

Both stopped breathing. The light from the lantern revealed and the flashlight highlighted the iron container filled with gold coins. They hugged each other, she squealing in excitement. They were completely without composure and nearly insensible with shock; and it was minutes before they could collect themselves to move in a concerted manner to survey what they had discovered. If the other containers, now determined to be ten more, were similarly filled, the value of their find was beyond their comprehension.

Their emotional responses encompassed a full spectrum of reactions from stupefied wonder to avarice, the two not necessarily sharing the same reaction at the same moment. Marna got control of her voice and spoke in quiet tones. "I'll never understand what's happening to me, Jim; all of this was in my dream. You might say I helped place these boxes here. The prize blew up and sunk in the cove. I saw men killed in battle. I killed some myself. I was in command of a vessel in battle. Jim, it was so real. We prevented a savage plot by the British from coming to pass. I…"

"Sweetie, easy on yourself. You knew this was here. I can handle that. I want to hear the whole thing from the start, but holy sweet love, Honey, what lies in front of us men and women have died for. It has invoked every kind of lie and cheating. Nations have gone to war, populations enslaved and murdered." He grasped his head between both forearms. "Where am I going with this? What in hell are we going to do?"

"Can we get this much to the house?"

"Sure, in several trips. I wouldn't trust the box. We could find some baskets and boxes, I guess. The skiff would hold it. The others we haven't wracked around…we can make a derrick with one of the oaks. Water comes near at high tide. We could lower them down to the boat. Yeah, we better get moving."

"Sweetie, they're beautiful. Look, here's one like I have. There's the "A".

"Looks like crowns and nobles. Here's a pound piece, a rose noble." He frowned mockingly. "What's this gold Louis doing here? Good God, Marna, this could be the fabled treasure of King John that was lost in the mud flats."

The many trips ended with their having confiscated every type of container in the house and sliding them with their precious contents under beds. Jim estimated they had nearly a quarter ton of dead weight in the house with the contents of the first box. Their labors exhausted the shortened day far too quickly for Marna even though every muscle ached and perspiration beaded her forehead.

"Are we nuts? How can we leave the rest of it out there all night without standing guard?"

"I don't think we attracted much attention. Besides anyone that might be about is pretty busy with the storm damage. They're not looking at us."

"Just the same I...well, how are people supposed to act when they're in a situation like this? I mean..."

"We haven't changed. We're not supposed to act. We've had a little luck..."

"Like the riches of the world dropped on us. We haven't changed. Look at you and me. We're nuts. We're trying to figure how to move however many tons of gold into this house without attracting attention when anyone knows it'll go through the floor. The two of us..?"

"You want someone else in on it?"

"No!"

"All right, let's quietly think this over and get to work."

They made supper together, and in the growing chill he made a fire while putting some ideas together out loud. "First, we build a little garage handy to the turn-around and back from that huge spruce. I don't know why that didn't go over with the others. While we're cleaning up the broken trees, we have this little stone garage built, part of your restoration project. You are absolutely right. The house will not hold the load. We'll put the boxes back in the garage and build a work bench over them."

She looked straight at him as if she expected him to pull links of sausages from his sleeve. "..And the IRS takes my house..."

"While the garage is being built...that's your project...I'll erect a derrick, bring in a chain falls and construct an oak pallet. Once I have the boxes on the pallet, the next.... "

"Jim, this is freakin' crazy. We've got to get this stuff out of the house tomorrow and back in the cave where it's been safe all these years, apparently. Then, we can think this over calmly." He knew exhaustion was taking its toll of both of them, but what she uttered made a degree of sense. They were being overwhelmed by the magnitude of the discovery. But Marna's state of mind was a concern to Jim, as the find was a virtual epilog to a wild dream.

She picked some of the more attractive coins from the collection and placed them on her bedside table. Then both succumbed to a night's sleep, snug, while outside, a wind grew and punctuated the dark.

24

Jim woke fretfully from nothing less than a nightmare. In his nocturnal misadventure he had been ambushed while journeying to his home in Virginia. A musket ball had grazed his head, robbing him of memory. His dream intellect, however, kept him aware of the identity of his companion who, after gunning down two of the three marauders, went in pursuit of the third, but not before placing Jim in the care of a householder who promised good care for the wounded man. He knew he possessed a different name, and the period of the dream was strange to him

On sitting up, he was concerned only with waking and collecting his thoughts, disturbed at the slow pace at which his life seeped back into its wakeful mode. Young daylight outlined the form of his companion beneath the covers. Of course, he knew her intimately but was confused at the state of their relationship.

His motions and the resulting movement of the bed caused her to sit bolt upright and cry out, "Got to return to the schooner..the wounded..the prize." She'd been through this before, and with the web of the night world clearing from his mind, he knelt to her and touched her hair.

"Easy, Pumpkin, easy. Where've you been, Marna?" She knew the name and knew she was called by it somewhere...sometimes, but it was strange to her. Jim suspected she had been far off in another dream and spoke softly and slowly. The wounded were mending splendidly. They were fed. What of her plight? Slowly he helped her back to the world he thought he inhabited, but wasn't completely sure anymore.

"Jim, " she sighed. "You know me, but you're not Jim, but Comfort, and you're safe."

Jim saw his life going round a curve. Obviously, hers had already entered the curve and was, even now, headed in a new direction. The shock of revelation of their vast treasure had been too much after a dream cognition of involvement with it. He wanted her back with him. He was Jim Starr, and he wanted Marna right now, not Sarah. He was not Comfort MacLean, didn't give a damn about Comfort MacLean. He'd had it with dreamlife.

She asked him about the treasure, and he had no reason to believe any alternate reference was emerging other than to the gold they had just found. He replied it was still safe in the dam. This satisfied her. One of the last recollections Sarah's shade bore as it faded from Marna was taking the heinous orders from the English brig, placing them in the pouch, and putting it into the emptied gold specie container along with her mother's gold bracelet minus the one charm.

"Am I still dreaming?" She reached for Jim's face.

He was still kneeling and facing her. "You've been on one hell of a journey, I'll wager." She had come out of the dream easier the previous morning. He realized the impact of its influence on her. This might take days settling down. If only Roni were around. She was coming back to him. He was hopeful.

"God, Honey, you look good to me. We've been through so much together. Be patient with me. I don't think I can tell you in ten years all that has happened to me," said Marna.

"Can you remember we uncovered one hell of a treasure yesterday? Look on your bedside table. No, right there."

"It's so different here." Where was she, he wondered?

"Your bed table, look at those coins. You picked those out yourself. Aren't they beautiful? Better tuck those in your hiding place tomorrow."

"We're not poor anymore."

"I don't think we ever were poor, but we're certainly well off, now…or, rather, you are," he corrected.

"We share alike. Besides, I think I should tell you the whole story behind this treasure."

"My ears are yours."

"Who's getting breakfast?"

Echo Horizon

"I will," he replied. "You can tell me all about it while I put my clothes on and start breakfast."

"You'll never believe the tale I have for you. What a battle. Look at me real close. I can feel the sunburn. I had command of the *Archer* in a sea fight. We beat 'em, by God, and what a treasure we found on the prize! Oh, good Lord...they're moving the gold off the boat today. I've..."

"Calm down. I don't see anyone, no ships. You know it's already there in the dam and safe. Wow, you do have a burn. I'll be a minute...gotta put something on that. How is it I'm not sunburned? We worked all day together. I've figured out how it can be moved the easiest to the house."

"...All day together...no, don't move it!"

"Don't move it? Couple echoes in here, I think

"No, we mustn't, the others should have a chance at the division."

"Others. Then you were serious about taking the gold we moved yesterday back to the cave."

"It'll work out, Jim, you'll see. Oh, gee, I don't think anything will ever be the same again."

"You may just be right, but now, my girl needs feeding and..."

"Jim?"

"...And tender loving care...what?"

"Hold me, please?...like you've never held me before. I need to know you...to be close to you. Good God, Sweet, I wonder if you'll ever know how much..." Her voice trailed off into sobs. Breakfast would wait, and it did, a long time, a very long time.

"You want your eggs scrambled? How about with tomato. Flapjacks?"

"Jim, can you make a martingale stew?"

"A what?"

"And fig pie?"

His face appeared around the corner. "You doing a crossword, or what?"

"Get real. Can you?"
"Probably not."
"I hope I can remember how I did it."
"When?"
"A long time ago, I think. More like, where?"
"Do I dare ask? Whoops, butter's burning. Coffee's done. Did I ever tell you you're unique?"
"You mean strange, don't you?"
His face again at the corner, "Honey, would I ever say anything like that?"
"Are you squeezing oranges?"
"No, but I will."
"We don't anyone aboard to come down with scurvy."
"No, we don't."
"I'll be out in a minute," she offered.
"Forgive me, do I know you?"
"What a thing to ask," she riposted.
No, seriously, I get the feeling you've been on a long trip."

It was serious, she told herself. How would she ever tell him all that had happened, things of historic importance that *couldn't* be known. Truly a gulf of centuries separated them, and she must fight a battle that probably had never before been fought to close that rift. He had stood by her through all up to now. Not many men would have. Now, she must be certain it wasn't just the gold that was the attraction.

"All right, a high five, this smells yummy, Hon. Anyone ever tell you you're a magician in the kitchen, and that's not all; but that can wait 'til after breakfast." She knew that an influence had worked a change in her being. She couldn't help but know. The lifetime of social restraint on Sarah was eased in this twentieth century environment, and she hadn't even ventured outside this day. She was on the move to eat Jim alive, yet she knew she must not allow excessive physical desires to damage the precious bond between their persons. Then, she remembered Sarah was also engaged. What had Roni Dayan said about the window on the past viewing both ways? If she knew what he meant, she'd have to say they had come full circle.

"Jim, this is very good, and I'm starved." She had climbed into a dressing gown and sat opposite to him.

Bert Howe

25

Breakfast usually brought forth a lively riposte between them, but today Jim found difficulty phrasing comments and questions. At times he felt as though he were calling to her on a far off shore. She no sooner asked for the milk pitcher than she drifted off once more in a reverie, nor did her eyes focus on him, more like she was three drinks up on him.

Jim was well aware she had visited some far off realm in her sleep two nights past and more than likely languished in that never-province last night and no Roni Dayan to help in this widening puzzle. She had been animated when he presented her with her engagement ring, but this was more like already being married. He was perplexed.

She went outside for a stroll and stayed close to the house while he cleared away and stacked washed dishes in the drainer. If they were to return the box of gold to the dam they would need most of the day, so he decided to get right at some chores before calling her attention to the now. He called his realtor in Staunton to check on a closing date, then called Sylvanus Beal and Erick Lehn. The search for airplane wreckage was fruitless. He wasn't surprised but was allowing cracks to develop in his secure wall of logic.

More than an hour had slipped by when he heard Marna entering at the back door.

"That you, Sweetie? Wondered where you'd gone." She walked to him and touched his face with one finger, then buried her face in his chest.

"Where shall I start, Jim? I've had the wildest time, and I'm being a bitch about it. I don't know what to say."

"Tell me where you've been."

She looked up into his eyes. "You weren't there."

He didn't quite know whether to take that as an indictment or disappointment.

"You weren't in my dream."

"You did dream."

"Oh, my God, did I dream! You were gone back to Virginia. My father had gone off.."

"Honey, wait a minute. Sit over here with me. I don't know how to behave when you're as distant as you've been this morning. I hope I didn't say anything…"

"No..no, after I came to…after we…I came out here into the kitchen, breakfast was all ready. I had trouble with the here and now, realizing I'd come back to you…where we are. Dammit, I don't even know what day it is! I don't think I know the year for sure. I went for a walk, just around the house. The next I knew I was at the old homestead. I know that old farm. I've been there…Jim, I am there. My spirit…my whatever is there. I scratched some weeds away from the stones in the little burial ground. God, I must fix that up with a white fence."

"We'll fix it up, Sweetheart."

"I couldn't read any letters…all worn…weathered away, but I had a dreadful feeling I was walking on my own grave. It was like talking to my own ghost. Jim, hold me. I'm frightened out of my tree."

"Marna, my love for all life, we're together in this all the way. You're not alone, and I won't have you shaking with fear. Tell me, have I been in your other dreams, or rather this alter ego you say is my double?"

"Every one until now."

"Do you think you can tell me what went on in your dreams this last time? Won't it help to share it?"

"Can you stand another narration?"

"Try me."

"We were tied up at Newburyport in the Merrimac River. Mother's brother was a privateer who had been captured by the English and executed on board ship by its captain. Father was ready to set sail and hunt down the Englishman but was waiting for a fair wind. For three days the wind howled out of the southeast against the current of the river over sandbars. Comfort had since traveled to his home in Virginia to be with his ailing father. My father had gone off to Essex to view a new chronometer which was reported to be an improvement in maintaining accurate time at sea..."

"Don't stop."

"Jim, I know I was dreaming, because if I weren't I wouldn't be here now. In the dream I *knew* I was dreaming, but I couldn't wake up...and, Honey, it was serious. Here we are the finders of a Fort Knox size treasure, directly a result of my dream. But where's the excitement? We're exhausted from moving a small part of it. How do we convert it, spend it, invest...whatever? I'll be goddamned if I'll see one cent of it go to the IRS to be thrown down a million political ratholes, squandered on useless projects as fast as pencil-necked geeks can think them up. I'll see it go over the side in 2000 fathoms first! That's it. It's useless to us. On the other hand, my dream adventure at sea might explain where it came from. Oh, I don't know what to think. I know I've got to tell Nancy our theory about a British plot to end the rebellion may have happened and be provable. No, she'd think I've lost my senses."

"Marna.."

"No, don't you start. You think I'm crazy as a loon at this point."

"Marna, look at me. That's it, right here. Look in my eyes. This is Jim, the man who wants to marry you. There may be substance to these dreams. The deteriorated papers you found in a container at the cave had enough legibility to convince me we're on to something. Now, tell me what took place."

"OK." She stood and began walking around the room. "I can think better while I walk. A rider came from Salem and warned that a man o' war was moving close along the coast to pick up on any blockade runner. Course, that was us, *Archer*. We were blockade runners. My mother set out to bring Father back, and the wind shifted northwest. So, we had to take advantage of improved conditions; and I took command of the schooner. The men gave me their support. A man named Mr. Lane had served aboard my uncle's privateer and offered to fill in as sailing master. Since he could recognize the vessel we were after, he was welcomed aboard."

She went on in minute detail of the voyage: the encounter and ensuing battle with *H.M.S. Apollyon*, the heroism of the crew and officers and the intervention of the apparition in the sky which defoliated the rigging of the Englishman, killing its officers and half the crew before disappearing into the sunrise.

"It could only have been an airplane with machine guns. I mean, what are dreams for if you can't let your fancy roam?"

She told of the treasure and finding the military orders of perfidy, the treachery of the new sailing master, and that she shot him down.

"Jim," she started breathlessly, "I let the crew divide one whole container of loot, then placed the pouch with the orders for killing the Congress, along with my mother's bracelet in the empty container. I thought it was placed on the top of the stack in the cave..oh, you know...dreamed it was. I gotta get back there and look in that box again for the bracelet."

"Bracelet?"

"Remember? I left it last spring in my wet clothes on the schooner of those people who rescued me? Jim, don't look at me like that. That was real. Two nights ago I dreamt I found it, for God's sake."

"I don't believe I'm hearing this. Sweetie, that's too much detail for a dream, I mean your description of the repairs to the rudder, the crew's reaction to getting into the water in the night...never mind the repatriates who spiked the guns on *Apollyon*. Yes, let's start packing our riches back in the cave. I want to see, too."

On the trip in the skiff, he talked Marna into rowing. "I guess my dream was effect and not causal. I'd have put money on the notion the empty money box had the bracelet in it."

"Let's get the rest of our gold hidden, then pack for a trip to Virginia."

"What?"

"The closing on my farm is set for next Thursday. I could show you around. It's a state for lovers, absolutely beautiful, and it'll be a lot warmer. My fingers are about numb. How about it?"

"But what about..." Oh, why not? Deal." She reached her lips to his. "What's that you've done to your head, Jim? You've banged into something."

"Yeah, on one of our beam supports over the entrance to the cave. Does it look like a musket ball skun my gourd?"

"Could be." They chuckled.

"We pull that timber out the whole cave'll collapse."

"Have to chance it..maybe a good thing."

By late in the afternoon they were tired out, each grasping an oar to paddle back to the dock, their task completed. The reality hit them as humorous; they were no richer than they had been the week before. The treasure might as well not have existed, and they had hidden the entrance well. She had shuddered when the final pry against cut stones had caused three to slide down parallel and stand in what they supposed was the plane of the face of the dam.

As for Marna's dream experience, though the details gave credence to a reality, she was gaining control of her convictions sufficient that she could credit her own active imagination with the dream production. But one thing she couldn't explain was how a vessel would embark from Newburyport past Plum Island and numerous sandbars. The changes taking place within her psyche were subtle. Then there was the question that haunted her subconscious from the wings of a stage named *circumstance*. Why was she rewriting history?

They both gave in to a lack of desire or energy to make supper and agreed to dine at the Cuddy. Besides, they would be gone a week or more, and it would be wise to ask someone to check on the house once in a while.

Summer exuberance was long gone, but conversations in the restaurant were animated as they will be in a small community. Feeling still raged over the warped journalism the media exhibited in reference to the assault by terrorists on the campus.

The assassins had been given victim status in the press with cries for diplomatic immunity and demands for criminal charges against the Continental Militia as well as outright banning of such groups. Local sentiment was outraged with such bald faced biased and opinionated editorials masquerading as reporting.

"What do you think you'd like for supper, Sweet?" Jim whispered behind his menu.

"I thought I might have one of Syl's Caesar salads, but I feel more like having a steak."

"Me, too. Here comes Katie."

"Where do you guys manage to hide? We haven't seen you for what seems months."

"Can't be more than days, Kate," replied Jim. "How about a couple of your prime steaks. Marna will tell you what she wants for a wine."

"Marna, let me look at that chunk of ice again. Wow, guys, go for it. Oh, look what the cat dragged in."

"Good, Katie, ask Erick and Nancy if they would like to join us, will you?"

"Sure thing, Marna."

"Well, you two, what's goin' on?"

"Hi, Marna," chirped Nancy. "Hi, Jim."

"Hi, Nan, cold out. Let me have your hands and I'll warm 'em for you. Erick can blow on his own hands for a while."

"What an offer, Jim. Here," said Nancy

"Yeow! Have you guys been having a snowball fight?"

"We almost could," replied Nancy."Just this moment started to snow."

Marna looked at Jim and mouthed, "Just in time."

"What will it be, Erick? Join us for a steak?"

"Yo, I'm ready. Hey, why not a Chateau Briand for the four of us?"

Katie returned quickly from the kitchen. "Chateau Briand. Chef's right on it," she promised.

"Katie's right on the spot with the wine, Erick. Why don't we let the ladies send the bottle back or make Katie smile?"

Echo Horizon

"I'm OK with that. Marna?"

"I bow to Nan. She's our oenologist," riposted Marna.

"Oh, you guys," demurred Nancy. "All right, Katie, do your duty."

Katie tipped a little wine into a glass. Nancy acted out the whole drill, twirled the glass Katie dampened, inhaled, took a sip, swallowed and urged Katie to continue pouring. "I hope there's another bottle of the same year ready to follow this."

"No problem. You know you get a Caesar salad with the Chateau. Sylvanus will want to come out to do the honors."

"Thanks, Katie," responded Jim. "You know, this place really puts on the dog after the tourists are gone. I never saw the equal. Guess we called off operations at just the right time, Erick."

"What do you make of it? We combed this bay, checked with every fisherman we could talk to in order to pin down a zero point. I hope you're not…"

"No way, Erick, we win either way. What we've done is eliminate a possibility….maybe a probability, which is starting to make the game more appealing."

"How's the book coming, Nancy?" Marna was obviously changing the topic of conversation.

"You really want to know, Marn? I'm stumped. I mean, what did the British have in the way of armament or force that they didn't employ against the colonies? And the terrorism, the cruelties imposed on prisoners of war, for God's sake?"

"You still going with historic fiction? Why don't you consider infiltration and the establishment of a fifth column kind of move against the Continentals? Remember what General Francisco Franco boasted at the time of his siege of Madrid? Well, don't look at me like that. We read about him in History 56. He said he had four columns of troops including an armored column surrounding the city and a fifth column of saboteurs inside the gates. Try that on with the Brits, a fast ship loaded with gold and carrying orders to bribe anyone in high office and to assassinate as many as would not be bribed."

"Are you kidding? When would they have tried that?"

"Try 1777 right after the battle of Saratoga. Burgoyne was history, and General Howe was diverting a large force south to Philadelphia, by way of Chesapeake Bay. The time was ripe for mischief before the French sent their forces."

"Marna, that could be it. That sounds great. Thanks. Where'd you come up with such a fantastic idea?"

"That could be something she dreamed up, Nan." Jim looked over his wine glass at Marna. "Didn't you dream that up, Hon?"

"Yeah, right. I think it'll work, Nan. Oh look what's coming."

Sylvanus approached the table walking backward and pulling a table on wheels on which was loaded enough salad and meat for a small brigade. "What a treat to have you four at my tender mercy on a slow night."

"What do you mean, slow? Show me an empty table," exclaimed Erick.

"Who wants the well done and who wants the rare? Speak up. Don't none of you be bashful, now." Syl had prepared the salad in the kitchen, a demonstration which he would normally carry out at tableside.. He loaded up each plate, and when he reached Jim, he asked, "What's this going around about you resigning from the navy?"

"Not resigning, Syl, early retirement."

"You got twenty in, a young feller like you?"

"Will have after about six months of terminal leave. This young thing across from me has taken my unconditional surrender; and I tell you, Syl, I don't cotton to no chasing off to the ends of the Earth and leaving her unattended by the hearth." Cheers rang out.

"Marna need never sit alone and unattended, Jim."

"That's what I know, Old Man, and with more'n one like you around I intend to be at home." More cheers. Marna covered her face with her hands while Nancy patted her on her back

"Serious, now, what do you plan to do? We can probably find something for you to do right around here. Course it don't pay much."

"That sounds all right. It doesn't make a whole lot of sense to earn much these days."

"It sure as hell don't. Syl was interrupted before he could launch into a tirade on government looters and spenders by a call from the kitchen. Orders were piling up.

"What you got there, Marna?" Nancy's curiosity could stand no more. Marna had been toying with a trinket that looked like it was made of gold.

"This? Oh, it's from my mother's bracelet. It's a zodiac piece. This here's Sagittarius. It fell off some time ago. Remember? I told you back in the spring I'd left the bracelet with my wet clothes on that boat. This was hiding all the time in the wooden boat model Dad made."

"Can I see it closer, Marn?"

"Sure, Erick." She handed it across.

"What a little treasure. I'd like to have seen the whole article."

Marna looked up and met Jim's eyes and smiled.

"On the subject of antiquity, Jim, I never did learn. Didn't you tell me a while back about a piece of timber from a ship found in the mud at Marna's place? Weren't you having it analyzed, carbon dated, that sort of thing?"

"Submitted it to mass spectroscopy. It's very simple, really. We have a two centuries old chunk of oak buried in Maine mud for most of that time. The oak was a common variety growing in England when it was cut. We found a multitude of small, round holes punched in the wood, all at the same angle with residues of copper, high carbon steel and in some holes, molecular traces of phosphorous."

"What was the conclusion?"

"The timber and, probably the ship, was riddled with fifty caliber machine gun bullets, armor piercing and tracer." Silence.

"Christ!"

"That was my exact comment, Erick."

"This is paradoxical."

"That's what it is, but that's what we've got."

"Hey, you lumps are letting us get way ahead of you, which means we girls will have to wait around for dessert again."

"Marna, sometimes I think you were born three drinks ahead of me. Wade in, Erick, we got our orders. Oh, man, this is delicious. Get Katie back here so I can give her a kiss for Syl."

Snow was coming down hard when they were ready to leave. Jim stopped just inside the door. "What is it, Hon, a tummy ache? You have a funny look that I don't like."

"He knows."

"What? What are you talking about? Who knows?"

"Have Nancy and Erick gone outside?"

"Yes, they're getting in Erick's car."

"Rankin...he knows. I've got a feeling I don't think I can explain to you. He knows we've found the treasure. Marna, he's borderline. I don't trust him, and I've worked for him all these months. He knows me like he knows his trigger finger. Let's go home."

"Jim, I'm frightened."

"I don't know what to think, what his move will be."

"Well, we're safe with this snowstorm...must be four inches on the ground."

"Don't count on it. This is made to order for someone of his mindset simply because any move would be the last thing anyone would suspect. C'mon, let's get home to a fire. We can talk about it some more, but I'm getting bad vibes."

They had driven Marna's Blazer because bad weather threatened; and by the time they entered the driveway back home, the wind off the ocean was a gale already driving snowdrifts. This time of late autumn could produce a blizzard in Maine one day and balmy air the next.

They soon had a fire roaring, and Marna made tea and brought it to the fireside. "Why don't we just put a few clothes in a suitcase and leave in the morning as soon as the snow is over?

Echo Horizon

Am I ready! Got to get away from here. Maybe I can find a normal life yet."

"It occurs to me you have an idea, Ladybug. Let's see if anyone on TV thinks the snow will stop any time soon."

"I'm going upstairs to see if my black slacks are up there. Be down in a minute."

"I could look at you in black slacks from now 'til...Hey, let's don't pack heavy. We can buy you some real nice clothes in Richmond, or Washington if you prefer. Here it is...snow's going to stop in an hour. Let's leave right now."

Just as she was returning to the stairs to ask him what he had said, an explosion rocked the house and threw her onto the floor. Then the beat of helicopter rotors could be heard. Jim was dazed but got to her in a flash. Something heavy was hitting the house. They were under attack, and no doubt existed that the whole top floor had been blown away when snow came drifting down what remained of the staircase. Flames appeared at the windows.

"Christ! Rockets! Now, he's going after us with a 30 millimeter cannon. We gotta get to hell out of here, but where?" yelled Jim.

"Grab a flashlight and our jackets!"

"What are you doing?"

"Jim, Honey, I don't want to die. I want a long life with you. Trust me!" She ran to the mantel and opened her hiding place, took out Roni's notebook and felt for the coins. Not there. She'd moved them. No time. She picked up her notes. The coins by the bed upstairs were history; the house was being obliterated. "You ready? Let's have that light. You follow close." She took his hand and led him into the tiny entrance to the secret stairs.

"We hiding in here? This house is fast turning into a pile of hot embers."

"We're going out. Trust me." An explosion punctuated her last statement., and Jim halted for a brief moment. Flames illuminated the snow, and through the living room windows they could see both cars engulfed in flames.

"He's got us. I don't know what we'll do afoot."

"Maybe we can reach the boat. Hurry, Jim, no time left. Oh, God, I hope he doesn't find the gold. I think we hid it quite well."

"Most likely he's seen a big magnetic anomaly on his monitor. We going down those steps? Good Lord!"

"Our only hope."

"Where do they lead?"

"I don't know, for Christ's sake! Trust me! Hurry!"

By the light of the wavering flashlight they placed their feet, in turn, precariously on the stone steps. They were hard to distinguish, and the descent seemed interminable. Cold and damp clutched them, and both knew they weren't prepared for an extended stay outside in the storm. A crash from above told them retreat was now unthinkable. They had cast their lot. Marna held the light in one hand, and with the other, gripped the two notebooks which insisted on twisting in opposite directions. She still wore the green, wool dress she wore to dinner which seemed ages ago.

A tunnel continued from the bottom step, and they ducked to enter, wasting no time with conjecture over the why and the who. The tunnel was simply their only route. Jim bumped his head again and swore. The next few hundred feet were as miles, but they had no plan of action should they ever emerge. Time of night was of no matter when a killing machine hovered low in the snow laden air...one with every device known to man for hunting, seeking out, tracking and destroying whatever quarry regardless of weather. If Jim had taken time to rationalize, he would have realized the killer possessed the infra-red means of detecting body heat, and they would be struck down seconds after they popped from their burrow.

"The boat, where in hell will we go in a skiff tonight?"

"You come up with anything better, I'll listen, Jim. Ouch!. Oh hell, my shins!"

"What did you do?"

"Ran into something heavy in the path."

"Shine the light down here, Marn." He groped in the dim light. "Two of the same kind of boxes we've been dealing with today. Uungh! This one's heavy as hell. Other one's light enough. I wonder what...cover's loose."

"Jim, we don't have a minute to waste. We'll come back sometime. Someone has to see the fire. Where's the militia when you need them? Oh, hell, I'm going to drop this stuff into the box, keep losing everything. There it goes. Missed. Leave it."

"You OK? Militia wouldn't stand a chance against a Huey. That's what that son of a bitch Rankin has done. He's stolen him a Huey. We're dog meat."

"Well, we can't stay in here. Let's go."

Thirty or forty paces farther on the light showed a pile of rocks and earth in their path, blocking their way. "We've had it."

"No, Jim, I'll hold the light. You grab that stone up there, and I think you can wrench it free. Should give us room."

"Who built this passage?"

I'm not sure, Hon. It just feels like I've been in here before." She gripped her shoulders with crossed arms. "Kinda spooky, really."

"I'll show you spooky if we ever get out from here. Watch it below." A huge rock rolled to the floor, and they could feel the cold night air on their faces as they clambered over the top.

"We made it. Wow, what snow!"

"Yeah, now what?"

"I guess we run like hell for the dock, Jim."

"Guess it's our only move." They paused in a depression ringed by foundation stones, and both realized they were in the old cellar hole. Wind blew snow in their faces, and the beat of rotor blades was barely audible above the roar of wind in pines and the crash of surf. A bright searchlight probed the scene, and tree tops shown in its glare.

"The bastard's looking for us. Prob'ly already found the gold. He'll plan on using a sky hook to move it first thing after the storm. Stay down, Sweetie." A flat blast of sound detonated in their ears, and a jet of fire stabbed the night and reflected briefly off the water, followed by another. Then, the night vanished in the light of a ball of flame which swirled alarmingly close to their position. The fireball was punctuated by a cacophony of explosions as something fell out of the sky in a final raging blast.

26

Nancy's head came off her pillow as alarming flashes of red light stabbed into the bedroom. Hadn't sirens wailed the whole night through? The Saxtons Volunteer Fire Company had never mustered so much equipment at one time, it seemed. She winced. Her head felt like a football recently kicked. She needed to sit up. It was the middle of the night. The digital clock had to be wrong…couldn't be 5:00 am. A red glow on the horizon had not yet caught her attention.

"Erick…Erick, you awake?" She made two more tries before she heard a groan. Slowly the pieces of consciousness came together. She heard him stumble across the room shortly after her exit.

"Nancy, look out the window," he exclaimed as he burst through the bedroom door. "No, the other way. Isn't that just about the direction of Marna's place where that red glow is?"

Her reply was a shriek. "Call the dispatcher, Erick. That has to be Marna's house! Oh, God, what's happened?"

The sun hadn't yet risen when they turned in at Marna's lane. Nothing was as it should have been. Erick's headlights joined those of several trucks in lighting up the scene, showing hoses snaking every which way and a great, lonesome chimney standing surrounded by glowing embers and debris. The remains of two burnt out vehicles sat at the foot of a totally scorched skeleton of a once proud tree. They sat, neither able to speak. The blackened and trampled snow was mute testament to what must have been a scene from Hell. Nancy gripped Erick's arm until he demanded release.

Once out of the car, Erick held his wounded side and picked his way to two nearby fire fighters. He was acquainted with them all. She remained in the car in stunned disbelief. The notion was just taking hold that she had not seen either Marna or Jim. Of whatever her friendship with Marna meant, of all the times they had spent together at work or play, this might be all that was left. The thought nauseated her. Had they escaped? Where were they?

Erick was asking Bob Harvey the same questions and not liking the supposition he was receiving in response.. They had not driven off in their vehicles, and the company hadn't seen any sign of them on the road. Erick was told the fire marshal would be on hand come first light. One good sign..no smell of burned flesh. He then splashed over to the rusted looking car bodies and released a whistle that Nancy could hear. She crawled from the car and joined him.

"I'm looking at them, Erick, what is it?"

"These two have been riddled with automatic cannon fire or I'll eat your hat!"

"Cannon…fire, Erick, what are you talking about?"

"I don't know what else could have put those holes in the cars. That one's Jim's."

"But who? What? Where are they, Erick?" The panic gripped Nancy's voice as she slowly lost control.

A pickup truck bounced along the lane and came to a stop beside Erick's car. Katie had spied them and walked toward them, alarm showing in her expression. Sylvanus walked over to the firemen. Katie had trouble with the words. Had they gotten out? When asked if she had seen Marna or Jim in town, she shook her head, and tears fell.

Tide was up, and the pumper was taking water from the cove. Syl walked beside a fire fighter who was checking the intake. "What do you make of it, Sid?"

"Too much debris way off from the house site for easy explanation, some of it scorched but not burned…like there was an explosion."

"Fire marshall will want to look at that."

"We got some of the debris secured in the truck…left some more where it was."

Sylvanus was looking around, searching the scene, when in the growing light, he saw something. "What's smoke doing over there, Sid? You fellers knock down a fire at the swamp?"

"No, what you got? Yeah, we better have a look. Watch your footing."

Sylvanus made no riposte at the younger man's tender regard for his elder's safety, a singularity in itself. They splashed, tripped and trudged through new fallen snow headed for the far end of the cove until they broke through underbrush into a clearing or what was left after the burnable vegetation had been consumed and blasted back from the center where lay the twisted remains of an obvious helicopter. What was left of a human form sprawled on the ground fifty feet in their direction from the aircraft.

"Jesus Christ!" Sylvanus exploded. I didn't reckon on this!"

"That's a Huey, Syl…gunship. Suppose we can get a closer look?"

"It's a chance. Prob'ly still hot, and unless I miss my guess, some ordnance exploded in that thing, maybe not all."

Quite gingerly they closed in on the wreck and saw the remains of another person plastered to what was left of the interior and, as in the case of the first body, did not disturb it.

"Better get on your horn and call somebody in here, Sid."

"Right. Look at that thirty millimeter. S'pose that was what took out the cars and the house?"

"That and some three inch rockets." Syl was scratching his head. This was not starting out as one of his better days. "This is a lot bigger than we can handle, Sid. The whole thing is beginning to stink. Now, what on Earth brought down that 'copter?"

Sid rummaged near a wrecked seat and straightened with something in his hand, something round.

"What in hell? Syl, look at this here, heavy little bastard."

"Sid, that's a cannon ball. Where'd you find…Naw…Couldn't be. Are we supposed to think someone threw that sucker at the 'copter and brought it down? No way."

"Right here inside the wreckage, and I don't think either of these guys would have been carrying it around to play catch. It's about six pounds. Yah, yer right, no way, Syl."

"Besides, six pound round shot probably hasn't been fired since the 1860s."

"This is weird. Why would that be in there? Hell, let's get back to the radio. That was a long, rough tramp the way we came in. Let's bear closer to the shore on our way back. I think Marna has cleared there some. Where in the hell are those two? I'm worried. This looks awful bad, Sid."

They tramped back on the suggested route, and it was easier. As they approached an old cellar-like depression, Sid let out a shout. "Tracks, Syl. Good God, look! There, leading right out of that hole in the ground and on up to the mound. I think right past it. And that's where they stop. The goddamn tracks stop right up there and no tracks coming back! What in hell goes here?"

When Erick and Nancy viewed the pair of foot tracks leading out of the cellar depression, they back tracked; and Erick, with a pained side, lowered himself and traced the prints back to a wall and found the exit. He ventured inside and lit a match which revealed the blocking pile of earthen rubble. After lighting several more matches he made out a passage at the top and returned to the car for a light. "Nan, please stay back with Katie."

By removing some earth he was able to slither over the mound and entered a tunnel which was amazingly dry. He was quick to notice it had been burrowed through clay which was impervious to surface water., and no spring had made it through the floor. A scraping noise behind him stopped him with a chill. A frail beam of light showed him his shadow on the ground and wall.

"Why are you here? I asked you to stay back with Kate."

"Oh, Erick, not now, don't. I gotta be here. What've you found?" As she spoke her light outlined some square forms ahead on the floor.

He started for them and dropped his light as he stooped to pick up a towel wrapped bundle and a couple notebooks. "They must have come this way in a hurry…must've tried to drop this stuff in that empty box. Strange looking containers. This other one is heavy. I'll put this in the light one. Can you manage it. I"ll wrestle with the other. We ought to save this material for Marna, whenever she shows up. Good God, apt to find anything in this place. Let's boogie before people start gathering and get suspicious."

Sun was just breaking the horizon when the two muscled their burdens into the car and cast a last look on the desolation. Tears welled in Nancy's eyes as the absence of her friend bore in on her. They were still reddened from crying as she shrank from the reflection which greeted her in the mirror behind the bar as she mixed drinks for Erick and herself. Erick encouraged a fire. Day's end had brought no word of their friends.

Nancy had spread out on a table the papers and other articles found in the lighter of the two boxes while Erick labored at the hearth with tools and some skin and blood. His intake of breath at sight of the contents of the box was piercing.

"What?"

"Put your hand in there. You may never see anything like this in your life."

"What...where did they come from?"

"Who could guess?" Erick let a number of the coins slip through his fingers. "Maybe we have a clue in the stuff you have poured out there." Nancy put her hand in the box and pulled it out with a beautiful gold bracelet with charms suspended all about.

"Whoops, missing one. It's the zodiac. Marna had one of these, the missing one I bet. But why leave this all lying about?"

"Bingo, you've got the log of a ship..quite old, I wager. Notes..What's this? This is old. I wonder if we can get at it to read it. Looks like some sort of marching orders. Wait a minute..on the boxes, the rampant lion. These are English! Better take it easy with these old parchments. What do you have?"

"A notebook of Marna's. It was on the ground beside a box. She's got all sorts of weird stuff here. Take time later to read it. This other notebook...Roni Dayan for Heaven's sake, but it's in Hebrew. Her name's in it."

"Hold on, Nan, I gotta take it easy for a bit. I'm really hurtin'."

"Well, it's no wonder, the way you went at it. That box of gold must weigh two hundred pounds. Listen to me. I refer to a treasure as valuable as the whole town like it was an extra pair of boots."

"We're saturated…take a while for all this to sink in, but one thing."

"What?"

"The snow won't last long. We did both see two sets of foot prints end abruptly on the slope to the water, didn't we? Am I dreaming?"

"I saw them. It blows me away."

Only exhaustion could part them from the newly found treasures of the tunnel even if they hadn't as yet made proper sense of them. The vessel's log was that of a schooner named *Archer* and recorded a sea battle fought with an English armed brig during the American Revolution. *Archer's* master was named Sarah Alport.

"Where are they, Erick? I've heard Marna speak of these things. How could she have such intimate knowledge of the past? What is it she's trying to tell us? Who in hell is Sarah Alport?"

All the while Nancy inveighed against a conclusion, Erick thumbed through parchments from the brittle leather pouch and said, "How can this be? We've got bribery and assassination here. Who could have known of this? Where are the historians?" Neither could tear themselves away from the table. "Nancy, for the love of Jesus, we've got a pilot's log for a Piper Navajo." He swung to his feet, scrambling for words. "We've been combing the god damned Atlantic for that airplane, and here's the christless log. What in God's green Earth is it doing here?!"

Near collapse from exhaustion and the gravity of their discoveries finally forced them to surrender to their bodies' need for sleep.

The Next Morning

From the half destroyed pouch, Erick removed the old papers with writing still legible on much of them. It revealed specific order from the Council of War for a clandestine campaign against the continental government and referred to tonnages of gold specie to fund the mischief. A figurative light bulb above Erick's head flickered and glowed, but little was coming together. It was all too fantastic.

When he took up the final offering from the tunnel and began to read, Nancy had to remove his cup of coffee from one trembling hand and John Gantry's flight log from the other. The aircraft listed was a twin Piper Navajo. It's last entry checked with what was known about his and Betsey's departure, but this log shouldn't have been where it was found, but, rather, in the aircraft. This was beyond belief, and he saw, now, how his hands were shaking. "Nancy, what are we doing?"

"Erick, we've got to stop. We have to wake up. This is a bad dream. None of this is happening. Please, tell me it's not happening."

They remained in the house that day and spoke with no one. On the next day, information received by phone only deepened the mystery. No trace of human remains had been located in the residue of Marna's house. Nancy was badly strung out with the ordeal and sank into a depression after reading the manuscript she picked off the floor of the tunnel. Marna had told Nancy she had found some fascinating historical accounts in her attic and was trying to write a story that seemed to materialize from the information in the old documents.

Erick studied the military documents, just three sheets, assembled and laid out beside their battered leather container. Whoever had issued the orders had wasted few words, but so much time and damage made it impossible to discover the identity of the signer. Nancy read Marna's story. The phone rang, and when Erick answered, she could overhear Syl's voice speaking about a helicopter.

"That was Sylvanus, Nan. He's run down a report of a 'copter similar to the one he found…released to some high brass and equipped for support of a drug interdiction just off the coast here…no names, of course."

He resumed his perusal. "The damned effrontery of those English bastards! Can you believe this, Nancy? '…move without delay to discover which and several of men loyal to our Sovereign and display those amount of specie sufficient to move these same to seek out and separate those men as can be from position of leadership in the late rabble government of the rebellion…to strike down those who will not and including officers and members of the outlaw continental congress.' I can make out the year, 1777."

He looked up at Nancy's face, more pale than before, breath labored. She was speaking, but barely audibly.

"It happened, Erick. It really happened."

"An idea Marna and I had. My granddad had made the same suggestion to me when I was very young and facing some very boring history classes in grade school. I told Marna what Gramps had suggested after she'd had that weird experience with the schooner whose crew pulled her out of the water. Come to think on it, she started to change right after that. Some off-the-wall things began happening."

"How well do you know Marna? You do know she is a very rich lady judging by the quantity of gold coins in that box. Some of those pieces are worth thousands as individual items."

"Well, nobody would have ever known, not from that girl. I know we hit it off well, both into the history thing. I convinced her she should take the job with the university."

"OK, time to try to get it together." But try as they would, they couldn't put the pieces together. All they were sure of was that everything was related, and Marna was the common fitting. Nothing in their experiences prepared them for the puzzle they faced.

The phone rang. "He told you what, Syl? Right up against a tree by his barn? That's at least a half mile from where you and

Sid found the 'copter. What? Wait a minute. Did you and Sid find any snow on the body outside the helicopter? Practically none..?"

"What was that all about?"

"Syl says Ed Gale found a cannon ball in his yard where it had bounced and slid through the snow."

"So-o-o?"

"Well, Honey, who's going around firing cannon balls in the snow?"

"Why did you want to know about snow on the body?"

"That simply suggests the snow had stopped when the helicopter crashed or was...or whatever."

"You were going to say 'shot down', weren't you, Erick?"

"I guess I...I don't know. That would imply...no, no, no damn it, that's too crazy!"

"Is there anything about this goat picnic that isn't? Back up, Erick. Marna and Jim are among the missing. We have no exit by auto unless a third car was available. That's unlikely. Why would they leave in a storm and set fire to the house?"

"...and shoot their other cars full of holes? No way."

"Connections..we're looking for a connection. A fortune in gold and Marna's story notes, a ship's log and a pilot's log, all together. We think they had to pass through the tunnel, from the evidence."

"How about another helicopter, Nan? Didn't you tell me a 'copter woke Marna up one morning that Jim ordered sent in to pick up a timber? That must have been some piece of wood."

"She and Jim dug up some old ship out of the mud flats in the cove." Nancy decided she wouldn't clutter the conversation with an account of the strange illusion she, Marna and Roni had seen in the stars back in the spring. "I'll bet that's where the gold came from."

"Nan, this makes me wonder how well we really know that pair. Who in the world is going to walk away from a fortune in gold?"

"How do we know she knew about it?"

"Get real. We know she came through the tunnel.."

"Stop right there. The bracelet, Marna told me she left her wet clothes and that bracelet in her jeans pocket on the schooner after her ducking in the Atlantic."

"Then, what's it doing where we found it?"

"Exactly!" Where does this fit with a pilot's log from the 1980s and the log of the *Archer* from the 1700s? You finished reading from it? Sarah Alport, Master. Marna showed me an old letter written to a girl named Sarah. She was very protective of it. Sarah was in love with a boy named Comfort MacLean. Well, love triumphed. But a woman in 1777 is master of a fighting ship, a privateer, and takes on an English ship of war and stomps it. Do you realize what this could mean, Erick? My old grandfather was on to something, and here in our possession could be the evidence that it happened. The Brits really tried some dirty tricks we didn't know about...and the gold in the box..you don't suppose..?"

"I'm just about ready to believe anything, Nan, but why the flier's log? Her father didn't crash, it seems. On the last page that contained writing, someone states a VFR landing was made on a grassy meadow behind a barn. Seems Jim and I searched the bay for a ghost in Syl's *Charming Sally*. There was no downed aircraft to be found. But why did Marna hide the log in the tunnel with this other stuff? What didn't she want anyone to know?"

"She didn't, Erick. Trust me, I know. If she had known these things were down there, she'd have told me."

"Wish I could free up this page in Master Alport's log."

"How about vinegar?"

The vinegar did its work, and Erick studied the page, finally emitting a shrill whistle. He stood, nearly upsetting the table. "Thirteen chests of gold in the prize towed by *Archer* and brought home, the gold to be placed in the foundation. Crew paid off to sustain them temporarily and all to meet on the next blue moon to divide the balance."

"Erick, these gold pieces must have come from the same boat. Foundation...foundation, what foundation?" she mused. She rose and dizzied herself about the room. "Only a small portion...Good God, what foundation? The house?" She grasped the sides of her head as she paced.. "Not that house..too recent. Cellar hole? No, Erick, a dam...the dam. Marna spoke to me about a dam. She thinks the sum of the events described in her trove of documents took place right by her property. There was a very important dam...foundation...tons of gold."

"Nancy, cool it for crying out loud. You don't think anything like that could exist after what, two hundred years? Let's concentrate on finding Marna and Jim. Didn't they say something about driving to Virginia the other night at dinner? Maybe they reached Virginia some other way. We ought to be hearing from them...Nan...Nan! What is it? Why are you looking like that?"

"A blue moon, Erick...Marna told me that was what her mother said just as she was climbing into the airplane. 'We'll see you in a blue moon'." She stepped to a window facing seaward. "They've gone, Honey, and I think they've gone a lot farther away than Virginia."

Erick got up from the table and put his arms around her, felt her shiver. "What's left is the notebook we have with Marna's name in it and Roni's notes in Hebrew. There's got to be a perfectly good explanation why two modern day works, a diary and a flight log, are found together with an old ship's log and God knows how much worth in gold. Nancy, they had to be fleeing for their lives. What we found at her place was no accident. I'll carry that scene from Hell to my grave." He reached for the notebook and stated, "They left enough wealth behind to buy all of Virginia west of the Blue Ridge. The whole thing's in Hebrew. Do you suppose...?"

"What, that Roni was seeing her professionally? Well, he is a kind of psychiatric doctor. Why not?"

"Might tell us a lot, give us a clue where Marna is. But who could translate for us?"

Dr. Jerome Levi's Office

"Come in…come…watch your step with that carpet. Can I offer you some refreshment? Why don't we sit over there where all can enjoy comfort?" Nancy's eyes roamed from one spectacular astro picture to the next, nebulae, galaxies and colorful cloud shapes. On tables stood bronze measuring devices and sighting instrumentation from the middle ages.

"No, nothing, thanks. Professor Levi, thank you for seeing us on such short notice."

"Nonsense, Ms Marsh, a pleasure." He led them across his spacious office decorated to enhance light. They passed assorted charts and graphs on the walls.

"I think you've met my friend, Erick Lehn."

"We have run across one another on occasion. Good morning, Mr. Lehn. Oh, enough, should we not all be of first names?"

"I'm OK with that," agreed Nancy.

"Good to see you again, Jerome. I've attended your lectures," reminded Erick.

"So, how is it I may help you?"

Erick seated himself after assisting Nancy, then listened in silence. He noted the diminutive size of Jerome Levi; but what called his particular notice, something he had forgotten, was the falsetto trailing of the final consonant of a sentence. It was disconcerting at first, then he wondered if his face would crack.

"We wonder if you would be willing to do some translating for us," ventured Nancy.

"So, we'll have a look, see what it is. You have this with you?"

She reached inside her shoulder bag and withdrew the diary and handed it into Jerome Levi's waiting grasp. He was quiet as he thumbed through several pages.

"A modern script…private notes of Ronen Dayan concerning our friend Marna Gantry. Forgive me. May I ask how you come by this?"

Nancy opened her mouth, prepared to invent and improvise a reply when Erick interrupted "Professor Levi...Jerome, I'm sure you're well informed concerning the tragic goings on at Marna's home..."

"Trouble on trouble, when will it end? Yes, terrorists again, I am led to believe."

"We're...well, no one's certain what happened. Circumstances point to terrorists for sure. What we are concerned about most is that Marna and Jim Starr have not been seen by anyone since the night the house was destroyed."

"They must show up. We must believe...surely the police..."

"Jerome, we are desperate," urged Nancy. "Marna and I are the closest of friends. She's the nearest to a sister of anyone in the world. There's so much we can't explain, but we think everything will be made known in good time."

"Yes, and the notes will be turned over to the authorities. A search is underway, but Nancy and I, because of some peculiar developments, believe these notes have some information that may help find them."

"To be sure." Jerome selected another pair of spectacles and opened the book to continue. He excused himself and bore into the writings. From time to time he set the book aside and stared into space as if digesting some context.

Nancy and Erick traded off looking at each other, then at the celestial extravaganzas. Finally.

"My friends, no ordinary notes these. Marna's visits were not clinical in scope...at least as I gather so far. Ronen states early on he had no intention to make notes, but rather, to counsel a friend. He goes on, and this is utterly fantastic."

> Marna Gantry presents the model
> of a physically well young woman,
> composed as to her role in society
> but restless. The one inordinate

> departure from an otherwise normal
> outlook on the world is her dreams.
>
> A total transportation to the persona
> of another girl in another time is
> repetitive, the experience enervating.
>
> I find no precedent for the totality
> of change in form and venue via
> a dream experience. She presents
> an observer with an example of
> mental construct beyond earthly
> experience and wakens with knowledge
> and recall beyond anything she could
> know in the present.

"Oh, dear me, my colleague has gone deep. This is indeed a rarity."

"What? Oh, excuse me Jerome." Nancy was sitting on the raw edge of anticipation.

"Marna's dreams present an enigma for us all. Apparently, she is possessed of all five senses, and her dreams are in serial." He turned pages for several minutes.

Nancy's gaze returned to the splendid astro-photos, and she became engaged with study of their detail. Slowly, she was aware of Dr. Levi's countenance. He was looking at her, and his facial expression projected awe.

"Nancy, engrossed in history as I know you to be, can it be possible you and Marna have discussed any of it? Has she engaged you in discussions of any particular period in history?"

Nancy's reverie was broken. "Yes, we've talked a lot about the period of the American war for independence. We both find it fascinating and have a theory involving that struggle."

"That may be singular. Ronen writes that Marna describes what must be considered an alter ego living in that period and somewhere on this coast. Marna is seeing events unfold as through the eyes of another, actually as if she were that other. She feels; she hears…"

Nancy went pale. Erick got up and walked toward the professor.

"There is apparently a lot more in that book. I can't for the life of me understand how Marna came to possess it…unless Roni discussed with her openly what he has written."

"He may not have. Yes, there is more…much more, something wondrously exciting in these pages. Ronen may have broken new ground." He trailed off with, "…though who will be ready to accept?"

"Please go on."

"Yes, Nancy, but I caution, it could be distressing. The dreams progress in time with an ever increasing violence. A disturbance exists. Ronen refers to an influence, a shade; but, for the love of God, he states he has no doubt of the existence of the influence!"

Erick was aware the professor no longer let his sentences trail off as before, and a change appeared in his countenance. "Jerome, we are rational people here, but I've had a most uneasy feeling these past several days. I'm sure a lot more exists in those notes, and the book had to be one of the last items Marna had with her when she fled the house while it was burning to the ground."

"There is no possibility she…they are still…?"

"Nothing in the ashes."

"C'mon, Erick, Jerome, I want to hear more! This may be our only chance of picking up their trail. Did I just say what I think I said?"

"Where Ronen is going with this, I am not sure. He is a scientist of reputation, but…"

"Couldn't we just contact him in view of what's happened?"

"Nancy, no one in authority would acknowledge his existence. I cannot divulge more."

"OK."

Erick wasn't satisfied. His expression belied acceptance of that statement. Even though he sensed the professor didn't wish to pursue the issue further, he made the plunge.

"Dr. Levi, what in hell is going down here? We're rational and open minded, but enough smoke. What's in those notes you're not telling us?"

The professor gave him a long hard look. Erick sensed he was sizing him up.

"All right, but hear me through, for I am serious. You may not be ready for the ideas I will place before you. You say you are open minded. We shall see."

Nancy detected a tremor in the voice and looked at Erick. "We really want to know anything which may help us find them."

"It is well we can talk so. What is being said here by Ronen goes beyond your wildest thoughts unless you have been following a theoretical development which has caught the attention of many men and women of science of diverse disciplines the world over.

"The philosophies and teachings of many old, traditional sects, as well as the writings of the ancient world, possess a common theme…

"Two states of being exist, the void or implicate order of the universe in which thought and consciousness alone exist, and time and dimension do not. Beginning at that end of an energy continuum, a procession through awareness to a more substantive reality of material solids results in a non void or explicate level of universe…the illusion of a substantive reality as we have come to know it. All time is a construct, goes the theorem. All events in explicate existence are preserved on the plane of the implicate and can be drawn on and repeated.

"Ronen has stated that he believes Marna possesses the interconnectedness in her genes which manifest an ability to construct an alternate reality and virtually step into it…probably involuntarily. The concepts as Ronen relates them fit together if one accepts the invitation, growing in urgency, to regard the universe as a hologram, a virtual existence projected by an energy field beyond time and space. The possibility exists that influences in this altered state of Marna's are working in this direction. In essence the two planes of existence are in dialogue. He continues with respect to his own concerns that the progression to greater violence in her dreams is placing her in harm's way, that…"

Erick watched Nancy with alarm as he saw her motionless and pale as a sheet. "Honey..Honey, you all right?"

She came to with a sudden exclamatory fusillade of questions. "Does he mean he's afraid Marna might be killed…die in a dream? Good God! But, instead, has she gone into another time plane? What am I supposed to believe?"

"Not to worry, Nancy," Jerome assured her. "Our reality is very real to us regardless of ancient philosophies. We have been born into it, and our consciousness has become accustomed. I will grant that the brain interprets every sensation transmitted to it. We are electromagnetic beings. The brain takes what amounts to no more than interference wave fronts of light and transforms them into a beautiful today and everything else.

"What Ronen is doing, I believe, is comparing what Marna has, perchance, reported, to what one would surmise to be characteristic events under the condition of the universal construct offered by ancient philosophies. If there be substance to all this, what may have befallen Marna and probably her friend, Commander Starr, could affect us all equally.

"Quantum physicists report a wild variety of paradox, subatomic particles which appear to be created by the observer, particles while observed, then reverting to wave motion. How can we argue, then, with the ancients who profess that consciousness creates the stars and galaxies, the sun, the rain, the tiny snowflake and the grain of sand?"

"Then if any of this is applicable to Marna, and that would be a stretch of my imagination save for some things to which I have been privy…if they reside on another plane, we'll never see either of them again. I assume Jim is with her. All we have is multiple witness to two sets of footprints in the snow which end with no possible rhyme or reason."

"If in fact Roni's interpretations of the theorems have substance, Erick, you may see them sooner than you expect and under circumstances you never dreamed."

"Enough! Enough," complained Nancy. "I've got to catch up. This is too much. I mean none of this is proven, right?"

"Nancy, most of our knowledge in science is unproven. Rather, the concepts have been around under foot so long, and they seem to work for us, we make them natural laws. One day an observation with contrary data comes along, and we start all over."

Then, the way we look at the universe, we have become used to," Erick started.

"We perceive. Our brain takes signals from this field of energy we think of as reality and paints our picture for us. Ronen has gone on to note that the mind may not reside in the body corporeal, but on another plane. It is high in a hierarchy of continuum which includes the electromagnetic field of energy, awareness, consciousness and things substantial, air, water, plants, minerals and all other life forms. Ronen is a magnificent mix of intellect; but as a theorist, he shines."

"All theory?" Nancy sagged in her chair. "This is all theory, so we're right back where we started?" Tears welled. "They're gone, Erick; they're not coming back."

"I do not like to see you so disheartened, Nancy. I have attempted to translate, not raise hopes. As to the fate of your friends, it would not be unwise to think on what Ronen has put forth here. What else have we? Is it not like standing on new ground, the discoverers?"

"But mental constructs? We're not ready for this."

"Think, my friend, Erick. You have seen the laser, no? Have you been present at the demonstration of the hologram?"

"You mean where a beam of laser light is split, one part probing the subject, both halves diffused and coinciding at a photographic plate and generating an exposure?"

"Precisely! Then, when the plate is illuminated by laser light a three dimension virtual image is produced."

"Well, yes."

'All right, use that model as a parallel to the process of the brain in presenting reality to us every day. Think on it."

"Thank you, Professor Levi, I think." Nancy was on her feet. "May I continue to read his notes? I will return promptly."

"Sure. Erick, we gotta go home. We've taken a lot of Jerome's time." She was quiet at first on the ride back, then, "Erick, will you start a fire, a good hot fire, in that old wood stove in the kitchen? I'm going to bake you some biscuits and make a supper you'll never forget. Tomorrow, I'm going to give the cottage a thorough house cleaning."

Bert Howe

27

"What a freakin' fireball..hell, we shouldn't look at it! We won't be able to see a thing. What do you suppose did that?"

"You didn't hear the cannon, see the stab of the powder ring?"

"No, I was scrambling over those damn rocks. Well, they won't be shooting at us anymore. But what a way to mess up a life! What do we do, now, hitch into town and try to rent a car?"

"I think it's a little late for that."

"Yeah, better wait 'til morning, which shouldn't be long coming. Look at the dawn light."

"I mean, it's too late to try to hitch into town or rent a car."

"I don't get you. What do we do, wander around in the snow and…?"

"What snow?" Marna was doing her best with the impossible task of explaining to Jim that their level of reality had been inexorably altered. "Try to relax, Sweetheart. I've been here before, and we have friends who are waiting for us. You'll see."

"Relax? Hey, you know you probably left some gold coins by the bed, but…"

"All gone, now, but no matter; this is all a dream, Hon. Let's keep walking. Getting lighter."

"We're in a newly mown field. Hell, it's summer. What's happening to us? I know, you've caught me up in one of your dreams. I want to wake up. This has all been a dream."

"Look behind you." She directed his gaze to a handsome house with central chimney and the front roof sloping steeply down to the friezeboard over the tall front windows. She pointed to a dormer and told him it was her room. A well sweep stood in the yard. "This is her dream, Love, and we won't be waking from it. This is all as real as it gets. Your level of reality, mine…we're who we are. Sometimes I used to dream of Sarah's world. Sometimes she dreamt of mine. We met, and Sarah went away to find you. You want to get used to calling me Sarah, and you're Comfort. Remember, we're together."

He stopped still for a moment. "This is weird, Marn..Sarah. I am experiencing no compulsion to understand, but where are we?"

"Where we've been for the past months. We're going to love it here. You'll really love being you. After the war, there will be so many things for us to do. We'll never need to worry about money.."

"After the war..right! You know, I can remember a lot of things. I think I'm going to be comparing things to what I remember. Can you remember how it was with us?"

"Of course, we'll always be able to remember. That's OK, because no one here with the exception of Mom and Dad will know what we're talking about. You can tell any of the neighbors anything you want. They won't have a clue, nor believe a thing you say beyond their experience."

"I want a hug before we start meeting neighbors. How do you feel, Sarah, you going to be all right with me? I sure haven't changed in my feelings for you even if you changed your name…and your hair color. What a gorgeous auburn shade!"

"There's the sun, and there's Archer at that quay. Somebody's coming ashore to meet us, and I think it's Mr. Dighton. He replaced you as first officer when I was skipper. Now, you'll be captain."

"What?!"

"Well, what do you expect with your experience?"

"It's kinda sudden."

"The men will expect it. Oh, there's Mom and Dad with Mr. Dighton."

"You know, Love, I may just be able to carry it off; but one thing I know. We will not be sailing in Skimpe's downeaster to China."

"You won't feel any more anxiety about leaving our previous plane of reality than a lobster does leaving an old shell

Echo Horizon

behind or a snake shedding a skin too small. Glad you decided against that."

"We'll need to talk about this someday." He greeted the three coming toward them as if he had departed moments before to find a drink of water. "Captain Alport..Madam Alport...Mr. Dighton, it's been a time, hasn't it; and my lady has told me of the grand victory over HMS Apollyon. So good to see all looking so well..." Sarah kicked him.

"Don't overdo it," she cautioned

"Comfort," said Betsey, "So good you are among us once more, and your father, pray tell?"

"Passed on these two months, I'm afraid."

"Comfort, you're a sight for sore eyes," John Alport croaked as Comfort gave him a bear hug.

"Happy to be shipping with you again, Mr. Starr. Mistress Alport, you have been sore missed. There be those of us who would sail to the lintels of hell with you if you bid. Mind, if we needs fire on any more demons in the sky, a six pounder carriage should be altered for elevation and sighting."

"Mr. Dighton, as we have told, Betsey and I will remain ashore while the rest of you track down the *Sea Damsel* and destroy it or take it as prize. Sarah will command if she shall choose."

"Thank you, Father, no, I yield to Captain MacLean."

"Well, it is good; come, Bets, they have not a moment to waste."

"I shall have officers' call, Captain. Here be a report on supplies taken on and armaments."

"Thank you, Mr. Dighton, let's plan our voyage."

"John, they made it by the blue moon. They know, don't they?"

"We four know. It will be difficult living in this reality and knowing what they know, but they will flourish, dear."

"Have you nearly finished getting rid of that airplane, John? How would you explain one of those engines to Caleb?"

"Matter of fact, Caleb helped me bury the two engines and never was even curious. I put a wing in the passage with the box of gold. Almost done."

I love our home, John. The mill prospers. Did we have it as good on the other side?"

For two days and nights *Archer* sailed to the south and west. The skies were cloudless, and a steady wind from the north sped them on their way. Morale was high; the food was excellent. On the third day Sarah had the watch and saw a sail still hull down. The glass discovered it to be a brig bearing a resemblance in sail pattern to the description given of *Sea Damsel*. She called the bearing when of a sudden a rip started in the blue canopy of sky surrounding them. Portions of waves crumbled before her, and, then another tear in the sky.

She thought she heard voices which suggested she was going mad. Hurriedly she attempted to climb back down the shrouds, but her legs wouldn't move. Something beyond the reality of the schooner supported them. The sky began to crumble as did the water so that the scene about her was deteriorating. Next the sails started to dissolve, and another voice assailed her ears.

"Looks like she's coming around." She had the faintest impression of faces in the rents in the sky; and slowly the blues of sky and water dissolved to a bright sun washed wall in an enormous room. She lay covered in a four poster bed. Details of the room assumed definition as a handsomely appointed period bedroom bathed in sunlight. Figures took form, as faces bore smiles. Words flowed. Where she was she hadn't a clue. She knew only that she was conscious and possessed a headache.

She knew a middle aged couple were familiar to her, but her energies were focused on the younger man sitting by her on the bed and holding her hand. She knew him immediately and spoke, "Comfort, where have you taken me, now?"

"Comfort?" queried his familiar voice. "Comfort?"

"I'm sorry, Jim. Oh, don't play games with me while I have this headache."

"Doctor Barnes left something for your headache, Darling," cooed the woman's voice. "Oh, Marna, you've been unconscious so long, we've been worried out of our minds."

"You got quite a bang on the head when *Arcturus'* main boom took you over the side, and..."

"And Jim pulled me out?"

"No, ah...well..."

"Jim, don't do this to me. I've lived with this man these last months; we're engaged and he's still the biggest tease. Mom...ah, Mom?"

"Yes, Dear."

"Want to give me that something the doc left for me? I'd sure like to feel better. Jim, you have a lot of explaining to do. Where are we, and what have we been doing?"

The man she knew as Jim spoke low and slowly. "I'll explain everything when you're feeling better, but you should know what happened to you. I was sailing near your dad and mom when the boom knocked you off your dad's schooner. I saw you go in and knew you were knocked cold, so I went in after you."

"He saved your life, Sweetheart," said her dad.

"You're not Jim, are you?"

"I think I wish I were. Whoever he is, I'm jealous already."

"You're my Jim in every detail but name, then. What is your name?"

"You can call me Dale...or anything you want to call me."

"Dale hasn't left the house since he brought you in here."

"I think we should all leave and let Marna have some rest, John."

"If you guys leave me, I'll never forgive you. Or, at least, Dale, you stay with me. I'm going to be quite frank. I'm in love with a man who is your twin, I swear. We're engaged."

"You never let your mother in on that little detail, Marna. What in the world?"

"Well, I don't think there's anyone in Saxtons Harbor who doesn't know, Mom. I mean, it's hardly a secret."

"Saxtons...where?"

"My God, we still live in Saxton's Harbor, don't we. It's on all the charts."

"Do you know where Saxtons Harbor is, John?"

"Never heard of it."

"Oh-h, c'mon."

"Dear, we've always lived here in Lanesport. Certainly...ohh, the blow to her head..."

"You've eaten at the Cuddy...you know, Sylvanus Beal's wharf and restaurant?"

"Marna, you must rest, then we'll talk some more."

"Dale, you stay with me."

"Your mother and I will go outside if you want us."

"OK, Dad. Dale, what in the name of all that's holy is going down. I've let my hair down to you. Have I just come in with the tide?"

"All right, Marna, if you can stand it. I'll be just as candid with you. From the moment I took hold of you in the water, I was so afraid I'd lose you, I was near out of my mind. Why don't you just ramble and tell me what's on your mind. My guess is you have had one whale of a dream; and if that's so, I might just be the vehicle to help. Want to try?"

"Dale, you could be the answer to a maiden's prayer. Here goes.." She did ramble on for at least an hour, feeling better by the minute. When she had exhausted her recall, they sat and looked at one another.

"Wow, a parallel lifetime.."

"All my friends and acquaintances, they are so real. I can't let go. I feel like I'm falling from somewhere very high. They're all gone. I must have dreamed it all. Oh, Dale, please, if you have any human compassion left, don't walk away from me."

"Do you really mean it? You'd like me around? Well, it so happens I have no place I have to be. I'll help you back into your life."

"And then what?"

"I think I'd like to stick around after that."

"Tell me about yourself?"

"OK, your dad and my dad flew together in the Navy in Nam; and, of course, they survived, and when it was all over went into business in electronics and later computers in a big way. But you should know that."

"Wait a damn minute. You're that brat that used to tease me whenever your folks brought you to visit.."

"I never could find a way to get to know you. I wanted to, always wanted to, but you were so sassy."

"I wanted you to just say to me, 'Marna, I want to get to know you and be friends.' But you never did."

"I know, but I do, now. Marna, I really want to get to know you."

"OK, you saved my life. Traditionally, my life is yours, but not Jim's. He doesn't exist. Oh, God, Dale, I'm throwing myself at you."

"I don't think you can throw yourself at me hard enough, Marn. Why in hell do you think it is I never married. I've been my dad's overseas agent for years, now. For God's sake, tell me you're my girl. I'll never forsake you." He took both her hands in his. I thought I'd never get to you quick enough when you were face down in the water. My life was ready to end."

"Dale, there's more to your name...Ty..Tyr."

"Dale Ellison Tyree from Roanoke, Virginia."

"I'll be damned. OK, out. I gotta get dressed and have a look see around this palace. Is this really my home?" He escorted her as if this were her first view.

"And that, Marna, is the view from the ocean side. Look at those old cannon there."

"What are the yachts in the cove?"

"You know that one, your dad's.."

"And the black one..ohh-h, she's a beauty, a Baltimore clipper, isn't it?"

"How did you know?"

"I was skipper of one a long time ago. I told you about the dream."

"Whoa, Marna."

"Is the mill working?"

"You don't remember? Your mom made it into a restaurant and gift shop. Guess it's been there a long time."

"I hope to shout it has."

"Isn't your house familiar to you, yet?" They walked around the solidly constructed manse, the tiny panes in its windows, the well sweep, the barns."

"That's where Gantry and Tyree started business, that old barn, fixed up quite a bit."

"My God the place is beautiful, and this is my home?"

"You're going to have to live with that fact."

"Where do your and my dads do business, now?"

"Down the coast a way in Portland. They believe the time is right for international expansion or be killed by their competition, but it's slow raising the capital."

"Capital, Dale?"

"They're lining up investors."

"They don't need investors. Dad has all the capital he needs. By the way, that beautiful black schooner is yours?"

"My pride and joy."

"OK, work with me, Dale."

"You're feeling better, Marna."

"I am. I've dreamed of doing with this old place what Mom and Dad have done. I've got to find my father."

John Gantry was quick to inquire of his daughter's well being, and once assured was ready to be shown what it was that agitated her so.

"OK, I'm looking at three granite blocks standing on end. What then?"

"We pry 'em out for starters."

"No way.?

"Dad, I know what I'm saying. Your capital is in there. Two crowbars, and what will it cost for a back hoe to put the rocks back in the dam. We're back from the water...won't interfere with a thing."

"All right, if this is what it takes to humor you."

"Humor me, Dad." He did, and two workmen helped pry the stones loose, exposing a cave above water level and dropping back in the dam toward the anchor in the hillside. "OK, guys, you can quit, now." Marna dismissed the men and poked a flashlight into the recess. They were there. She knew the lid on one was loose and pried it off. She returned with the light shining on a handful of sparkling gold coins. Dale had to steady the older man who was near to fainting dead away at the sight. Dale was speechless.

"You guys got to get it together. There's about three tons of this stuff in there. Let's get to work, Dale, on the rest of our lives. A girl like me only comes around once in a blue moon."

Any similarity between persons dead or alive or events real or imagined is coincidental.

Bert Howe

About The Author

Bert Howe is a veteran of World War II and has been married to his wife Jean for 47 years. In addition to years as a high-tech salesman, he has been a schoolteacher, builder, farmer and woodsman. When in their fifties, Bert and Jean carved a homestead and farm out of a wilderness and lived much as did the early settlers in Maine who inspired much of *Echo Horizon*. Bert lives today with Jean in Boothbay, ME and enjoys four young people, five grandchildren and a great grandchild. The sea and the mountains are as much their home as the tranquil wooded area in which their homey Cape Cod dwelling sits. Wildlife, plants, hiking and traveling occupy much of their time.

Printed in the United States
2100